WebLogic Diagnostic Framework
Understanding and Using WLDF through Practical Examples and Profiles

Oracle In-Focus Series

Martin Heinzl

RAMPANT
TECHPRESS

Dedicated to my wonderful wife Lourdes.

WebLogic Diagnostic Framework
Understanding and Using WLDF through Practical Examples and Profiles

By Martin Heinzl

Printed in the United States of America.

Published in Kittrell, North Carolina, USA.

Oracle In-Focus Series: Book #51

Series Editor: Donald K. Burleson

Production Manager: Janet Burleson

Editor: Jennifer Kittleson

Production Editor: Jennifer Kittleson

Cover Design: Janet Burleson

Printing History: February 2015 for First Edition

Oracle, Oracle7, Oracle8, Oracle8i, Oracle9i, Oracle10g, Oracle 11g, and Oracle 12c are trademarks of Oracle Corporation.

ISBN 13: 978-0-9861194-0-8

Library of Congress Control Number:

Table of Contents

Part IV: WLDF Profiles

Part V: Using and Visualizing WLDF Data

Chapter 17: Getting access to diagnostic data 247

Using the Online Code Depot

Purchase of this book provides complete access to the online code depot that contains sample code scripts. Any code depot scripts in this book are located at the following URL in zip format and ready to load and use:

rampant.cc/WLDF.htm

If technical assistance is needed with downloading or accessing the scripts, please contact Rampant TechPress at rtp@rampant.cc.

Conventions Used in this Book

It is critical for any technical publication to follow rigorous standards and employ consistent punctuation conventions to make the text easy to read. However, this is not an easy task. With database terminology there are many types of notation that can confuse a reader. For example, some Oracle utilities such as STATSPACK and TKPROF are always spelled in CAPITAL letters, while Oracle parameters and procedures have varying naming conventions in the database documentation. It is also important to remember that many database commands are case sensitive, are always left in their original executable form and never altered with italics or capitalization. Hence, all Rampant TechPress books follow these conventions:

- **Parameters:** All database parameters will be lowercase italics. Exceptions to this rule are parameter arguments that are commonly capitalized (KEEP pool, TKPROF); these will be left in ALL CAPS.

- **Variables:** All procedural language (e.g. PL/SQL) program variables and arguments will also remain in lowercase italics (*dbms_job*, *dbms_utility*).

- **Tables & dictionary objects:** All data dictionary objects are referenced in lowercase italics (*dba_indexes*, *v$sql*). This includes all *v$* and *x$* views (*x$kcbcbh*, *v$parameter*) and dictionary views (*dba_tables*, *user_indexes*).

- **SQL:** All SQL is formatted for easy use in the code depot, and all SQL displayed in lowercase. The main SQL terms (select, from, where, group by, order by, having) will always appear on a separate line.

- **Programs & Products:** All products and programs that are known to the author are capitalized according to the vendor specifications (CentOS, VMware, Oracle, etc.). All names known by Rampant TechPress to be trademark names appear in this text as initial caps. References to UNIX are always made in uppercase.

Foreword

My name is Martin Heinzl and since 1998 I have been working with Enterprise (Middleware) Systems based on Common Object Request Broker Architecture (CORBA), Java Enterprise Edition (JEE) and other similar technologies. During my assignments in many different companies and various sectors as principal consultant and architect, I have frequently observed administrators busily writing their own shell scripts, tinkering with configuration files or even using graphical configuration tools to repeatedly alter the same settings across multiple servers in production environments.

Have you ever tried to monitor a complex environment like a WebLogic domain with all its subsystems? The WebLogic runtime MBeanServer offers thousands of MBeans, depending on the amount of configured services, servers, and applications. And what about analyzing a problem situation? The second topic is even worse because it is always difficult to determine the right level of details to be collected in order to have enough data for problem analysis and the impact these collections have on the overall performance. What about activating data collectors just in case the system is in a problematic state? Usually the collectors and parameters are set at startup time.

Well WebLogic offers an integrated solution to that. The WebLogic Diagnostic Framework (WLDF) offers a large number of subsystems and components which can be used to collect data, analyze data, create metrics, and much more. These collectors can be added or activated at any time during the server lifecycle without restarting the server. Even your own application code can be instrumented so that monitoring data can be collected.

Oracle has a comprehensive documentation on WLDF, but it looks like the complexity of WLDF is scaring a lot of potential users. This book does not want to replace the Oracle documentation at all. This book wants to use a pragmatic and practical approach. After an introduction to WLDF and the different components and structures, this book discusses the notion of so-called profiles with many practical examples. Based on these examples, the reader should be able to start quickly with WLDF diagnostic activities. This book has no intention of discussing all the features of WLDF in detail, as it is not a replacement of the official documentation. Instead, this book is intended to enable users to easily understand WLDF using the WebConsole, WLST, or JMX, and most importantly, to break the complexity of WLDF into small pieces and easy-to-understand examples.

This book is based on WLDF for WebLogic 12c. As there are differences between WebLogic 12.1.1, WebLogic 12.1.2, and WebLogic 12.1.3, a lot of effort has been made so that all scripts and programs run against all versions. Where appropriate,

WLS 12.1.2 and 12.1.3 extensions will be discussed in the book. All statements about features coming in versions 12.2.1 and beyond are based on actual information and are subject to change at any time as long as these versions are still under development by Oracle.

September 2014
Martin Heinzl
wldf_book@mh-enterpriseconsulting.de

Preface

Scope of this book

This book is all about the WebLogic Diagnostic framework (WLDF). The scope of this book is restricted to Oracle's WebLogic Server version 12.1.1, 12.1.2, 12.1.3, and above. If possible, upcoming features in 12.2.1 will be mentioned. The WLDF subsystem of WebLogic 10.3.x (especially 10.3.5 and 10.3.6) is very similar to WebLogic 12.1.1 and I was able to run all scripts I have tested without change to these versions as well, but no effort was made to verify all scripts and codes against 10.3.x versions.

The scripts and programs are specific to WebLogic, as WLDF is a WebLogic-specific subsystem. The applications detailed in this book serve as a guide for diagnostic and automation approaches for WebLogic, and the reader must understand that adapting the scripts provided in this book to products other than WebLogic is not possible.
Please note that this book is NOT only about automating WLDF. It is also a very good entry point for anybody who needs to learn about WLDF, as the first chapters introduce the main WLDF components step-by-step.

Prerequisites

In order to fully appreciate the contents book and all the scripts, a good working knowledge of WebLogic is required. WebLogic administration experience will also benefit the reader. The scripts presented within the book are written in the Jython programming language or in Java. Introductions to Jython and Java-JMX are out of scope of this book. Please see suggested readings as provided in the appendix.

How to read this book

This book is divided into 6 major parts. After an introduction, this book describes the principle concepts behind WLDF and its main components. After that, the book discusses different concepts of "Profiles," which really helps to leverage the power of WLDF. After a discussion about usage of the data gathered by WLDF, the last part will touch on the more advanced features of WLDF.

Part 1 is a very brief introduction to the main technologies beside WebLogic, which are Jython and JMX. Please refer to the appendix for suggestions on learning Jython and JMX. Please also see my book about WLST for a deep discussion about WLST.

Part 2 is a general discussion about WLDF and its architecture. The author discusses best practices and lessons learned in real situations, including how WLDF should be used to really benefit from its features. The second half of this section provides a high-level component overview and discusses the MBean structure of WLDF, as this knowledge is required in order to automate based on Jython or WLST.

Part 3 of the book discusses the main artifacts of WLDF. Starting from the diagnostic module and the archives, the following chapters will discuss everything needed in order to create common WLDF profiles. This part provides a good basic understanding sufficient to create and work with most profiles.

Part 4 of the book introduces the idea of WLDF profiles, which are very useful in structuring WLDF components and working with them in complex system environments.

Part 5 discusses possible ways to access, use, and visualize the data collected by WLDF. The main topics discussed here are the data accessor, the flight-recorder integration, and the dashboard

Part 6 is a discussion about advanced concepts around instrumentation and dye injection.

For readers new to WLDF, is it advisable to read the book section by section, as the sections are building on each other, meaning that later sections require the knowledge of previous sections. Advanced users can of course jump directly to the chapters of their interest.

Who should read this book?

WLDF offers benefits to all people involved with WebLogic, therefore everybody using WebLogic should benefit from this book. This book is primarily targeted to administrators, operators, and architects who have identified a need to use or automate WebLogic Server diagnostics and troubleshooting. This book is also meant to be read by developers and all people who have to do diagnostic every now and then, as the first part introduces the main WLDF components step-by-step and also explains how to configure those using the administration WebConsole.

Source Code and Scripts

Every effort has been taken to provide ready-to-run scripts and examples. Important note for all code examples: Please always make sure to change path names, server names, file locations and any other aspect which depends on your local machine prior to testing the scripts. This note applies to all code examples and there won't be a reminder at every code listing.

Acknowledgements

I would like to thank David Cabelus from the Oracle WebLogic Product Management Team who is responsible for the WLDF subsystem for this support.

I would like thank the company Oracle for granting me the permission to quote or use some listings of the official documentation, and especially for using one of the code libraries for component profiling.

Also I would like to thank Philip Aston and René van Wijk for the permission to use parts of their work for this book.

And also thanks to everybody helping me with the review.

Part I

Introduction and Technology Overview

Introduction to WLDF

Introduction

As this book is a about WLDF and therefore this chapter only provides a very brief overview over the WebLogic concepts. Please refer to the extensive WebLogic documentation from Oracle, all the different (administration) books or all the other websites and blogs which are available for a detailed introduction about WebLogic.

Introduction to WebLogic

WebLogic is a complex, professional application server environment with a complex and powerful security environment. WebLogic server at its core implements the J2EE specification stack and its main purpose is to offer a hosting environment for J2EE applications. But WebLogic is much more than that. Like most professional J2EE server WebLogic also offers a large number of extended features like comprehensive management, clustering and failover functionality on different levels, plus a number of extended enterprise features not required by J2EE but very useful in the enterprise world, enterprise features that are required by many companies.

A *domain* is the basic administration unit for WebLogic. This administration unit consists of one or more server instances and is managed by one of the server with a special role, the so called administration server (=AdminServer). This server hosts the management console and manages zero or more managed servers which may be hosted local to the AdminServer or remote on different physical machines. Managed servers may be grouped into cluster.

If managed servers are located on remote machines, separate NodeManager instances can be used for lifecycle operations (*start, stop,* and *monitor*). You can define multiple domains based on different system administrators' responsibilities. You may also (although this is definitely not recommended) use a single domain to manage and monitor all WebLogic Server instanced. The central configuration file is called *config.xml* and it will play a major role in the further understanding of the scripts and management tasks. This *config.xml* file is stored on the Administration Server together with other files such database configuration files and security files.

Each AdminServer manages exactly ONE domain and all changes or activities will only apply to this domain. Note that all the scripts and source code in this book runs against one AdminServer (unless states otherwise) and therefore targets one domain. For more information on domains, see e.g. the Oracle Documentation

Every domain must contain at least one the administration server. For development and testing this might be sufficient as this server can also host applications but this setup is strongly discouraged in production and production like systems.

Jython and WebLogic

The WebLogic Scripting Tool (WLST) is a toolkit that administrators and operators can use to monitor and manage WebLogic domains. It is based on the Java scripting interpreter Jython. WLST does not only offer WebLogic-specific scripting features. As it is based on Jython, it is also possible to use all common features of the Jython language like local variables, conditions, or flow statements. Administrators can extend WLST for their own needs by providing features, functions, and classes based on the Jython language syntax. Three different forms of executions are available: scripting, interactive, and embedded. WLST can be enabled for online and offline connection modes and can act as a JMX client.

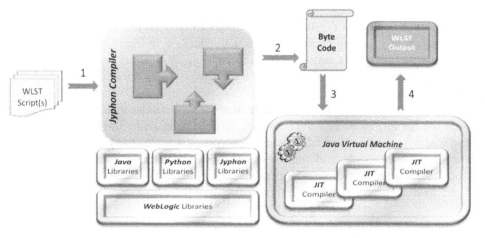

Figure 1.1: *Depiction of the Jython/WebLogic compilation process*

The source code for the WLST script is written as a Jython script. It is recommended that the WLST program file should have the file extension *.py*, which is the default extension for Jython/Python source code files. This source code is going to use a

JVM machine when it is instructed to RUN the script, and its invocation internally generates Java byte code to interpret the JVM to produce the desired output.

JMX and WebLogic

WebLogic makes heavily use of JMX. In fact, everything is organized in a different MBean server and different MBean trees. In sum, the WLST (WebLogic scripting environment) is just a Jython interface to the complex MBean structure (besides the other WLST features of course).

In order to understand the administration and monitoring of WLST, it is essential to understand the WLS MBean structures. It is also essential to understand the differences between Runtime- and Edit-MBeanServer and the concepts WebLogic is using for their JMX layer (Figure 1-1):

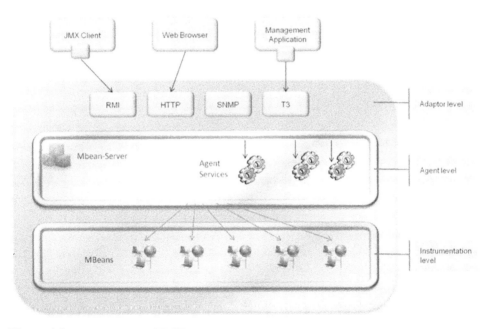

Figure 1.2: *Different levels of JMX*

Summary

WebLogic is the technology stack used for hosting J2EE applications. WebLogic consists of many different APIs and features for developers but also a rich set of features for administrators, which includes WLST based on Jython and JMX.

WLDF (WebLogic Diagnostic framework) is an integrated part of WebLogic. It can be configured and used by using either the WebLogic console or WLST scripting or JMX. All three approaches will be discussed throughout the rest of the book.

For a better understanding of the reach feature set provided by WLST and JMX, I recommend reading my book *Advanced WebLogic Server Automation* by Rampant TechPress.

Part II

WLDF Overview

The second part of the book discusses the main idea behind WLDF and provides architecture overviews and recommendations for how to work with WLDF.

WLDF Architecture and Components

WLDF Architecture and Components

The following chapter of the book provides an introduction into WLDF and the WLDF architecture. Our main goal is to provide an understanding of the overall architecture and the different parts of WLDF. As this book is oriented on practical use, this section also discusses the MBeans that are provided by WLDF.

Introduction to WLDF

The WLDF (WebLogic Diagnostic Framework) is an integrated framework in WebLogic that is used in order to collect, save and analyze runtime data for monitoring or troubleshooting. The WLDF provides a number of services which will be executed within the WebLogic server VM, and using these services, you will be able to gather information which will help you to get a detailed view into the runtime performance of our server instances and also inside the performance of deployed applications. In sum, WLDF is a very valuable tool for error location and diagnostic operations.

WLDF offers a set of features and configurations that can be composed from a number of components. One of them is the integration with JRockit which means that WLDF can add information to the JRockit Flight Recording file. The Capture Diagnostic Image function allows the administrator to record a live snapshot which can later be used to analyze problems. The archive feature capture and archives information. Code instrumentation allow the user to collect data at the time of specific operations. The harvester feature also allow the data collection from standard and custom MBeans. There is also a feature to send out notifications when certain events occur.

WLDF consists of the following components:

- Data creators
- Data collectors for the logger and the harvester components
- Archive component

- Accessor component

- Instrumentation component

- Watch and Notification component

- Image Capture component

- Monitoring Dashboard

Data creators collect diagnostic data which is then passed to the Logger and the Harvester components. The main *server state* can also be captured using the *image capture* component. The *logger* and the *harvester* use the *archive* feature in order to persist the collected information. In case there are *notifications* or *watched* configured, these components will also inform these parts of WLDF. In order to query and use the data, the *accessor* subsystem will be used.

The WebLogic Diagnostics Framework (WLDF) is provided by Oracle as an integrated set of components which offer powerful features for analysis and monitoring. Let's take a close look.

First, WLDF is a powerful subsystem of WebLogic. It is neither a separate product nor does it have to be installed separately. WLDF is integrated into WebLogic, and runs in each WebLogic server instance and provides components and APIs which enables the user to access runtime information from WebLogic MBeanServer.

Note that it does not provide access to the ConfigurationMBeans, only to the runtime MBeans. WLDF is not meant to be a tool for creating reports about the configuration. Instead, WLDF is targeted to work with runtime information. WLDF can be used to collect data from different MBeans or create state snapshots, and other WLDF components can perform certain analysis or actions based on the collected data. This data can be access via external tools or displayed using the integrated dashboard. The main goal of WLDF is it to provide access to insight information into the runtime state of servers and applications in order to monitor health or detect and analyze problem situations.

One very important aspect of WLDF is that the data collection can be started/stopped at any time without restarting the WebLogic instance. Furthermore, the amount of data (collector definitions) can be changed at any time without restarting the WebLogic instance.

WLDF Components

WLDF is a very powerful functional framework. The side effect is that the WLDF structure and component dependencies are quite complicated, by their very nature. The following simplified and higher level overview shows the main artifacts and components of WLDF.

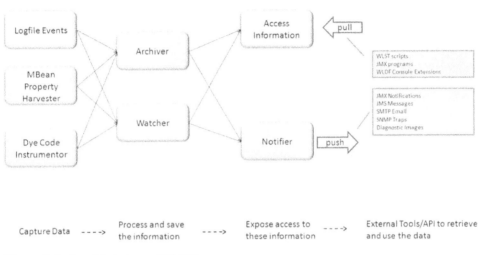

Figure 2.1: *Simplified view on WLDF*

(Based on the blog of Paul Done
http://pauldone.blogspot.com/feeds/posts/default)

WLDF consists of the following components:

- Data creators (basically the standard and custom MBeans available in WLS)
- Data collectors (the Logger and the Harvester components)
- Image Capture component
- Archive component
- Accessor component
- Instrumentation component
- Watch and Notification component
- Monitoring Dashboard

The Logger, Harvester (and also the image capture feature) collect and consume runtime information which is created by the different data creators. Normally data creators are the different runtime MBeans inside the runtime MBeanServer of the WebLogic instances. The collected data is used by the Archive component for persistence and by the *Watch* and *Notification* components for monitoring and analysis.

The data access subsystem communicates with the *harvester* and the *logger* for getting real time information and with the archive for historical data.

The WLDF Data Collectors

Many components in WebLogic are collecting runtime information simultaneously. As already mentioned the two major components which are important for WLDF are runtime MBeans (standard and custom MBeans) and also the WLDF's own instrumentation. It is impossible (or at least it would be very time consuming, and a waste of space) to collect all possible runtime data. The different data collectors in WLDF are designed to collect only the attributes and data which are important for your actual monitoring or investigation goal. The components which are used to gather the diagnostic data are called harvester and logger. In addition the diagnostic image feature can collect a complete snapshot.

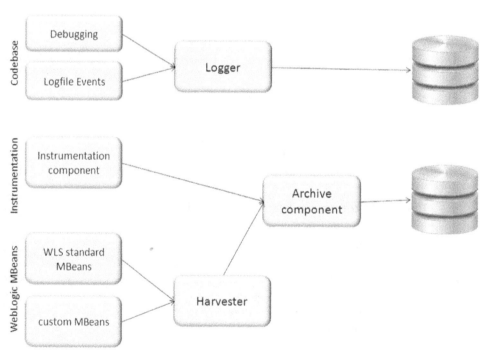

Figure 2.2: *Relationships between data collectors and data creators*

(http://docs.oracle.com/middleware/1212/wls/WLDFC/architecture.htm#i1083839)

Data Processing and Archiving

Because it is impossible for administrators to sit in front of many different screens, pressing *refresh* all the time so that they do not loose important data event, WLDF provides components which can analyze the data and react to certain predefined events. The notification and the watch subsystems of WLDF have to be configured if automated reactions on certain events are required. Reactions can be based on rules, which have to be configured in the WLDF configuration MBeans.

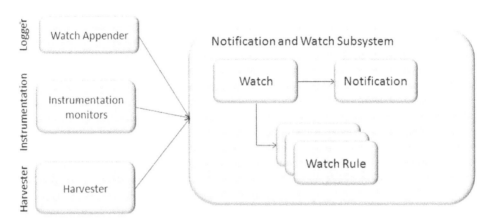

Figure 2.3: *Relationship between data collector and the watch/notification subsystem*

(http://docs.oracle.com/middleware/1212/wls/WLDFC/architecture.htm#i1083841)

It's important to note that every watch supports multiple notifications. Beside the default method (log entry in log file of the server) the four main management and messaging standards are also supported: JMX and SNMP management as well as JMS and SMTP messaging.

Data Access

Collecting data is the necessary prerequisite for monitoring and troubleshooting. But the data is useless unless it can be access and used by appropriate tools. The data accessor component is the subsystem of WLDF which implements access to all the data collected by WLDF. Two different flavors of data can be accessed. This includes historical data from the *archive* subsystem and runtime data from *harvester* metrics
.

The *data accessor* component provides different features required for data access. This includes filtering based on different strategies and also an offline access tools in case

---

data from an archive file is requested but this server instance is not running at the moment.

Complete Picture of WLDF

The following picture from the official oracle documentation shows the full complexity and dependency of the WLDF implementation and its various subsystems.

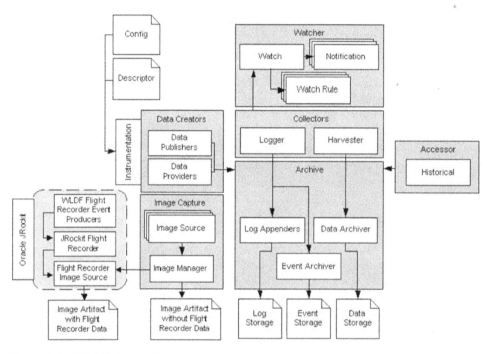

Figure 2.4: *WLDF Detail View*

(http://docs.oracle.com/middleware/1212/wls/WLDFC/architecture.htm#i1085986)

Target vs. Activation

Up to WebLogic release 12.1.1, WebLogic did not allow the administrator or user to target more than one diagnostic module to one single WLS server instance. Instead, the WLDF modules could be activated by targeting them to one or more server instances and deactivated by untarget them from all server instances.

With WLS 12.1.2 this has been changed and it is now possible to target multiple WLDF modules to any server instance. Oracle has added control actions to WLDF modules with allow the administrator to activate/deactivate the modules

Summary

As we have seen, the WLDF is a complex framework with offers a lot of components for collecting data, analyzing data, creating notifications based on conditions and much more. Due to this many features the internal structure in WebLogic which is based on JMX MBeans is rather complex. In order to use the power of WLDF automation it is important to understand the MBean structure.

Working with WLDF

Working with WLDF

Like any other technology framework, working with WLDF is not trivial and if it is done wrong you may have a massive impact on overall system behavior, stability and performance. The following guidelines are not based on recommendations from Oracle but are based on practical experiences from the author with WLDF.

General Guidelines to work with WLDF

Most of the projects and guidelines work and give good results, but this cannot be considered as a rule of thumbs. If we read the complete setup requirements and apply it carefully, there is no 100% guarantee on them because the setup for each project varies. This applies because every project, every setup and every application has different requirements for resources like threads, heap, connections, throughput and response times.

Starting with WebLogic 12.1.2 Oracle, has added built-in default WLDF modules which can be used out-of-the-box or which can be used as templates for own WLDF diagnostic modules.

In general, WLDF is a data collection and analyzing framework. Collection data and persisting data have allows a performance and resource penalty. Therefore it must be carefully considered, which data will be collected, which data will be persisted and how long this persisted data must be kept. Especially with instrumentation it might be possible that the data collector will see business critical and confidential data which otherwise would be invisible for administrators. Security aspects w.r.t. data access must also be considered.

WLDF Profiles

A very useful approach (which will be discussed in detail later in this book) is it to define a set of diagnostic modules. Throughout this book we will call them "profiles". This is not WLDF terminology and could also be called a "setup", "collection" or

---

"library". A profile in this context a collection of WLDF configuration artifacts (harvester, watches, notifications, archives and others) which together allow the collection and analysis of certain data artifacts.

Possible profiles my include "Web Application profile", "Enterprise (EJB) profile", "Integration profile", "Messaging profile", "data access profile", "internal server profile", "application profile" or any other special compilation of WLDF artifacts depending on the nature of your application and environment setup. It is recommended to not create comprehensive profiles. It is better to create multiple, specialized profiles.

From experience it is absolutely recommended to provide profiles always with automated setup routines written in WLST or JMX. It is also advisable to provide scripts or programs which may create new profiles as a combination out of existing profiles. It is also advisable to create automations to activate (target) and deactivate (un-target) profiles. All of these activities will be discussed later in detail.

Lifecycle of WLDF Artifacts

In production and production like systems data collection usually either happens all the time if the user wants to continuous monitoring or must capture immediately in case of error situations. In both cases the WLDF configurations must be available all the time. In case of development systems, monitoring will change constantly over time depending on actual development and actual issues.

Production and production-like systems:

- In production systems it is highly recommended that we create all WLDF diagnostic modules at a well-defined point-in-time without activating (target to one or more servers. This will dramatically speed up the process in case monitoring and data collection is needed. In this case only a target command via WLST or Web Console (or JMX) is needed.

- The setup of diagnostic modules and all WLDF configurations must be done via WLST or JMX in order to do it in an automated and repeatable way.

- It is highly recommended that we remove all WLDF diagnostic modules as soon as they are no longer needed by the application.

Development systems

- In development systems monitoring and diagnostic is far more common and changes happen more often. Therefore it is often just the best way to define the WLDF components using the WLS console and do your diagnostic on the fly.

- It is recommended to use the "WLST record" functionality in order to record the setup steps you are doing. This helps to re-setup a WLDF modules much quicker and it also helps to share common and useful WLDF modules among other developers.

- Also in development environments it is recommended to delete all WLDF modules which will not be used any more.

Summary

Working day to day with WebLogic in all stages of the lifecycle has shown the importance of high quality monitoring and analysis tools. All tools - especially in production systems - have to be used carefully. This section has provided proven guidelines based on practical experiences.

Starting with WebLogic 12.1.2 it is recommended - especially for beginners - to have a look at the built-in WLDF modules as those might be sufficient for your need.

Configuration and Usage

Configuration and Usage

WLDF is an out-of-the-box tool that is available with WebLogic. Nevertheless, there are a number of different ways to configure and use WLDF. Configuration can be done via the WebLogic console, using automated scripts (WLST) and programs (JMX) and also by doing direct configuration in the WebLogic XML configuration files. The data created and collected by WLDF can be used either with the integrated Dashboard combing with WebLogic, by using MissionControl or other tools which get notifications or collect data using one of the various APIs.

Using the WLS Console

The most obvious way to configure WLDF is with the WebLogic console, and every configuration activity can be done using the WebLogic console. As we have already mention, these configurations will be lost when the domain gets deleted but for a short test period, using the WebLogic console is a very useful approach. Regardless which approach is used, the WebLogic console is very useful to verify and control if all of the settings are done and activated as needed.

Figure 4.1: *Sections in the WebLogic home area dedicated to WLDF*

A whole section in the domain structure view is dedicated to WLDF and diagnostics, and all of the settings can be found within these sub trees.

The following screenshot shows an example of the configuration of a harvester section of one diagnostic module:

Figure 4.2: *Example of a harvester configuration*

Using the Dashboard

While the WebLogic console can be used to define the diagnostic modules (the WLDF profiles), it is not meant to display the data. WebLogic is equipped with an integrated dashboard in order to display WLDF recorded data. The dashboard can be reached from the home screen by selecting "Monitoring dashboard".

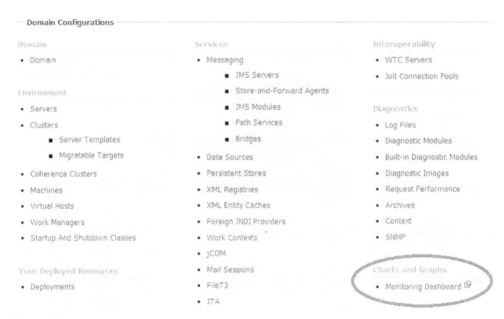

Figure 4.3: *Using the Dashboard*

The dashboard comes with a number of built-in views, but of course own views can be added, depending on your own project needs.

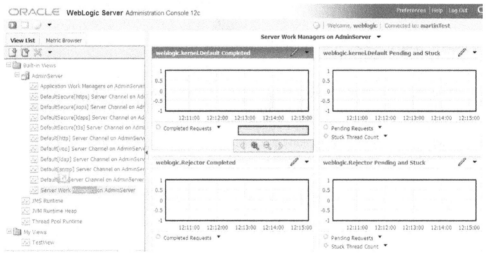

Figure 4.4: *WebLogic dashboard, with one of the built-in views*

Using WLST / JMX

The most common usage of WLDF is with automated processes based on WLST or JMX. WLST is the best choice for administrators who want to setup WLDF configurations, activate or deactivate them or modify configurations. It is script-based and therefore easier to use than JMX.

For automated environment setup based on java or even for tools setting up WLDF configurations on-the-fly as needed it is better to use the JMX API directly from java code. For main focus of this book will be on WLST and JMX.

The following script create a simple WLDF module. The different steps will be discussed in detail in the subsequent chapters.

```
# connect to the admin server
connect(...)

# switch to edit mode and start editing
edit()
startEdit()

# change to the diagnostic module with the name "HarvesterTest"
cd('/WLDFSystemResources/HarvesterTest/WLDFResource/HarvesterTest/Harvester/HarvesterTest')

# create a metric for the mbean type JVMRuntimeMBean
cmo.createHarvestedType('weblogic.management.runtime.JVMRuntimeMBean')

# change to metric MBean
cd('/WLDFSystemResources/HarvesterTest/WLDFResource/HarvesterTest/Harvester/HarvesterTest/HarvestedTy
pes/weblogic.management.runtime.JVMRuntimeMBean')

# configure which attributes (2 in this exampel) should be harvested
set('HarvestedAttributes',jarray.array([String('HeapFreePercent'), String('HeapSizeMax')], String))

# configure on which WebLogic server instances this metric should be executed
set('HarvestedInstances',jarray.array([String('com.bea:Name=MS1,ServerRuntime=MS1,Type=JVMRuntime'),
String('com.bea:Name=MS2,ServerRuntime=MS2,Type=JVMRuntime')], String))

# finally set the MBeanServer to be used (usually always ServerRuntime)
cmo.setNamespace('ServerRuntime')

# save and activate the changes
save()
activate()
```

Using the Configuration Files

Because all of the configuration items are saved in the config.xml file of the domain or in separate XML files which are referenced by the *config.xml* file of the domain, it is also possible to modify the XML files directly.

We strictly discourage you from doing this for the following reasons:

- **It is error-prone:** and errors will not be detected until WLS restarts and a restart of the AdminServer with errors in the configuration file in almost all cases results in a server which cannot restart.
- **Hard to debug:** Mis-configurations are hard to find as there are no checks. If done over the WLS console, the console does some checking for you.
- **Domain must be offline:** The domain must be offline and the user must have access to the machine where the AdminServer is running and must have write access to the domain folders on the file system.
- **Errors:** Syntax may change in every WebLogic version which may lead to errors in your setup.

Example configuration for a simple WLDF module. As you can already see, the XML notation is not easy to create or modify by hand.

```
<wldf-system-resource>
  <name>HarvesterTest</name>
  <descriptor-file-name>diagnostics/HarvesterTest-7992.xml</descriptor-file-name>
  <description></description>
</wldf-system-resource>
```

In the file diagnostics/HarvesterTest-7992.xml which in this case ist he outsourced configuration fort he diagnostic module (note: not only the harvester):

```
<?xml version='1.0' encoding='UTF-8'?>
<wldf-resource xmlns="http://xmlns.oracle.com/weblogic/weblogic-diagnostics"
xmlns:sec="http://xmlns.oracle.com/weblogic/security"
xmlns:wls="http://xmlns.oracle.com/weblogic/security/wls"
xmlns:xsi="http://www.w3.org/2001/XMLSchema-instance"
xsi:schemaLocation="http://xmlns.oracle.com/weblogic/weblogic-diagnostics
http://xmlns.oracle.com/weblogic/weblogic-diagnostics/1.0/weblogic-diagnostics.xsd">
  <name>HarvesterTest</name>
  <harvester>
    <harvested-type>
      <name>weblogic.management.runtime.JVMRuntimeMBean</name>
      <harvested-attribute>HeapFreePercent</harvested-attribute>
      <harvested-attribute>HeapSizeMax</harvested-attribute>
      <harvested-instance>com.bea:Name=MS1,ServerRuntime=MS1,Type=JVMRuntime</harvested-instance>
      <harvested-instance>com.bea:Name=MS2,ServerRuntime=MS2,Type=JVMRuntime</harvested-instance>
      <namespace>ServerRuntime</namespace>
    </harvested-type>
  </harvester>
</wldf-resource>
```

Summary

WLDF is a powerful and comprehensive framework which offers many ways to use it. Depending on the environment some methods are more useful than others. In production and production like systems only automated technologies based on WLST and JMX should be used. In no situations the author can recommend editing the configuration files directly.

Understanding
WLDF MBeans

WLDF MBeans

The following chapter discusses the different MBeans which WebLogic uses in order to represent the different WLDF configuration artifacts. Due to the complexity of WLDF, WebLogic uses a rather complex system of MBeans. Understanding this structure is essential for any automation of WLDF.

Introduction to the WLDF MBeans

Every configuration item in WebLogic as well as all runtime state is represented as a JMX managed bean (MBean). The same also applied for every aspect of the WLDF configuration. The configuration MBeans are stored in the domain configuration and/or in outsourced additional xml files which are referenced in the main config.xml file. Whenever you create WLDF artifacts by either running WLST scripts, running JMX programs or creating configuration items using the WLS Console, WebLogic will create configuration MBeans. Even if you edit the config.xml files directly WLS will create MBeans after the admin server has been restarted.

WLDF MBean Types

WLDF is a feature rich diagnostic module. Each feature itself may have a number of possible configurations. WLDF acknowledge this by structuring the configuration into many different MBean-types, which allows an easier usage and configuration. The following list will provide only the names of the different MBean types used for the WLDF framework.

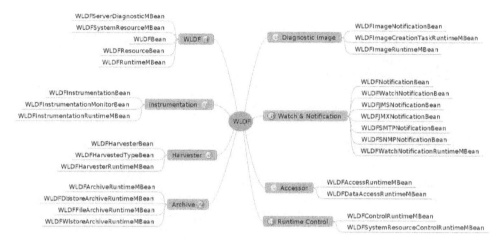

Figure 5.1: *WLDF MBeans grouped by subsystem type*

Core WLDF system:
>   WLDFBean, WLDFServerDiagnosticMBean, WLDFSystemResourceMBean,
>   WLDFResourceBean, WLDFRuntimeMBean

Diagnostic Image subsystem:
>   WLDFImageNotificationBean, WLDFImageCreationTaskRuntimeMBean,
>   WLDFImageRuntimeMBean

Instrumentation subsystem:
>   WLDFInstrumentationBean, WLDFInstrumentationMonitorBean,
>   WLDFInstrumentationRuntimeMBean

Harvester subsystem:
>   WLDFHarvesterBean, WLDFHarvestedTypeBean,
>   WLDFHarvesterRuntimeMBean

Watch & Notification subsystem:
>   WLDFNotificationBean, WLDFWatchNotificationBean,
>   WLDFJMSNotificationBean, WLDFJMXNotificationBean,
>   WLDFSMTPNotificationBean, WLDFSNMPNotificationBean,
>   WLDFWatchNotificationRuntimeMBean, JMXWatchNotification,
>   WatchNotification

Archive subsystem:
>   WLDFArchiveRuntimeMBean, WLDFDbstoreArchiveRuntimeMBean,
>   WLDFFileArchiveRuntimeMBean, WLDFWlstoreArchiveRuntimeMBean

Data Accessor subsystem:
WLDFAccessRuntimeMBean, WLDFDataAccessRuntimeMBean

Runtime Control subsystem:
WLDFControlRuntimeMBean, WLDFSystemResourceControlRuntimeMBean

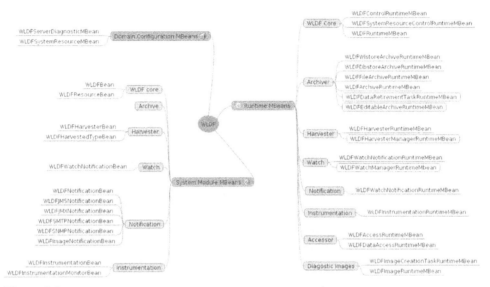

Figure 5.2: *WLDF MBeans grouped by function (configuration / runtime)*

All these MBeans are organized in a hierarchical fashion, and Figure 8.2 shows the hierarchy. Understanding the hierarchy make is much easier to navigate using the interactive WLST shell mode or writing JMX programs. Users who intend to use the WLS console only do not benefit much from the hierarchy as the WLS console hides the complexity.

For a complete reference to all these MBeans please consult the Oracle documentation. The following section will only provide a brief description of the most important MBean types.

Browsing WLDF using the WLST shell

The following example will show how to navigate in such a WLDF structure using the interactive WLST mode. While browsing MBeans the user has to distinguish if he wants to browse the configuration part of WLDF or the runtime part of WLDF.

Browsing the Configuration tree

The configuration MBean tree is being used in order to create WLDF artifacts, look at the configuration or change it.

After the connection to the WebLogic server, it is important to switch to the configuration MBean tree

```
connect('weblogic','<pw>','<url>')
serverConfig()
```

The WLDF configuration can be found under the WLDFSystemResources subtree:

```
# change to the WLDFSystemResources' subtree
cd ('WLDFSystemResources')
# change to your diagnostic module (unless you want to create a new one)
cd ('TestModule')
```

Now you have reached the root of your diagnostic module. From here, you can inspect, change, add or delete resources, sub deployments and targets. Note that the "Resource" and "WLDFResource" subtrees are identical.

```
wls:/testdomain/serverConfig/WLDFSystemResources/TestModule> ls()
dr--   Resource
dr--   SubDeployments
dr--   Targets
dr--   WLDFResource

-r--   CompatibilityName                      null
-r--   DeploymentOrder                        100
-r--   DeploymentPrincipalName                null
-r--   Description
-r--   DescriptorFileName                     diagnostics/TestModule.xml
-r--   DynamicallyCreated                     false
-r--   Id                                     0
-r--   ModuleType                             null
-r--   Name                                   TestModule
-r--   Notes                                  null
-r--   SourcePath                             ./config/diagnostics/TestModule.xml
-r--   Type                                   WLDFSystemResource

-r-x   freezeCurrentValue                     Void : String(attributeName)
-r-x   getInheritedProperties                 String[] : String[](propertyNames)
-r-x   isInherited                            Boolean : String(propertyName)
-r-x   isSet                                  Boolean : String(propertyName)
-r-x   unSet                                  Void : String(propertyName)
```

Now let us switch to the resources section and examine the configured resources:

```
cd ('WLDFResource/TestModule')
ls()
dr--   Harvester
dr--   Instrumentation
dr--   WatchNotification

-r--   Id                                     0
-r--   Name                                   TestModule
```

As you can see the resource section is the WLST root for all harvester, instrumentation, watches and notification configurations.

First of all let us examine the harvester section. You will see that the harvester root allows you to enable the complete harvester and define a sampling interval:

```
cd('Harvester/TestModule')
ls()
dr--    HarvestedTypes

-r--    Enabled                              true
-r--    Id                                   0
-r--    Name                                 TestModule
-r--    SamplePeriod                         60000
```

You can also list the configured harvester types:

```
cd ('WLDFResource/TestModule/Harvester/TestModule/HarvestedTypes')
ls()
dr--    weblogic.management.runtime.EJBCacheRuntimeMBean
dr--    weblogic.management.runtime.EJBLockingRuntimeMBean
dr--    weblogic.management.runtime.EJBPoolRuntimeMBean
dr--    weblogic.management.runtime.EJBTimerRuntimeMBean
dr--    weblogic.management.runtime.EJBTransactionRuntimeMBean
dr--    weblogic.management.runtime.JDBCDataSourceRuntimeMBean
dr--    weblogic.management.runtime.JMSConnectionRuntimeMBean
dr--    weblogic.management.runtime.JMSConsumerRuntimeMBean
dr--    weblogic.management.runtime.JMSDestinationRuntimeMBean
dr--    weblogic.management.runtime.JMSProducerRuntimeMBean
dr--    weblogic.management.runtime.JMSRuntimeMBean
dr--    weblogic.management.runtime.JRockitRuntimeMBean
dr--    weblogic.management.runtime.JTARecoveryRuntimeMBean
dr--    weblogic.management.runtime.JTARuntimeMBean
dr--    weblogic.management.runtime.JVMRuntimeMBean
dr--    weblogic.management.runtime.MessageDrivenEJBRuntimeMBean
dr--    weblogic.management.runtime.QueryCacheRuntimeMBean
dr--    weblogic.management.runtime.ServerRuntimeMBean
dr--    weblogic.management.runtime.ThreadPoolRuntimeMBean
dr--    weblogic.management.runtime.TransactionResourceRuntimeMBean
dr--    weblogic.management.runtime.WebAppComponentRuntimeMBean
dr--    weblogic.management.runtime.WorkManagerRuntimeMBean
```

The interesting information is of course configured for each harvester type. You can either *cd* into each type and do a list or just list them directly in UNIX/Linux:

```
ls('weblogic.management.runtime.EJBCacheRuntimeMBean')

-r--    Enabled                              true
-r--    HarvestedAttributes
java.lang.String[ActivationCount, CacheAccessCount, CachedBeansCurrentCount,
CacheMissCount, PassivationCount]
-r--    HarvestedInstances                   null
-r--    Id                                   0
```

```
-r--    KnownType                               false
-r--    Name
weblogic.management.runtime.EJBCacheRuntimeMBean
-r--    Namespace                               ServerRuntime


ls ('weblogic.management.runtime.JMSRuntimeMBean')

-r--    Enabled                                 true
-r--    HarvestedAttributes
java.lang.String[ConnectionsCurrentCount, ConnectionsTotalCount]
-r--    HarvestedInstances                      null
-r--    Id                                      0
-r--    KnownType                               false
-r--    Name
weblogic.management.runtime.JMSRuntimeMBean
-r--    Namespace                               ServerRuntime


ls ('weblogic.management.runtime.JTARuntimeMBean')

-r--    Enabled                                 true
-r--    HarvestedAttributes
java.lang.String[ActiveTransactionsTotalCount, SecondsActiveTotalCount,
TransactionAbandonedTotalCount, TransactionCommittedTotalCount,
TransactionHeuristicsTotalCount, TransactionRolledBackTotalCount,
TransactionTotalCount]
-r--    HarvestedInstances                      null
-r--    Id                                      0
-r--    KnownType                               false
-r--    Name
weblogic.management.runtime.JTARuntimeMBean
-r--    Namespace                               ServerRuntime
```

Now we will switch from the harvester configuration to the instrumentation configuration of this diagnostic module:

```
cd ('/WLDFSystemResources/TestModule/WLDFResource/TestModule')
cd ('Instrumentation/TestModule')
ls()
dr--    WLDFInstrumentationMonitors

-r--    Enabled                                 false
-r--    Excludes                                null
-r--    Id                                      0
-r--    Includes                                null
-r--    Name                                    TestModule
```

The last section of the resources contains the different watch and notification configurations.

```
cd ('/WLDFSystemResources/TestModule/WLDFResource/TestModule')
cd (WatchNotifications/TestModule')
ls()
dr--    ImageNotifications
dr--    JMSNotifications
```

```
dr--    JMXNotifications
dr--    Notifications
dr--    SMTPNotifications
dr--    SNMPNotifications
dr--    Watches

-r--    Enabled                             false
-r--    Id                                  0
-r--    LogWatchSeverity                    Warning
-r--    Name                                TestModule
-r--    Severity                            Notice
```

The subtree "Watches" contains all the watch configurations, including rule expressions, rule types and more.

```
cd ('Watches')
ls()
dr--    SERVER.HOGGING.THREADCOUNT
dr--    SERVER.JVM.PROCESSORLOAD
dr--    SERVER.LOG.SEVERITY
dr--    SERVER.PENDING.USER.REQUESTCOUNT
dr--    SERVER.WORKMANAGER.STUCKTHREAD
```

You can again either navigate into each watch for further actions or you can just list them for investigations.

```
ls('SERVER.HOGGING.THREADCOUNT')
dr--    Notifications

-r--    AlarmResetPeriod                    60000
-r--    AlarmType                           None
-r--    Enabled                             true
-r--    Id                                  0
-r--    Name
SERVER.HOGGING.THREADCOUNT
-r--    RuleExpression
${ServerRuntime//[weblogic.management.runtime.ThreadPoolRuntimeMBean]//Hoggi
ngThreadCount} >= 10
-r--    RuleType                            Harvester
-r--    Severity                            Notice


ls('SERVER.JVM.PROCESSORLOAD')
dr--    Notifications

-r--    AlarmResetPeriod                    60000
-r--    AlarmType                           None
-r--    Enabled                             true
-r--    Id                                  0
-r--    Name                                SERVER.JVM.PROCESSORLOAD
-r--    RuleExpression
${ServerRuntime//[weblogic.management.runtime.JRockitRuntimeMBean]//JvmProce
ssorLoad} >= 70
-r--    RuleType                            Harvester
-r--    Severity                            Notice
```

The last section of the resource tree are the different notifications. The resource root node has again subtrees for all kind of supported notifications.

You can either list all available notifications (sub-tree "Notifications") or you can list type specific subsets (see the different type specific subtrees).

List the "Notification" subfolder in WLST in order to get a list of all available notifications:

```
# change to the notifications section
cd ('/WLDFSystemResources/TestModule/WLDFResource/TestModule')
cd (WatchNotifications/TestModule')

# list all notifications
ls('Notifications')
dr--    MailNotification
dr--    SERVER.PROFILE
```

First we will look at the JMX notifications. This again can be done by either changing into the directory or by just list the content.

```
cd ('/WLDFSystemResources/TestModule/WLDFResource/TestModule')
cd (WatchNotifications/TestModule')

cd ('JMXNotifications')
ls()
dr--    SERVER.PROFILE


# list the content of this notification
cd ('SERVER.PROFILE')
s()

-r--    Enabled                          true
-r--    Id                               0
-r--    Name                             SERVER.PROFILE
-r--    NotificationType
weblogic.diagnostics.watch.defaultNotificationType
```

As another example, let's look at the configuration of an email notification. You will see that this type has different settings. As we will discuss in the notification chapter, this notification requires that an email session has been configured on WebLogic level.

```
cd ('/WLDFSystemResources/TestModule')
cd('WLDFResource/TestModule/WatchNotification/TestModule')
ls('SMTPNotifications')

dr--    MailNotification
```

```
cd ('Notifications/MailNotification')
ls()

-r--    Body                                        This is your desired
notification
-r--    Enabled                                     true
-r--    Id                                          0
-r--    MailSessionJNDIName                         mail/TestMailSession
-r--    Name                                        MailNotification
-r--    Recipients
java.lang.String[wldf@mh-enterpriseconsulting.de]
-r--    Subject                                     WLDF Test Notification
```

Browsing the Runtime tree:

The runtime MBean tree is being used in order to get WLDF runtime information. In order to browse the runtime it is necessary to switch to the runtime MBean environment. Note that WebLogic is using a different MBeanServer for configuration and runtime information.

```
# switch to the runtime environment
serverRuntime()

# change to the WLDF runtime environment
cd ('WLDFRuntime/WLDFRuntime')

ls ()
dr--    WLDFAccessRuntime
dr--    WLDFArchiveRuntimes
dr--    WLDFControlRuntime
dr--    WLDFHarvesterRuntime
dr--    WLDFImageRuntime
dr--    WLDFInstrumentationRuntimes
dr--    WLDFWatchNotificationRuntime

-r--    Name                                        WLDFRuntime
-r--    Type                                        WLDFRuntime

-r-x    preDeregister                               Void :
```

As you can see WebLogic offers a number of runtime section for WLDF related information.

The archive section is related to the diagnostic archives and provide further details about the different archives used in WLDF.

```
ls ('WLDFArchiveRuntimes')

dr--    DataSourceLog
dr--    DomainLog
dr--    EventsDataArchive
```

```
dr--    HTTPAccessLog
dr--    HarvestedDataArchive
dr--    ServerLog
```

One possible archive is the server log file (we will discuss details when we explore the log archives later in the book)

```
ls ('WLDFArchiveRuntimes/ServerLog')

-r--    IncrementalIndexCycleCount              0
-r--    IncrementalIndexTime                    0
-r--    IndexCycleCount                         0
-r--    IndexTime                               0
-r--    Name                                    ServerLog
-r--    RecordRetrievalTime                     0
-r--    RecordSeekCount                         0
-r--    RecordSeekTime                          0
-r--    RetrievedRecordCount                    0
-r--    RotatedFilesCount                       0
-r--    Type                                    WLDFFileArchiveRuntime

-r-x    preDeregister                           Void :
```

One of the most important archives is the harvester archive which will be used to store harvester events

```
ls ('WLDFArchiveRuntimes/HarvestedDataArchive')

-r--    DataRetirementCycles                    0
-r--    DataRetirementTotalTime                 0
-r--    DeletionCount                           0
-r--    DeletionTime                            0
-r--    IndexPageCount                          0
-r--    InsertionCount                          0
-r--    InsertionTime                           0
-r--    LastDataRetirementStartTime             0
-r--    LastDataRetirementTime                  0
-r--    Name                                    HarvestedDataArchive
-r--    RecordCount                             0
-r--    RecordRetrievalTime                     0
-r--    RecordSeekCount                         0
-r--    RecordSeekTime                          0
-r--    RetiredRecordCount                      0
-r--    RetrievedRecordCount                    0
-r--    Type
WLDFWlstoreArchiveRuntime

-r-x    performDataRetirement                   WebLogicMBean :
-r-x    performRetirement                       WebLogicMBean :
-r-x    preDeregister                           Void :
```

It is for example possible to get information about the time used to insert data or to retrieve data. This will also offer information about the amount of data records and more.

The second section of the runtime information provides information about the system resources or to be precise about the usage of system resources

This section has the two subsections HarvesterManagerRuntime and WatchManagerRuntime.

```
ls('WLDFControlRuntime/AdminServer/SystemResourceControls/TestModule')
dr--    HarvesterManagerRuntime
dr--    WatchManagerRuntime

-rw-    Enabled                                         false
-r--    Name                                            TestModule
-r--    Type
WLDFSystemResourceControlRuntime
```

The HarvesterManagerRuntime provides information about timing, about the amount of sampling cycles and the amount of data.

```
ls('WLDFControlRuntime/AdminServer/SystemResourceControls/TestModule/Harvest
erManagerRuntime/TestModule')

-r--    AverageSamplingTime                             0
-r--    CurrentDataSampleCount                          0
-r--    CurrentSnapshotElapsedTime                      0
-r--    CurrentSnapshotStartTime                        -1
-r--    MaximumSamplingTime                             0
-r--    MinimumSamplingTime                             0
-r--    Name                                            TestModule
-r--    TotalDataSampleCount                            0
-r--    TotalSamplingCycles                             0
-r--    TotalSamplingTime                               0
-r--    Type
WLDFHarvesterManagerRuntime
```

The WatchManagerRuntime provides information about notification timing, about the amount of alarms and as an interesting value about the amount of successful/total and failed.

```
ls('WLDFControlRuntime/AdminServer/SystemResourceControls/TestModule/WatchMa
nagerRuntime/TestModule')

-r--    ActiveAlarmWatches                              null
-r--    AverageEventDataWatchEvaluationTime             0
-r--    AverageHarvesterWatchEvaluationTime             0
-r--    AverageLogWatchEvaluationTime                   0
-r--    CurrentActiveAlarmsCount                        0
-r--    MaximumActiveAlarmsCount                        0
-r--    MaximumEventDataWatchEvaluationTime             0
```

```
-r--    MaximumHarvesterWatchEvaluationTime           0
-r--    MaximumLogWatchEvaluationTime                 0
-r--    MinimumEventDataWatchEvaluationTime           0
-r--    MinimumHarvesterWatchEvaluationTime           0
-r--    MinimumLogWatchEvaluationTime                 0
-r--    Name                                          TestModule
-r--    TotalActiveAutomaticResetAlarms               0
-r--    TotalActiveManualResetAlarms                  0
-r--    TotalDIMGNotificationsPerformed               0
-r--    TotalEventDataEvaluationCycles                0
-r--    TotalEventDataWatchEvaluations                0
-r--    TotalEventDataWatchesTriggered                0
-r--    TotalFailedDIMGNotifications                  0
-r--    TotalFailedJMSNotifications                   0
-r--    TotalFailedJMXNotifications                   0
-r--    TotalFailedNotifications                      0
-r--    TotalFailedSMTPNotifications                  0
-r--    TotalFailedSNMPNotifications                  0
-r--    TotalHarvesterEvaluationCycles                0
-r--    TotalHarvesterWatchEvaluations                0
-r--    TotalHarvesterWatchesTriggered                0
-r--    TotalJMSNotificationsPerformed                0
-r--    TotalJMXNotificationsPerformed                0
-r--    TotalLogEvaluationCycles                      0
-r--    TotalLogWatchEvaluations                      0
-r--    TotalLogWatchesTriggered                      0
-r--    TotalNotificationsPerformed                   0
-r--    TotalSMTPNotificationsPerformed               0
-r--    TotalSNMPNotificationsPerformed               0
-r--    Type                                          WLDFWatchManagerRuntime
```

The next section in the runtime information has detailed information about the harvester engine.

```
ls('WLDFHarvesterRuntime/WLDFHarvesterRuntime')

-r--    AttributeInfoForAllTypes                      {…}
-r--    AverageSamplingTime                           0
-r--    CurrentDataSampleCount                        0
-r--    CurrentSampleTimeAnOutlier                    false
-r--    CurrentSnapshotElapsedTime                    0
-r--    CurrentSnapshotStartTime                      -1
-r--    InstancesForAllTypes                          { … }
-r--    KnownHarvestableTypes                         java.lang.String[…]
-r--    MaximumSamplingTime                           0
-r--    MinimumSamplingTime                           0
-r--    Name                                          WLDFHarvesterRuntime
-r--    OutlierDetectionFactor                        0.0
-r--    SamplePeriod                                  0
-r--    TotalDataSampleCount                          0
-r--    TotalSamplingCycles                           0
-r--    TotalSamplingTime                             0
-r--    TotalSamplingTimeOutlierCount                 0
-r-x    getCurrentlyHarvestedAttributes               String[] : String(type)
-r-x    getCurrentlyHarvestedInstances                String[] : String(type)
-r-x    getHarvestableAttributes                      [[Ljava.lang.String; :
String(type)
```

```
-r-x    getHarvestableAttributesForInstance          [[Ljava.lang.String; :
String(instancePattern)
-r-x    getHarvestableType                           String :
String(instanceName)
-r-x    getKnownHarvestableInstances                 String[] : String(type)
```

This actually contains lists of all known harvester types and even all attributes. The "…" are quite large lists and have been removed from the listing for easier reading.

The next section of the runtime information is related to diagnostic images. There are also operations available for you to trigger an image creation using a WSLT operation (or via a JMX program).

```
ls('WLDFImageRuntime/Image')

-r--    Name                                         Image
-r--    Type                                         WLDFImageRuntime

-r-x    captureImage                                 WebLogicMBean :
-r-x    captureImage                                 WebLogicMBean :
Integer(lockoutMinutes)
-r-x    captureImage                                 WebLogicMBean :
String(destination)
-r-x    captureImage                                 WebLogicMBean :
String(destination),Integer(lockoutMinutes)
-r-x    clearCompletedImageCaptureTasks              Void :
-r-x    listImageCaptureTasks                        WebLogicMBean[] :
-r-x    resetImageLockout                            Void :
```

The last section is dedicated to watches and notifications and has very similar information as the system control section we have seen earlier

```
ls('WLDFWatchNotificationRuntime/WatchNotification')
dr--    WLDFWatchJMXNotificationRuntime
dr--    WLDFWatchJMXNotificationSource

-r--    ActiveAlarmWatches                           null
-r--    AverageEventDataWatchEvaluationTime          0
-r--    AverageHarvesterWatchEvaluationTime          0
-r--    AverageLogWatchEvaluationTime                0
-r--    CurrentActiveAlarmsCount                     0
-r--    MaximumActiveAlarmsCount                     0
-r--    MaximumEventDataWatchEvaluationTime          0
-r--    MaximumHarvesterWatchEvaluationTime          0
-r--    MaximumLogWatchEvaluationTime                0
-r--    MinimumEventDataWatchEvaluationTime          0
-r--    MinimumHarvesterWatchEvaluationTime          0
-r--    MinimumLogWatchEvaluationTime                0
-r--    Name                                         WatchNotification
-r--    TotalActiveAutomaticResetAlarms              0
-r--    TotalActiveManualResetAlarms                 0
-r--    TotalDIMGNotificationsPerformed              0
-r--    TotalEventDataEvaluationCycles               0
-r--    TotalEventDataWatchEvaluations               0
```

```
-r--    TotalEventDataWatchesTriggered          0
-r--    TotalFailedDIMGNotifications            0
-r--    TotalFailedJMSNotifications             0
-r--    TotalFailedJMXNotifications             0
-r--    TotalFailedNotifications                0
-r--    TotalFailedSMTPNotifications            0
-r--    TotalFailedSNMPNotifications            0
-r--    TotalHarvesterEvaluationCycles          0
-r--    TotalHarvesterWatchEvaluations          0
-r--    TotalHarvesterWatchesTriggered          0
-r--    TotalJMSNotificationsPerformed          0
-r--    TotalJMXNotificationsPerformed          0
-r--    TotalLogEvaluationCycles                0
-r--    TotalLogWatchEvaluations                0
-r--    TotalLogWatchesTriggered                0
-r--    TotalNotificationsPerformed             0
-r--    TotalSMTPNotificationsPerformed         0
-r--    TotalSNMPNotificationsPerformed         0
```

The above listing is provided as examples for you so that you will be enabled to have a look around the MBean tree and familiarize yourself with the WLDF structure and data. Note that this will look differently in each WLS domain as all the above listings depend on the WLDF configuration done on your domain.

Additional WLST commands for WLDF

Starting with WebLogic 12.1.2, additional WLST commands have been added for WLDF support. The following table just lists the different WLDF commands which are available for WLST.

WLST command	Description
captureAndSaveDiagnosticImage	Combines several steps into one. This command will capture the image and also download it to the local machine
createSystemResourceControl	Allows the administrator to create a new system resource. This command will operate with a descriptor file which has to be provided
destroySystemResourceControl	Opposite action to the previous one. It will enable the administrator to delete a system control
disableSystemResource	This command will deactivate a diagnostic resource. Be aware that it can only deactivate a control hosted on a server instance
enableSystemResource	Opposite action to the previous one which activates a resource.

dumpDiagnosticData	Interesting command which can read a harvester and copy the data from it into a local file
exportDiagnosticData	It is possible to specify a query which will then be executed against a log file
exportDiagnosticDataFromServer	This differs from the previous action as it executes a query on the server side
getAvailableCapturedImages	Lists the available images which are available for that server
listSystemResourceControls	Provides a list of available (deployed!) resources on a server.
saveDiagnosticImageCaptureFile	Allows an administrator to copy an image file from the server to the local file system
saveDiagnosticImageCaptureEntryFile	This is an interesting option if only a part from an image is required (e.g. for flight recorder). This command will download only a part – which means one file out of the image zip – to the local machine.

Summary

This chapter has introduced the MBean structure of WLDF. For a better understanding of how to use WLDF with the JMX and WLST APIs and the powerful automation capabilities provided, it is important to have a good understanding of the different MBeans and MBean relationships.

WLST offers a very convenient way to browse the configuration and runtime MBean structure and in some cases (like diagnostic images) also offers operations which can be used from automations.

Part III

WLDF Main Artifacts

The third part of the book discusses the main artifacts of WLDF. Starting from the diagnostic module and archives, the following chapters will discuss everything needed to create common WLDF profiles.

Configure
Diagnostic Modules

Diagnostic Modules

The first artifact you will have to work with is the diagnostic module. It is basically the container which contains all configuration artifacts for WLDF.

Introduction

A diagnostic module is the main configuration artifact for WLDF. A module contains all WLDF configuration items which belong together.

Why do we need diagnostic modules? A diagnostic module has no own functionality but provides a bundle facility to combine a number of configuration elements together. The diagnostic modules could be viewed similar to the EAR package in J2EE. Just like an EAR package contains EJB-applications (*.jar), Web-applications (*.war), Resource-adapters (*.rar), a diagnostic module bundles all configuration items which belong together.

Creating a new Diagnostic Module

The first step when working with WLDF is the creation of a new diagnostic module. A module basically consists nothing else but a name and a description. The important aspect is that a module creates the container MBean inside WebLogic for the module configurations.

Using the WebLogic console:

In the console, you need to select "Diagnostic modules" from the domain structure menu.

Figure 6.1: *Accessing the main configuration view using the WLS console*

After selecting "new", the following dialog appears which allows the user to enter a unique module name and a module description. Especially in configurations where many modules are defined, it is highly advisable to use well defined names.

Figure 6.2: *Entering name and description in order to create a new diagnostic module*

Using WLST

The same creation process can be done by using the following small WLST script.

```
# connect to the admin server
```

```
connect(...)

# switch to edit mode and start editing
edit()
startEdit()

# switch to root and create a new module
cd('/')
cmo.createWLDFSystemResource('WLDFNewModuleTest')

# switch to the new module and set the description text
cd('/WLDFSystemResources/WLDFNewModuleTest')
cmo.setDescription('This is a new WLDF module')

# save and activate the changes
save()
activate()
```

Using JMX

Using java code with the JMX API, the module creation can be done using the following code snippet.

```
ObjectName myDomainConfigMBean = myJMXEditWrapper.getDomainConfigRoot();

// create MBean
ObjectName myNewDiagnosticModuleMBean = (ObjectName)myJMXEditWrapper.invoke(myDomainConfigMBean,
    "createWLDFSystemResource",
    new Object[]{new String("MyTestModule")},
    new String [] {String.class.getName()});

// set description
myJMXEditWrapper.setAttribute(myNewDiagnosticModuleMBean,
            new Attribute("Description","This is a test diagnostic module"));
```

Built-in diagnostic module

Starting with WLS 12.1.2 WebLogic comes with pre-build WLDF modules. These are called built-in diagnostic system modules. These modules are designed to collect common values from important WebLogic MBeans. Different modules (in this book called "default profiles") are provided to collect data for WebLogic runtime, virtual machine, WebLogic services like JDBC, JMS and also for application containers.

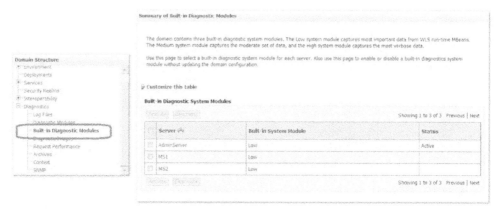

Figure 6.3: *Accessing the built-in section in WLS 12.1.2*

These default profiles or built-in modules can be accessed over the WebLogic console through a separate menu point in the domain structure window.

Three different default profiles are defined which are named "Low", "Medium" and "High". The name reflects the amount of data collected. "Low" means that only a minimum of data will be collected and high means that quite a lot of data will be collected. Even though multiple profiles - also multiple of the built-in modules (=default profiles) can be activated for each WebLogic server instance, in case of the built-in modules it is only possible to activate ONE for each WebLogic server instance. But it is possible to choose a different built-in module for each WebLogic server instance if required.

Built-in Diagnostic System Modules

	Server	Built-in System Module	Status
☑	AdminServer	Low	Inactive
☐	MS1	Low	
☐	MS2	Low	

Activate Deactivate   Showing 1 to 3 of 3 Previous | Next

Figure 6.4: *Each WLS server instance is configured to have a different built-in module*

Activating / Deactivating Built-in modules

It is very easy to activate or deactivate a built-in module for a specific WebLogic server instance. The main view of the built-in modules offer a "activate" and "deactivate" button. Below, we select the instance(s) first and press the appropriate button.

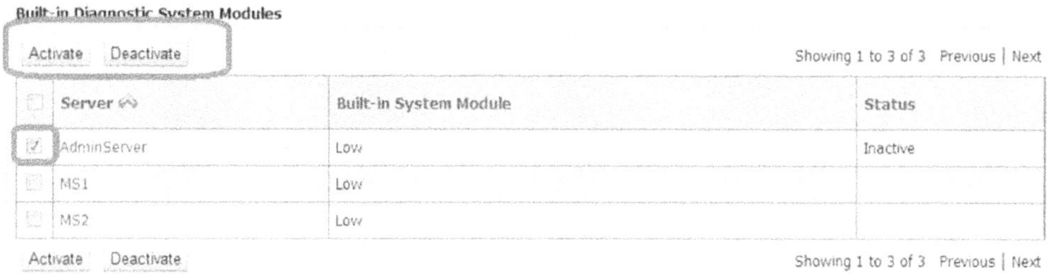

Built-in Diagnostic System Modules

Activate Deactivate		Showing 1 to 3 of 3 Previous | Next
☐ **Server** ↔	**Built-in System Module**	**Status**
☑ AdminServer	Low	Inactive
☐ MS1	Low	
☐ MS2	Low	
Activate Deactivate		Showing 1 to 3 of 3 Previous | Next

Figure 6.5: *Activating / deactivating built-in modules*

> *NOTE:* You can only activate/deactivate built-in modules for running instances. In the example above only the status for the AdminServer is shown. The reason is that - on purpose - for this depiction the managed-servers instances were shutdown. Therefore the status of the managed-server are not shown and also activation/deactivation for MS1 and MS2 is not possible until they are coming online.

This same process can also be done using WLST:

```
# connect to the admin server
connect(...)

# switch to edit mode and start editing
edit()
startEdit()

# switch to server runtime tree
serverRuntime()
# cd to the current built-in mbean of the server you want to change
cd ('/WLDFRuntime/WLDFRuntime/WLDFControlRuntime/AdminServer/SystemResourceControls/Low')
# enable it
cmo.setEnabled(true)
# use the following command in order to deactivate it
# cmo.setEnabled(false)

# save and activate the changes
save()
activate()
```

Please note that the "cd" command contains the name of the server ("AdminServer" in this case) and the name of the built-in module currently configured for this server ("Low" in this case).

Changing flavor of Built-in modules

It is also very easy to change the built-in module for a given server instance. In the same view as above you need to click on the name of the server instance you want to change.

NOTE: This is a configuration change and therefore changing the built-in module for a server can also be done when this server is not running.

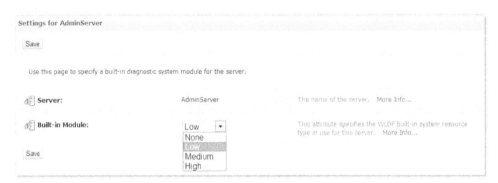

Figure 6.6: *Selection dialog for changing the built-in module of a server*

> *NOTE:* Selection of "NONE" means that no built-in module is configured for this server instance.

Of course, this function can also be done using a WLST command:

```
# connect to the admin server
connect(...)

# switch to edit mode and start editing
edit()
startEdit()

# navigate to server specific DiagnosticConfig mbean
cd('/Servers/AdminServer/ServerDiagnosticConfig/AdminServer')

# change the value
cmo.setWLDFBuiltinSystemResourceType('High')

# save and activate the changes
save()
activate()
```

> *NOTE:* While doing this, the runtime MBeans will be changed. Therefore the MBean names in the script of the previous section (activating/deactivating) has to be adapted.

Create Diagnostic modules from built-in templates

At the beginning of this chapter we discussed how to create empty diagnostic modules. Up until WebLogic release 12.1.1, this is the only way that diagnostic modules could be created. WebLogic 12.1.2 offers an additional feature which allows the user to base a new module on one of the built-in modules discussed in the last section.

The following screenshot shows how to create such a module. You need to activate this new WebLogic feature (checkbox) and then select the built-in module you would like to use.

Create a Diagnostics System Module

OK   Cancel

System Module Properties

The following properties will be used to identify your new system module.

" indicates required fields

What would you like to name your new module?

" **Name:**   TemplateTestModule

Provide a description for your new module.

Description:

This is a module which is based on the
medium template

Would you like to use a built-in diagnostic system module as template?

√ **Use a built-in diagnostic system module as template**

Built-in diagnostic system module: Low

Low
Medium
High

OK   Cancel

Figure 6.7: *Create module from template*

The same can be done of course also with native WLST using the following script:

```
# connect to the admin server
connect(...)

# switch to edit mode and start editing
edit()
startEdit()
```

```
cd('/')
cmo.createWLDFSystemResourceFromBuiltin('TemplateTestModule', Medium)

cd('/WLDFSystemResources/TemplateTestModule')
cmo.setDescription('This is a module which is based on the medium template')

# save and activate the changes
save()
activate()
```

After the module has been created, new module has all the components (harvester, metrics, watches, and more) which have been defined in the built-in template. See the list of inherited metrics for example:

Figure 6.8: *Access to all inherited template configuration items*

The important aspect now is that these components are COPIES from the template. This means that the administrator or user can now go ahead and delete unwanted metrics (or other components), modify them or add additional ones.

This is just a convenient way for users of the web console to use WLDF quickly as the built-in templates cover the most common scenarios. It can also simplify complex WLST scripts of JMX programs by using a template and then just perform the modifications which are special to the actual project needs.

Target/Untarget Diagnostic modules

Diagnostic modules can only be used if they are targeted to at least one managed-server. Every module can be targeted to many servers. Up to WLS 12.1.1 only one module could be targeted to a WebLogic server instance. Targeting a module a WebLogic instance up to 12.1.1 also automatically activated the module. Untargeting automatically disabled the module.

Even though targeting a module has an additional meaning up to WLS 12.1.1 the process is the same. Targeting/Untargeting can be done using the WLS console, WLST or JMX.

Figure 6.9: *Access to module targets*

On the main page of the diagnostic module you need to switch to the "Targets" tab.

The next dialog allows the user to select (or unselect) the desired targets for this diagnostic module.

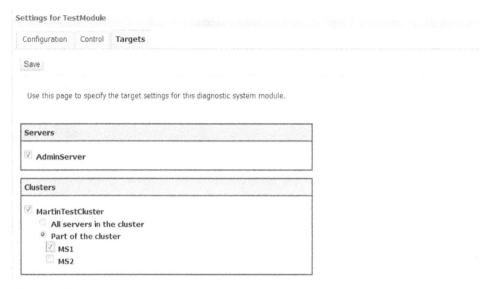

Figure 6.10: *Select targets*

Below we are using WLST to untarget a module from all servers. This basically means providing an empty target list.

```
# connect to the admin server
connect(...)

# switch to edit mode and start editing
edit()
startEdit()

# navigate to server specific Diagnostic mbean
cd('/WLDFSystemResources/MyTestModule')
# remove all targets
set('Targets',jarray.array([], ObjectName))

# save and activate the changes
save()
activate()
```

Targeting a module just means that you need to provide the list of target resources (server instances or cluster) instead of an empty array as parameter to the "Targets" attribute.

Activating / Deactivating Diagnostic modules

Since WebLogic 12.1.2 it is no longer necessary to target/untarget the diagnostic modules. It is now possible to activate/deactivate the module(s).

Settings for TestModule

Configuration **Control** Targets

Use this page to activate or deactivate a diagnostic system module without making a change to the domain configuration. Note that a change to the activation state of a diagnostic system module is not persisted across server startups. Therefore, if the corresponding server instance is restarted, it will revert to whatever diagnostic system module activation state that is configured in the domain.

Customize this table

Diagnostic System Module Status

Activate Deactivate   Showing 1 to 1 of 1 Previous | Next

✓	Server ⌄	Status
☑	AdminServer	Active

Activate Deactivate   Showing 1 to 1 of 1 Previous | Next

Figure 6.11: *Control action for WLDF since WebLogic 12.1.2*

The diagnostic module section in the WebLogic console has a new tab called "Control". This allows the administrator to enable/disable the diagnostic module on the actually running server. Note that only the server which are currently running are shown in this view as this is ONLY a runtime change. After a server restart, this change will be forgotten.

In order to use WLST to activate / deactivate a module, the new WLDFControlRuntime MBean must be used. Every server runtime instance has such a control MBean and if a module should be activated on multiple server then it must be activated on every WLDFControlRuntime MBean individually.

Example WLST script to activate "TestModule" on the AdminServer

```
# connect to server  (can be admin or managed)
connect(...)

# switch to server runtime
serverRuntime()

# change to WLDFControlRuntime of the current server
cd ('/WLDFRuntime/WLDFRuntime/WLDFControlRuntime/AdminServer/SystemResourceControls/TestModule')

# activate the TestModule
cmo.setEnabled(true)

#  use cmo.setEnabled(false)   for deactivation !!
```

Creation and Targeting of multiple Modules

Since WebLogic 12.1.2 it is possible to have multiple active diagnostic modules. The following WLST script discusses the creation of multiple modules with the same and/or different targets

```
# connect to the admin server
connect(...)

# switch to edit mode and start editing
edit()
startEdit()

cd('/')
cmo.createWLDFSystemResource('TestModuleDomain')

cd('/WLDFSystemResources/TestModuleDomain')
cmo.setDescription('Test Module to be targeted to the complete domain')
set('Targets',jarray.array([ObjectName('com.bea:Name=AdminServer,Type=Server'),
ObjectName('com.bea:Name=TestCluster,Type=Cluster')], ObjectName))

cd('/')
cmo.createWLDFSystemResource('TestModuleCluster')

cd('/WLDFSystemResources/TestModuleCluster')
cmo.setDescription('WLDF module to be targeted only to the cluster')
set('Targets',jarray.array([ObjectName('com.bea:Name=TestCluster,Type=Cluster')], ObjectName))

cd('/')
cmo.createWLDFSystemResource('TestAdminMS1')

cd('/WLDFSystemResources/TestAdminMS1')
cmo.setDescription('Last test module which will be targeted to he Admin Server and MS1')
cmo.setDescription('Next test module which will be targeted to he Admin Server and MS1\r\n')
set('Targets',jarray.array([ObjectName('com.bea:Name=AdminServer,Type=Server'),
ObjectName('com.bea:Name=MS1,Type=Server')], ObjectName))

cd('/')
cmo.createWLDFSystemResource('TestAdmin')

cd('/WLDFSystemResources/TestAdmin')
cmo.setDescription('This module will only run on the Admin Server')
set('Targets',jarray.array([ObjectName('com.bea:Name=AdminServer,Type=Server')], ObjectName))

# save and activate the changes
save()
activate()
```

After this script has been executed, the WebLogic console will show the following list of modules

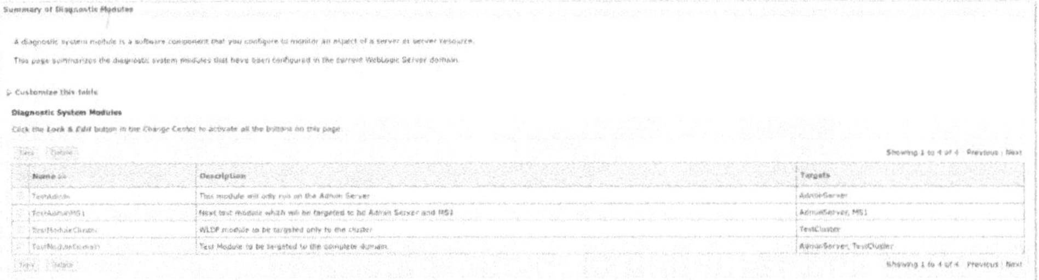

Figure 6.12: *Multiple diagnostic modules*

WebLogic creates its own XML configuration file for each module, which makes it easier to read the different modules. All outsourced XML files are referenced in the main *config.xml* file.

```
<domain>
...
  <wldf-system-resource>
    <name>TestModuleDomain</name>
    <target>AdminServer,TestCluster</target>
    <descriptor-file-name>diagnostics/TestModuleDomain-3442.xml</descriptor-file-name>
    <description>Test Module to be targeted to the complete domain</description>
  </wldf-system-resource>
  <wldf-system-resource>
    <name>TestModuleCluster</name>
    <target>TestCluster</target>
    <descriptor-file-name>diagnostics/TestModuleCluster-9308.xml</descriptor-file-name>
    <description>WLDF module to be targeted only to the cluster</description>
  </wldf-system-resource>
  <wldf-system-resource>
    <name>TestAdminMS1</name>
    <target>AdminServer,MS1</target>
    <descriptor-file-name>diagnostics/TestAdminMS1-3362.xml</descriptor-file-name>
    <description>Next test module which will be targeted to he Admin Server and MS1</description>
  </wldf-system-resource>
  <wldf-system-resource>
    <name>TestAdmin</name>
    <target>AdminServer</target>
    <descriptor-file-name>diagnostics/TestAdmin-0973.xml</descriptor-file-name>
    <description>This module will only run on the Admin Server</description>
  </wldf-system-resource>
</domain>
```

Note the different targeting of the different modules.

Summary

Diagnostic modules are the container building block for WLDF profiles. The container blocks must be targeted to one or more server in order to make use of them. Since WebLogic 12.1.2 the handling of diagnostic modules has been improved so that multiple modules can be targeted to the same server. Also starting with WebLogic 12.1.2 built-in modules provide configurations for the most common use cases and it is also possible to build custom modules by using the built-in modules as templates.

Keeping historical data for long term analysis

Data Archives

Data archives are important WLDF components which persists data and allow consumers to use both current and historical data for further analysis. Keeping historical data for long term analysis is a feature WebLogic does not offer for the normal Runtime MBean attributes, and all information offered from the Runtime MBean attribute are current state data. With data archives, WLDF extends this and allow historical data recording.

Overview

Whenever somebody needs to analyze a system or monitor system behavior it is vital to have access to the necessary data. The current data provides the current situation. Very often the past state is also very critical in order to do proper troubleshooting or reporting.

This of course means that metric data, events and potentially other source information must be kept over time – this is the "historical" data.

For WLDF modules, this is done by a component called *archiver*. Harvester metrics as well as events can be kept in a persistent store or database and can be provided by appropriate APIs for timeline (=historical) analysis and review. Archiver information is configured for each server individually and these configurations are stored in the config.xml file of the domain.

Figure 7.1: *Access to the archiver configuration is provided in the WebLogic console*

For WLDF data (archiving) we distinguish generally three different types of data:

- Standard logging which will be written into the log files.
- Harvester metrics will can be persisted by the archiver into data stores.
- Event information will can be persisted by the event archiver into an event store.

Basically WLDF supports two different ways to archive diagnostic data. Either in a file store or in a JDBC based database.

File based archives

The most common way to persist WLDF information is file-based. In this case the only configuration needed is the directory name (NOTE: not file name!). WLDF will then create all file required within this directory. The default directory used by WebLogic is: <domain>/servers/SERVER_NAME/data/store/diagnostics.

Benefits of using a file based store include:

- Faster speed
- Usually on the same machine (if not placed on NFS)
- Less dependencies (no DB connection needed, no network connection needed)
- Easy to copy and archive the created files

Disadvantages using a file based store include:

- Difficult file access if the user does not have a machine login
- Difficult to access remotely if the domain is not running
- Difficult to read without Oracle tools

Configuration using the WebLogic console:

The different configuration settings have to be for each server individually as the file-store will be configured on a per server basis.

Configuration   Diagnostics Store Monitoring

Save

Use this page to configure how and where the current server archives its monitoring and diagnostics data.

Server:	AdminServer	The name of the server. More Info...
Type:	File Store ▾	Determines whether the current server persists its harvested metrics and event data in a diagnostic store (file-based store) or a JDBC based archive. The default store is file-based. More Info...
Directory:	/data/diagnosticData/wls	The directory in which the current server maintains its diagnostic store. More Info...
☑ **Diagnostics Store File Locking Enabled**		Determines whether OS file locking is used. More Info...
Data Source:	(Required. Not Currently Specified) ▾	More Info...
Preferred Store Size:	1000	Return the preferred limit on the size of diagnostic store file in MB. More Info...
Store Size Check Period:	1	Return the period in hours at which diagnostic store file size check will be performed More Info...
☑ **Data Retirement Enabled**		This attribute controls if configuration based data retirement functionality is enabled on the server. If disabled, all retirement policies will be disabled. More Info...

Figure 7.2: *File based archives configuration using the web console*

Configuration using WLST

The following script shows how to set the directory. All other parameter can of course be changed in a similar way.

```
# connect to the admin server
connect(...)

# switch to edit mode and start editing
edit()
startEdit()

# navigate to server specific ServerDiagnosticConfig mbean of the admin server
cd ('/Servers/AdminServer/ServerDiagnosticConfig/AdminServer')

# set the directory name
cmo.setDiagnosticStoreDir('/data/diagnosticData/wls')

# example of setting other values
cmo.setPreferredStoreSizeLimit(1000)
cmo.setStoreSizeCheckPeriod(1)
cmo.setDataRetirementEnabled(true)
cmo.setDiagnosticDataArchiveType('FileStoreArchive')

# save and activate the changes
save()
activate()
```

As this setup will most likely always be done during domain creation it is very unlikely that these settings will be changed using JMX. Of course, it is possible to do the steps using pure JMX calls.

JDBC based archives

The second possible storage for the diagnostic data is a JDBC based database. This requires that the data source must also be targeted to the server where the data is collected. Please see the Oracle documentation for details about the schema and table layout. A detailed description about the creation of data sources (either single or RAC or Gridlink data sources) and data source security (either user/password or wallets) can be found in my book *WebLogic Automation* or in the Oracle documentation.

Note that WebLogic has a fallback mechanism implemented. If the data source that you want to use for persisting the diagnostic data is either incorrect configured or missing, then WebLogic will use the default file-based store to save the data.

Benefits using a JDBC based store include:

- Data centrally available.
- Many domains can save the data in the same database (but of course should use different schemas to avoid confusion)
- Easy to access via JDBC from other machines
- Easier to access and compare data from multiple machines
- No housekeeping needed on the local file system. The local file system has less IO

Disadvantages using a JDBC based store include:

- Slower (network traffic involved)
- Dependencies (DB connection needed, network connection to DB needed)
- More difficult to backup data (database backup instead of just file copy)

Configure a JDBC based archive for WLDF using the Web console

For the configuration of a JDBC based store it is important switch the type to "JDBC". In addition it is important to select an existing data source (which is targeted to the current sever!).

Settings for AdminServer

Configuration | Diagnostics Store Monitoring

Save

Use this page to configure how and where the current server archives its monitoring and diagnostics data.

Server: AdminServer

Type: JDBC

Data Source: WLDFdatasource

Preferred Store Size: 1000

Store Size Check Period: 1

✓ Data Retirement Enabled

Figure 7.3: *Configuration of a JDBC archive store*

Configure a JDBC based archive for WLDF using WLST

The same configuration can also be done using WLST.

```
# connect to the admin server
connect(...)

# switch to edit mode and start editing
edit()
startEdit()

# navigate to server specific ServerDiagnosticConfig mbean of the admin server
cd ('/Servers/AdminServer/ServerDiagnosticConfig/AdminServer')

# change type to JDBC
cmo.setDiagnosticDataArchiveType('JDBCArchive')

# set a datasource by getting the appropriate JDBC system mbean
cmo.setDiagnosticJDBCResource(getMBean('/JDBCSystemResources/WLDFdatasource'))

# example of setting other values
cmo.setPreferredStoreSizeLimit(1000)
cmo.setStoreSizeCheckPeriod(1)
cmo.setDataRetirementEnabled(true)

# save and activate the changes
save()
activate()
```

Data retirement policies

One important aspect which should never be forgotten is proper housekeeping of the data. Data collection - especially if a huge amount of data is collected - can very soon create huge amount of data. Furthermore analysis will take more time if more historical data has to be considered.

Configure a retirement policy using the Web-Console

In the archiver area, the last section of the page lists the different retirement policies which are defined for this archive. After switching to the "edit" mode, the "New" button is enabled and can be selected in order to create a new policy.

Figure 7.4: *Create a new retirement policy*

On the subsequent page the new policy can be configured. The configuration include the name of the policy, the data source (harvester or event or custom) and the different time period settings.

Figure 7.5: *Configuration of the new retirement policy*

Configure a retirement policy using WLST

In order to configure a new retirement policy it is necessary to switch to the server specific diagnostic configuration and create a new retirement policy for aged data. Then this policy can be configured.

```
# connect to the admin server
connect(...)

# switch to edit mode and start editing
edit()
startEdit()

# switch to the server specific diagnostic configuration
cd ('/Servers/AdminServer/ServerDiagnosticConfig/AdminServer')

# create a new retirement policy for aged data
cmo.createWLDFDataRetirementByAge('TestDataRetirementPolicy')

# change to the new policy and configure it
cd('/Servers/AdminServer/ServerDiagnosticConfig/AdminServer/WLDFDataRetirementByAges/TestDataRetireme
ntPolicy')
cmo.setArchiveName('HarvestedDataArchive')
cmo.setRetirementAge(144)
cmo.setRetirementTime(0)
cmo.setRetirementPeriod(12)
cmo.setEnabled(true)

# save and activate the changes
save()
```

```
activate()
```

Of course the same functionality is also possible using the standard JMX API, which might be useful if WLDF should be setup using automated processed based on Java.

JMX Example for a retirement policy:

```
public void createNewRetirementPolicy(ArrayList<String> serverNames,
                                String policyName,
                                String archiveName,
                                int age, int time, int period)
                                throws WLDFAutomationException
{
   try {
      for (int i=0;i<serverNames.size();i++)
      {
         ObjectName nextServerWLDF = new ObjectName("com.bea:Name="+serverNames.get(i)+",Server="
                                     +serverNames.get(i)+
                                     ",Type=WLDFServerDiagnostic");

         // create the policy:  createWLDFDataRetirementByAge(name)
         ObjectName myNewPolicyMBean = (ObjectName)myJMXEditWrapper.invoke(nextServerWLDF,
               "createWLDFDataRetirementByAge",
               new Object[]{new String(policyName)},
               new String [] {String.class.getName()});

         // set the different values
         myJMXEditWrapper.setAttribute(myNewPolicyMBean,
                     new Attribute("RetirementTime",new Integer(time)));
         myJMXEditWrapper.setAttribute(myNewPolicyMBean, new Attribute("RetirementAge",
                     new Integer(age)));
         myJMXEditWrapper.setAttribute(myNewPolicyMBean, new Attribute("RetirementPeriod",
                     new Integer(period)));
         myJMXEditWrapper.setAttribute(myNewPolicyMBean, new Attribute("ArchiveName",archiveName));
      }
   }
   catch(Exception ex) {
      ex.printStackTrace();
      throw new WLDFAutomationException(ex);
   }
}
```

Note that in both cases – WLST and JMX – the policy has be set for each server individually as each server has its own archive store.

Summary

For historical data analysis it is important to persist metrics and events, and WLDF uses the archiver component for that which can either persist into a file store into a database. Only one archiver per server can be defined. Especially for WLS 12.1.2 (when multiple diagnostic profiles are activated on one server) this should be kept in mind. In this case, data from all diagnostic modules will be mixed and saved in the same archiver.

Data housekeeping can be configured using retirement policies. Especially for long running data collections this is very important; otherwise there is a risk to run out of resources (file system space or database table space).

Harvesting Runtime Metrics for System and Performance Monitoring

The Harvester

Monitoring your system, controlling the health of your application and getting necessary information for troubleshooting require the user to collect data. Administrators may want to understand the current health of your application or the system on which it runs. WebLogic provides many runtime MBean attributes - runtime data points - that you can use to monitor your system. WLDF makes it easy to be efficient - you can capture only the data you are interested in, and not waste resources on uninteresting runtime data. The component that enables selective capture is called a Harvester.

Overview

The concept in WLDF of collecting metric data is called the "harvester". Data harvesters are configurations defined in WebLogic which describe which attributes from which Runtime MBeans need to be gathered at defined sampling rates. The collected information can then be used to analyze the metric for certain conditions or can be handed over to the archiving components in order to keep it as historical data. Collecting data with a harvester is especially useful for system state monitoring and for analyzing the performance of the complete server or a subsystem of the server.

WLDF distinguishes in its specification between Harvesting, Harvestable Data, and Harvested Data.

- **Harvesting:** WLDF calls the process of collecting the data "harvesting". This is based on the configured metrics.

- **Harvestable Data:** WLDF calls all attributes (only simple attributes are supported) which can be collected "Harvestable Data". Only MBeans which are registered in the runtime MBeanServer can be used.

- **Harvested Data:** All data items which are currently being harvested are called "Harvested data".

Harvesters are always configured as a child component of a diagnostic module. Every diagnostic module has exactly one harvester. In order to collect metrics from different MBeans, each harvester component can contain multiple metric definitions. Beside the different metrics, each harvester will be configured with a sampler interval.

Note that this sampler interval applies to all metrics as the sampler interval is configured on harvester level and not on each metric level. For each MBean type an own metric must be defined. Each metric can also include attribute expressions. Metrics also have target definitions which specify where this metric should be executed.

Using the WLS Console

The following example explains how to create a harvester using the WebLogic console.

The starting point for defining a harvester metric module is a diagnostic module. Note that multiple diagnostic modules can be defined in every WebLogic domain. If you want to use the same harvester in different modules, you need to define it in each module where you intend to use it.

After the desired diagnostic module is selected, the user will find several tabs. In order to define a metric the "collected metrics" tab has to be selected (see next screenshot). In this section of the diagnostic module metrics can be generally (will be applied for the complete module) enabled and a sampling interval can be configured. In the second part of this section the user can define the concrete metrics which are part of this harvester. Note that multiple metrics can be defined. Harvester usually consist of multiple metrics. At least one metric is needed otherwise no data at all will be collected.

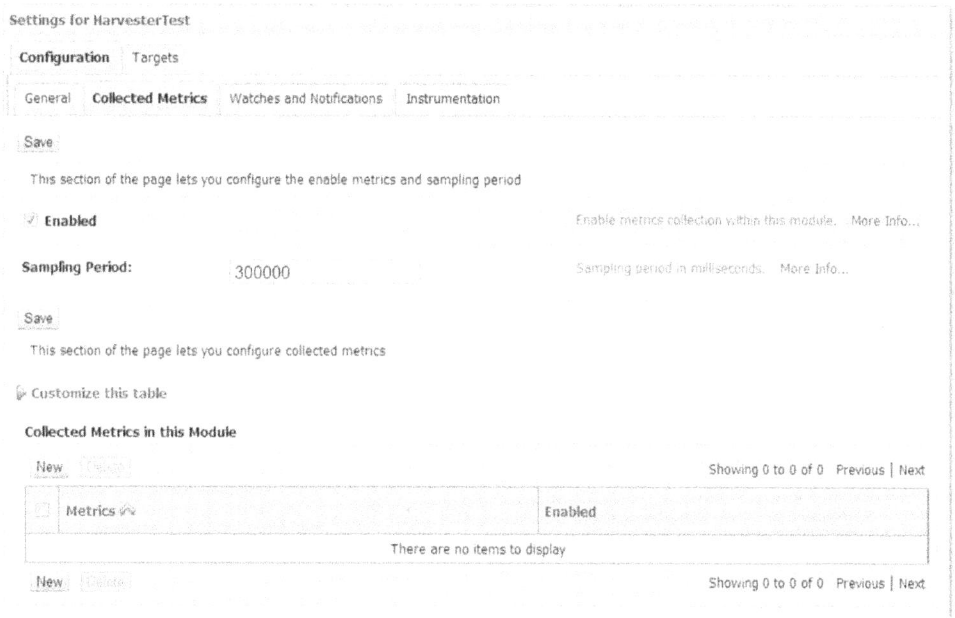

Figure 8.1: *A default and empty harvester module without any metrics*

We select "New" in order to create a new metric. In the first of the metric definition, the user has to select the runtime MBean which will be used as source the metric values. Note that only one MBean can be selected. This is also the main reason why a harvester usually consists of multiple metrics.

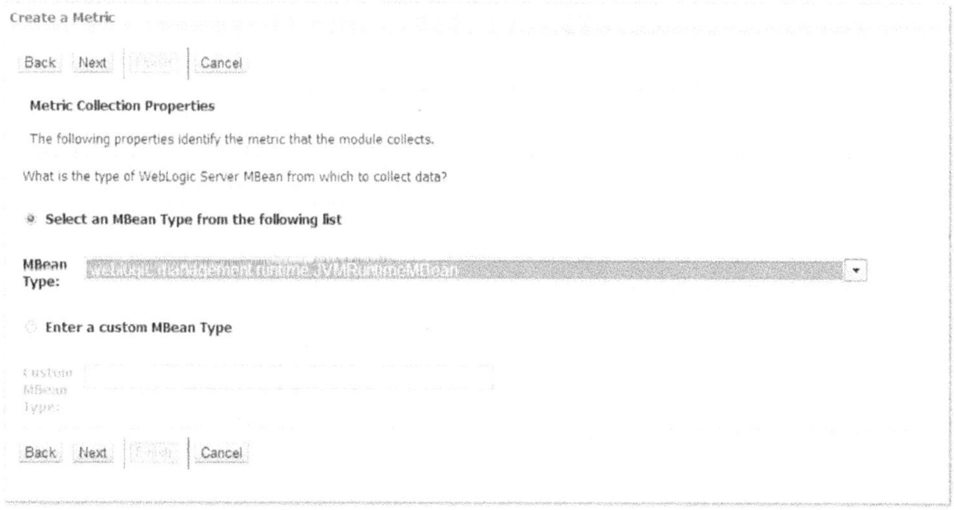

Figure 8.2: *Selection of MBean type for the metric*

Alternatively a custom MBean type can be entered das this wizard is not able to detect an offer a list of custom MBeans.

After a specific MBean is selected (in this case the JVMRuntimeMBean) the next step will offer a list of available attributes which are offered through the runtime MBeanServer. The user can select which of these attributes should be harvested during each sampling run, by moving these attributes to the "Chosen" list on the right-hand side.

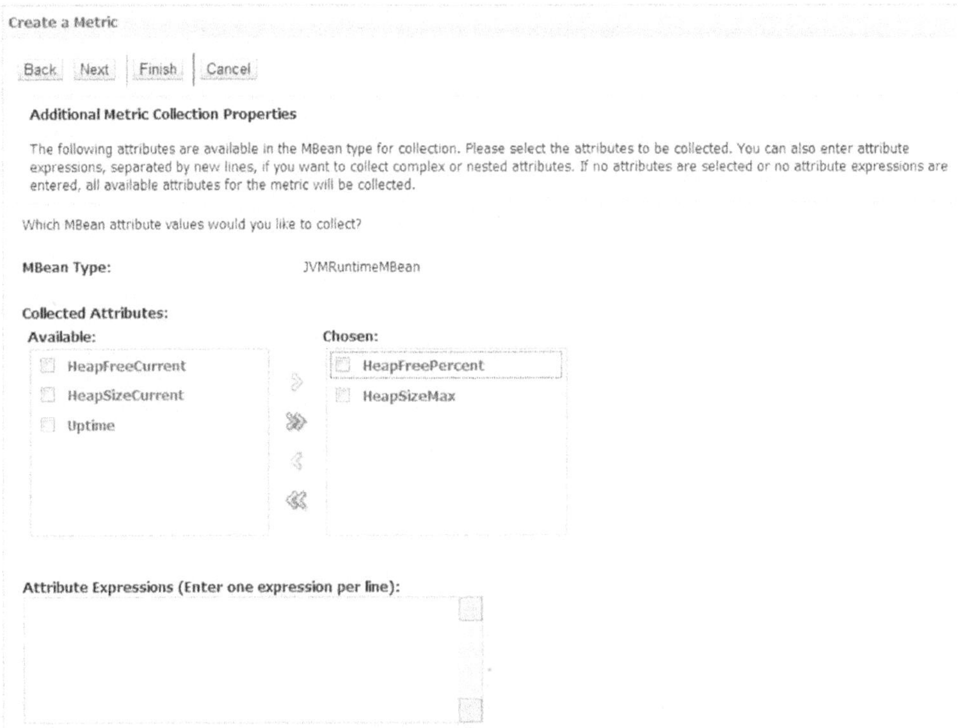

Figure 8.3: *Attribute selection for a metric*

It is also possible to provide attribute expressions. The expressions are not saved in the MBeans, but they are used to select the attributes to be put into the harvester list.

The third step allows the user to choose all WebLogic instances of the current WebLogic domain for which these values should be collected.

IMPORTANT: Do not confuse this selection with the targeting of the diagnostic module. Only if the server is selected in this configuration AND the diagnostic module is targeted to the specific WLS server (AdminServer or ManagedServer) the values will be collected.

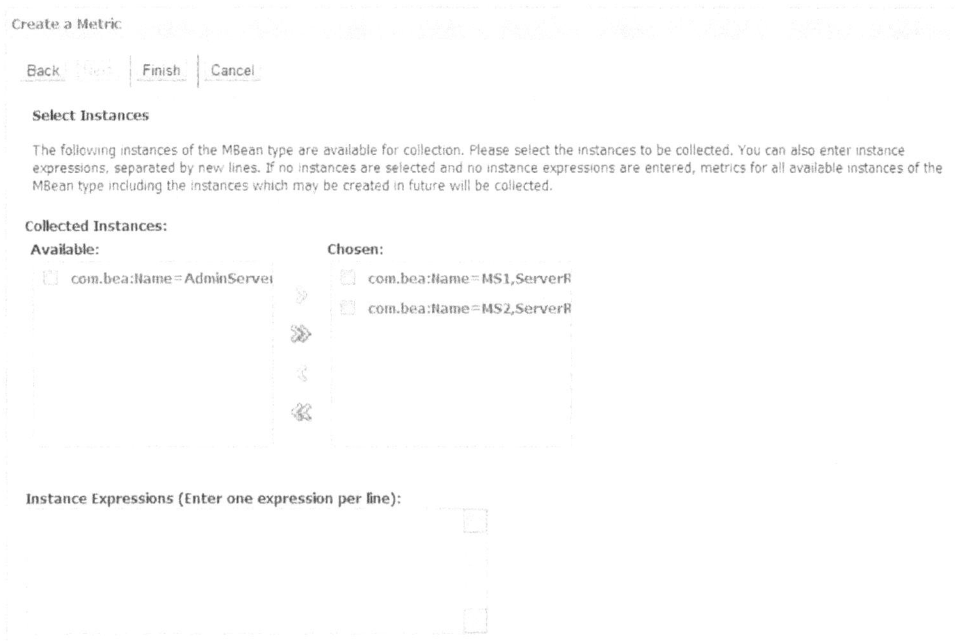

Create a Metric

Back   Finish   Cancel

Select Instances

The following instances of the MBean type are available for collection. Please select the instances to be collected. You can also enter instance expressions, separated by new lines. If no instances are selected and no instance expressions are entered, metrics for all available instances of the MBean type including the instances which may be created in future will be collected.

Collected Instances:

Available:	Chosen:
com.bea:Name=AdminServer	com.bea:Name=MS1,ServerR
	com.bea:Name=MS2,ServerR

Instance Expressions (Enter one expression per line):

Figure 8.4: *Select instances for a metric*

During this configuration step it is also possible to define expressions. This time the expressions apply to the selected instances.

After finally clicking "Finish", the new metric will be created. On the harvester page ("collected metrics" tab) the new metric will appear where the metric name is the MBean name.

Collected Metrics in this Module

Metrics ⌃	Enabled
JVMRuntimeMBean	true

Figure 8.5: *Metric listing after creation of the metric*

Next, let's look at using WLST.

Using WLST

The same harvester which was introduced in the last section can also be created using the following WLST script:

```
# connect to the admin server
connect(...)

# switch to edit mode and start editing
edit()
startEdit()

# change to the diagnostic module with the name "HarvesterTest"
cd('/WLDFSystemResources/HarvesterTest/WLDFResource/HarvesterTest/Harvester/HarvesterTest')

# create a metric for the mbean type JVMRuntimeMBean
cmo.createHarvestedType('weblogic.management.runtime.JVMRuntimeMBean')

# change to metric MBean
cd('/WLDFSystemResources/HarvesterTest/WLDFResource/HarvesterTest/Harvester/HarvesterTest/HarvestedTy
pes/weblogic.management.runtime.JVMRuntimeMBean')

# configure which attributes (2 in this exampel) should be harvested
set('HarvestedAttributes',jarray.array([String('HeapFreePercent'), String('HeapSizeMax')], String))

# configure on which WebLogic server instances this metric should be executed
set('HarvestedInstances',jarray.array([String('com.bea:Name=MS1,ServerRuntime=MS1,Type=JVMRuntime'),
String('com.bea:Name=MS2,ServerRuntime=MS2,Type=JVMRuntime')], String))

# finally set the MBeanServer to be used (usually always ServerRuntime)
cmo.setNamespace('ServerRuntime')

# save and activate the changes
save()
activate()
```

The script above actually does exactly the same steps as we have discussed in the Web Console setup section. The main difference is that the values which have to be used must be known. There is no "selection list" when using WLST.

Using JMX

The same steps can of course also be implemented in java using the JMX API.

```
JMXWrapperRemote myJMXEditWrapper = new JMXWrapperRemote();
```

```
myJMXEditWrapper.connectToAdminServer(true, // edit
                                      true, // domain
                                      user, password, url);


// direct code:
// e.g.: com.bea:Name=TestDomain,Type=Domain
ObjectName myDomainConfigMBean = myJMXEditWrapper.getDomainConfigRoot();

// javax.management.ObjectName  createJDBCSystemResource(name:java.lang.String  )
ObjectName myNewDiagnosticModuleMBean = (ObjectName)myJMXEditWrapper.invoke(myDomainConfigMBean,
    "createWLDFSystemResource",
    new Object[]{new String("MyTestModule")},
    new String [] {String.class.getName()});

// set description
myJMXEditWrapper.setAttribute(myNewDiagnosticModuleMBean,
                new Attribute("Description","This is a test diagnostic module"));

// get all configured server of the domain
 ObjectName[] servers = (ObjectName[])myJMXEditWrapper.getAttribute(myDomainConfigMBean, "Servers");

// set targets
 myJMXEditWrapper.setAttribute(myNewDiagnosticModuleMBean, new Attribute("Targets",servers));


// configure harvester

// get WLDF resource
ObjectName myWLDFresourceMBean =
(ObjectName)myJMXEditWrapper.getAttribute(myNewDiagnosticModuleMBean, "WLDFResource");

// from the resource => get the harvester
ObjectName myHarvesterMBean = (ObjectName)myJMXEditWrapper.getAttribute(myWLDFresourceMBean,
"Harvester");

// set harvester flag to true
myJMXEditWrapper.setAttribute(myHarvesterMBean, new Attribute("Enabled",new Boolean(true)));

// set harvester sampler interval in milliSec
myJMXEditWrapper.setAttribute(myHarvesterMBean, new Attribute("SamplePeriod",new Long(12345)));


// add metrics
// create new metric type (based on MBean type)
ObjectName myNewHarvestedTypeMBean = (ObjectName)myJMXEditWrapper.invoke(myHarvesterMBean,
            "createHarvestedType",
            new Object[]{new String("weblogic.management.runtime.JVMRuntimeMBean")},
            new String [] {String.class.getName()});

// set knownType flag to true
myJMXEditWrapper.setAttribute(myNewHarvestedTypeMBean, new Attribute("KnownType",new Boolean(true)));

// set attributes
myJMXEditWrapper.setAttribute(myNewHarvestedTypeMBean,
                new Attribute("HarvestedAttributes",
                new String[]{"HeapFreePercent", "HeapSizeMax"}));

// in this case targete to managed-server 1 only
myJMXEditWrapper.setAttribute(myNewHarvestedTypeMBean,
                new Attribute("HarvestedInstances",
                new String[]{"com.bea:Name=MS1,ServerRuntime=MS1,Type=JVMRuntime"}));
```

The steps in Java are exactly the same as in WLST.

Using configuration files

It is also possible to modify the WebLogic configuration files directly. This can only
be done when the domain and especially the admin server is stopped.

In *config.xml*:

```
<wldf-system-resource>
  <name>HarvesterTest</name>
  <descriptor-file-name>diagnostics/HarvesterTest-7992.xml</descriptor-file-name>
  <description></description>
</wldf-system-resource>
```

```
In the file diagnostics/HarvesterTest-7992.xml which in this case ist he outsourced configuration
fort he diagnostic module (note: not only the harvester):
<?xml version='1.0' encoding='UTF-8'?>
<wldf-resource xmlns="http://xmlns.oracle.com/weblogic/weblogic-diagnostics"
xmlns:sec="http://xmlns.oracle.com/weblogic/security"
xmlns:wls="http://xmlns.oracle.com/weblogic/security/wls"
xmlns:xsi="http://www.w3.org/2001/XMLSchema-instance"
xsi:schemaLocation="http://xmlns.oracle.com/weblogic/weblogic-diagnostics
http://xmlns.oracle.com/weblogic/weblogic-diagnostics/1.0/weblogic-diagnostics.xsd">
  <name>HarvesterTest</name>
  <harvester>
    <harvested-type>
      <name>weblogic.management.runtime.JVMRuntimeMBean</name>
      <harvested-attribute>HeapFreePercent</harvested-attribute>
      <harvested-attribute>HeapSizeMax</harvested-attribute>
      <harvested-instance>com.bea:Name=MS1,ServerRuntime=MS1,Type=JVMRuntime</harvested-instance>
      <harvested-instance>com.bea:Name=MS2,ServerRuntime=MS2,Type=JVMRuntime</harvested-instance>
      <namespace>ServerRuntime</namespace>
    </harvested-type>
  </harvester>
</wldf-resource>
```

Comparison

Modifying the configuration files is not recommended as the concrete syntax may easily change between WebLogic versions. It is also required to have physical access to the machine and write access to the configuration files. All other options should be preferred.

For one time activities and tests the configuration using the WebLogic console is usually the best way. Just keep in mind that repeating the activity requires to repeat all the steps manually.

For setting up "profiles" and test which should even be available up to production the WLS-Console approach is also inadequate. In these scenarios either WLST or JMX should be used. If the configuration is done by a system administrator and not by other tools, the preferred way (easiest to read and write) is WLST.

Complex example

The following example discusses a more complex metric collection which uses values from multiple MBeans (different metrics).

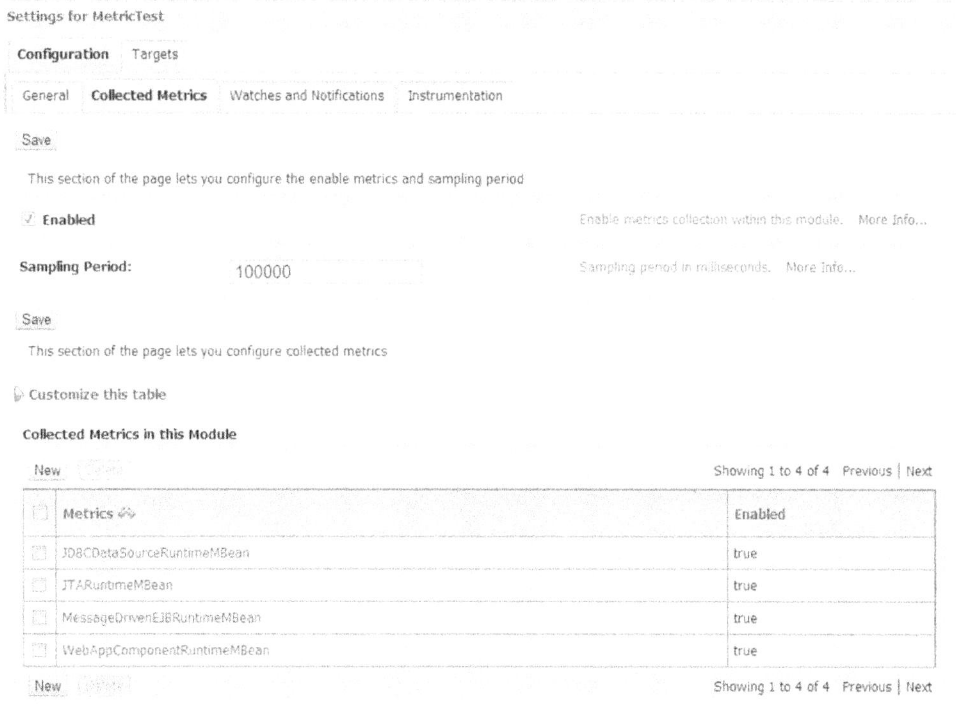

Figure 8.6: *Complex harvester example with multiple metrics*

WLST to setup this example:

```
# connect to the admin server
connect(...)

# switch to edit mode and start editing
edit()
startEdit()

cd('/WLDFSystemResources/MetricTest/WLDFResource/MetricTest/Harvester/MetricTest')
cmo.setSamplePeriod(100000)
cmo.setEnabled(true)
cmo.createHarvestedType('weblogic.management.runtime.JDBCDataSourceRuntimeMBean')

cd('/WLDFSystemResources/MetricTest/WLDFResource/MetricTest/Harvester/MetricTest/HarvestedTypes/weblo
gic.management.runtime.JDBCDataSourceRuntimeMBean')

set('HarvestedAttributes',jarray.array([String('ActiveConnectionsCurrentCount'),
String('CurrCapacity'), String('FailedReserveRequestCount'), String('FailuresToReconnectCount'),
String('WaitingForConnectionCurrentCount'), String('WaitingForConnectionHighCount')], String))
cmo.setHarvestedInstances(None)
cmo.setNamespace('ServerRuntime')

cd('/WLDFSystemResources/MetricTest/WLDFResource/MetricTest/Harvester/MetricTest')
cmo.createHarvestedType('weblogic.management.runtime.JTARuntimeMBean')

cd('/WLDFSystemResources/MetricTest/WLDFResource/MetricTest/Harvester/MetricTest/HarvestedTypes/weblo
gic.management.runtime.JTARuntimeMBean')
set('HarvestedAttributes',jarray.array([String('ActiveTransactionsTotalCount'),
String('SecondsActiveTotalCount'), String('TransactionAbandonedTotalCount'),
String('TransactionCommittedTotalCount'), String('TransactionHeuristicsTotalCount'),
String('TransactionRolledBackAppTotalCount'), String('TransactionRolledBackResourceTotalCount'),
```

```
String('TransactionRolledBackSystemTotalCount'), String('TransactionRolledBackTimeoutTotalCount'),
String('TransactionRolledBackTotalCount'), String('TransactionTotalCount')], String))
set('HarvestedInstances',jarray.array([String('com.bea:Name=JTARuntime,ServerRuntime=MS1,Type=JTARunt
ime'), String('com.bea:Name=JTARuntime,ServerRuntime=MS2,Type=JTARuntime')], String))
cmo.setNamespace('ServerRuntime')

cd('/WLDFSystemResources/MetricTest/WLDFResource/MetricTest/Harvester/MetricTest')
cmo.createHarvestedType('weblogic.management.runtime.WebAppComponentRuntimeMBean')

cd('/WLDFSystemResources/MetricTest/WLDFResource/MetricTest/Harvester/MetricTest/HarvestedTypes/weblo
gic.management.runtime.WebAppComponentRuntimeMBean')

set('HarvestedAttributes',jarray.array([String('OpenSessionsCurrentCount'),
String('OpenSessionsHighCount'), String('Status')], String))
set('HarvestedInstances',jarray.array([String('com.bea:ApplicationRuntime=martinTest,Name=MS1_/martin
Test,ServerRuntime=MS1,Type=WebAppComponentRuntime'),
String('com.bea:ApplicationRuntime=martinTest,Name=MS2_/martinTest,ServerRuntime=MS2,Type=WebAppCompo
nentRuntime')], String))

cmo.setNamespace('ServerRuntime')

cd('/WLDFSystemResources/MetricTest/WLDFResource/MetricTest/Harvester/MetricTest')
cmo.createHarvestedType('weblogic.management.runtime.MessageDrivenEJBRuntimeMBean')

cd('/WLDFSystemResources/MetricTest/WLDFResource/MetricTest/Harvester/MetricTest/HarvestedTypes/weblo
gic.management.runtime.MessageDrivenEJBRuntimeMBean')
set('HarvestedAttributes',jarray.array([String('ConnectionStatus'), String('MDBStatus'),
String('ProcessedMessageCount'), String('SuspendCount')], String))

cmo.setHarvestedInstances(None)
cmo.setNamespace('ServerRuntime')

# save and activate the changes
save()
activate()
```

XML Config file for this example:

```xml
<?xml version='1.0' encoding='UTF-8'?>
<wldf-resource … >
  <name>MetricTest</name>
  <harvester>
    <enabled>true</enabled>
    <sample-period>100000</sample-period>
    <harvested-type>
      <name>weblogic.management.runtime.JDBCDataSourceRuntimeMBean</name>
      <harvested-attribute>ActiveConnectionsCurrentCount</harvested-attribute>
      <harvested-attribute>CurrCapacity</harvested-attribute>
      <harvested-attribute>FailedReserveRequestCount</harvested-attribute>
      <harvested-attribute>FailuresToReconnectCount</harvested-attribute>
      <harvested-attribute>WaitingForConnectionCurrentCount</harvested-attribute>
      <harvested-attribute>WaitingForConnectionHighCount</harvested-attribute>
      <namespace>ServerRuntime</namespace>
    </harvested-type>
    <harvested-type>
      <name>weblogic.management.runtime.JTARuntimeMBean</name>
      <harvested-attribute>ActiveTransactionsTotalCount</harvested-attribute>
      <harvested-attribute>SecondsActiveTotalCount</harvested-attribute>
      <harvested-attribute>TransactionAbandonedTotalCount</harvested-attribute>
      <harvested-attribute>TransactionCommittedTotalCount</harvested-attribute>
      <harvested-attribute>TransactionHeuristicsTotalCount</harvested-attribute>
      <harvested-attribute>TransactionRolledBackAppTotalCount</harvested-attribute>
      <harvested-attribute>TransactionRolledBackResourceTotalCount</harvested-attribute>
      <harvested-attribute>TransactionRolledBackSystemTotalCount</harvested-attribute>
      <harvested-attribute>TransactionRolledBackTimeoutTotalCount</harvested-attribute>
      <harvested-attribute>TransactionRolledBackTotalCount</harvested-attribute>
      <harvested-attribute>TransactionTotalCount</harvested-attribute>
      <harvested-instance>com.bea:Name=JTARuntime,ServerRuntime=MS1,Type=JTARuntime
      </harvested-instance>
      <harvested-instance>com.bea:Name=JTARuntime,ServerRuntime=MS2,Type=JTARuntime
      </harvested-instance>
      <namespace>ServerRuntime</namespace>
    </harvested-type>
    <harvested-type>
      <name>weblogic.management.runtime.WebAppComponentRuntimeMBean</name>
      <harvested-attribute>OpenSessionsCurrentCount</harvested-attribute>
```

```
    <harvested-attribute>OpenSessionsHighCount</harvested-attribute>
    <harvested-attribute>Status</harvested-attribute>
    <harvested-instance>
        com.bea:ApplicationRuntime=martinTest,Name=MS1_/martinTest,
        ServerRuntime=MS1,Type=WebAppComponentRuntime
    </harvested-instance>
    <harvested-instance>
        com.bea:ApplicationRuntime=martinTest,Name=MS2_/martinTest,
        ServerRuntime=MS2,Type=WebAppComponentRuntime
    </harvested-instance>
    <namespace>ServerRuntime</namespace>
  </harvested-type>
  <harvested-type>
    <name>weblogic.management.runtime.MessageDrivenEJBRuntimeMBean</name>
    <harvested-attribute>ConnectionStatus</harvested-attribute>
    <harvested-attribute>MDBStatus</harvested-attribute>
    <harvested-attribute>ProcessedMessageCount</harvested-attribute>
    <harvested-attribute>SuspendCount</harvested-attribute>
    <namespace>ServerRuntime</namespace>
  </harvested-type>
 </harvester>
</wldf-resource>
```

dumpDiagnosticData

WLST offers a very useful command for getting a copy of the actual harvester data to a local file. This command will basically harvest all the data but instead of writing them to the archive file, these data will be written to a local file (local where the WLST script is running). This command is called dumpDiagnosticData.

Syntax:

```
dumpDiagnosticData(resourceName,fileName,frequency,duration,Server=None,date
Format="HH:mm:ss:SSS")
```

Where the options have the following meaning
- resourceName: System Resource name where data is polled from.
- fileName: file name where data will be dumped.
- frequency: polling frequency
- duration: total collection duration
- Server: name of the server
- dateFormat: date pattern

Example WLST script:

```
# connect to the server
connect('weblogic','<password>','t3://localhost:12001')

# server runtime
serverRuntime()

#dumps diagnostic harvester data
dumpDiagnosticData('myResource','/application/data/wldf/test.data',500,1000,Server='MS1',dateFormat="
HH:mm:ss:SSS")
```

Summary

This chapter has introduced the harvester component which is the WLDF subsystem for collecting metrics from runtime MBeans. In order to collect metrics from different MBeans, each harvester component can contain multiple metric definitions, execution targets and attribute expressions.

Taking snapshots of current state for analysis

Diagnostic Images

While metrics are configurations to gather specific sets of MBean attributes together as a metric, WebLogic offers the generation of state snapshots. These snapshots are called "diagnostic images".

Snapshots are a very important way to communication between administrator group or hosting provider, project group and developers. Usually developers do not have access to production environments and therefore the administrators can provide a copy of the current state – a snapshot – to the developers which they can analyze offline.

Another very common scenario is the requirement to compare the state in two different points in time. By taking a snapshot at each time it will be possible for administrators, architects or developers to compare different system states.

Introduction

While metric are configurations to gather specific sets of MBean attributes together as a metric, WebLogic offers the generation of state snapshots. These snapshots are called diagnostic images. Image capture can be triggered from different sources in WebLogic. Triggers can be events, actions on the administration console, a WLST script or a JMX program event.

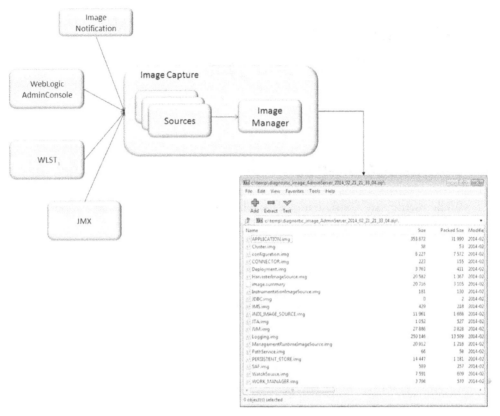

Figure 9.1: *Image capture process*

The WebLogic console offers an extra menu item in the domain structure section for diagnostic images.

The main screen depicts an overview of the configured directories and the last action. In addition it offers the possibility to configure the image capture settings for each server and also to raise an immediate image capture event.

Figure 9.2: *Main screen of the image capture WLDF subsystem*

Configuration of the image capture capabilities

By clicking on the server NAME, WebLogic will bring up a configuration screen which allows the user to configure for each server the path where the images are stored and some other settings like timing.

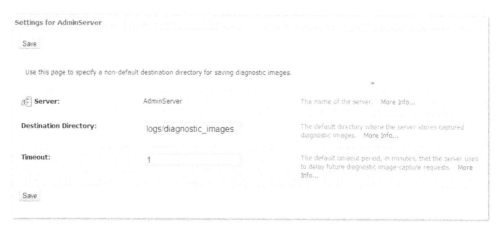

Figure 9.3: *Configure image capture settings using the WebLogic console*

The same configuration can be done using the following WLST script:

```
# connect to the admin server
connect(...)

# switch to edit mode and start editing
edit()
startEdit()

# navigate to server specific ServerDiagnosticConfig mbean of the admin server
cd ('/Servers/AdminServer/ServerDiagnosticConfig/AdminServer')

# set the image capture settings
cmo.setImageDir('logs/diagnostic_images_new')
cmo.setImageTimeout(2)

# save and activate the changes
save()
activate()
```

Issue an image capture request

By clicking on the server name, the configuration screen is coming up (see above) which allows the user to configure the diagnostic image behavior permanently. If a user would like to issue an active image capture request, the user must toggle the select box and then click on "Capture Image".

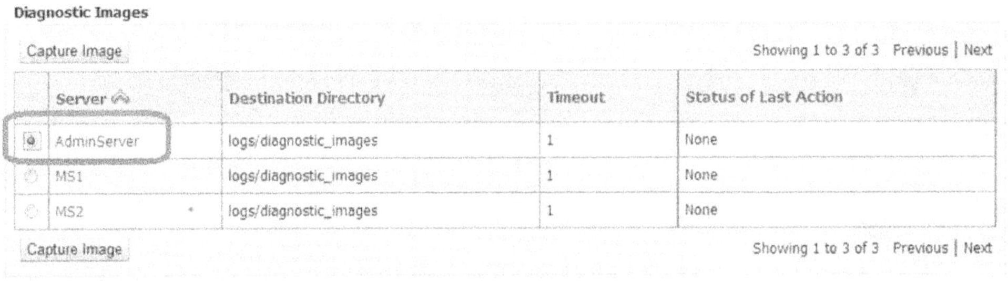

Diagnostic Images

Server	Destination Directory	Timeout	Status of Last Action
AdminServer	logs/diagnostic_images	1	None
MS1	logs/diagnostic_images	1	None
MS2	logs/diagnostic_images	1	None

Capture Image — Showing 1 to 3 of 3 Previous | Next

Figure 9.4: *Select the server instance for the image capture*

After clicking on "Capture Image" a dialog similar to the configuration dialog will appear. The only difference is that this time WebLogic does not require to open en edit session and finally click on save. This time the user can choose between "ok" and "cancel". By selecting ok, an image capture request will be raised.

Capture Diagnostic Image
OK
Cancel
Diagnostic Image Properties
This page provides the ability to overwrite the current Destination Directory.
The name of the server
Name:
AdminServer
Specify destination directory for the Diagnostic Image.
Destination Directory:
logs/diagnostic_images
Specify timeout period for the Diagnostic Image.
Timeout:
1
OK
Cancel

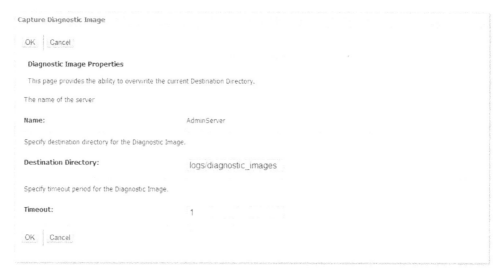

Figure 9.5: *Configure image capturing*

After clicking OK, the capture process will start:

Diagnostic Images
Showing 1 to 3 of 3 Previous | Next
Server
Destination Directory
Timeout
Status of Last Action
AdminServer
logs/diagnostic_images
1
Executing

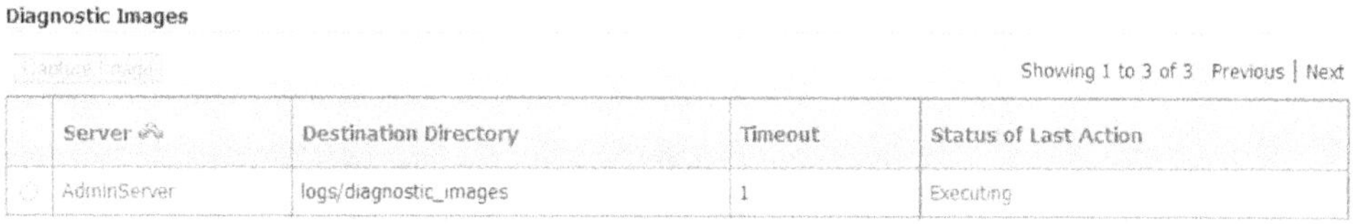

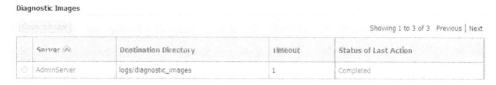

Figure 9.6: *Status update of the image capture process will be displayed in the console*

After the capture process has finished, the status will be updated on the web console:

Diagnostic Images
Showing 1 to 3 of 3 Previous | Next
Server
Destination Directory
Timeout
Status of Last Action
AdminServer
logs/diagnostic_images
1
Completed

Figure 9.7: *Capture process completed*

After the process has been finished, a zip file with the image can be found in the configured directory:

```
ls -l
<root>/martinTest/domains/martinTest_1/servers/AdminServer/logs/diagnostic_i
mages
-rw-r----- 1 martin martin 72130 diagnostic_image_AdminServer_xxx.zip
```

Issue an image request using WLST

```
# connect to the admin server
connect(...)

serverRuntime()
cd ('/WLDFRuntime/WLDFRuntime/WLDFImageRuntime/Image')

# issue image capture task
cmo.captureImage()
```

It is possible to list all image tasks

```
# connect to the admin server
connect(...)

serverRuntime()
cd ('/WLDFRuntime/WLDFRuntime/WLDFImageRuntime/Image')

# issue image capture task
cmo.listImageCaptureTasks()
```

The result may look like:

```
array(weblogic.management.runtime.WLDFImageCreationTaskRuntimeMBean,[[MBeanS
erverInvocationHandler]com.bea:ServerRuntime=AdminServer,Name=DiagnosticImag
eCaptureTaskRuntime_3,Type=WLDFImageCreationTaskRuntime,
[MBeanServerInvocationHandler]com.bea:ServerRuntime=AdminServer,Name=Diagnos
ticImageCaptureTaskRuntime_2,Type=WLDFImageCreationTaskRuntime,
[MBeanServerInvocationHandler]com.bea:ServerRuntime=AdminServer,Name=Diagnos
ticImageCaptureTaskRuntime_1,Type=WLDFImageCreationTaskRuntime])
```

The main reason is that also all completed tasks are kept in this list. If this is not
wanted, it is also possible to remove all completed task from this list so that only
ongoing tasks will be listed. This is possible with following WLST script:

```
# connect to the admin server
connect(...)

serverRuntime()
cd ('/WLDFRuntime/WLDFRuntime/WLDFImageRuntime/Image')

# issue image capture task
cmo.clearCompletedImageCaptureTasks()
```

Additional Tasks in WLST to work with diagnostic images

Starting with WebLogic 12.1.2, WLST has been extended with additional commands in order to handle WLDF diagnostic images. The most important functionality here is to download diagnostic images from the server to the machine where the WLST script is running. This is particularly useful if the WLST script is running on a remote machine or if the user which runs the WLST script does not even have read access to the directory where WebLogic writes the diagnostic images. The following commands are available in WLST.

captureAndSaveDiagnosticImage

Captures an image and then downloads it to the local machine where the script is running.

captureAndSaveDiagnosticImage(Server=None,outputFile=None)

- Server: name of the server where the System Resource is running.

- outputFile: The file to which image will be saved

Example:

```
# connect to the server
connect(…)

# switch to the server runtime
serverRuntime()

captureAndSaveDiagnosticImage(Server=MS1,outputFile=/data/ms1_image_data)
```

getAvailableCapturedImages

A WLST function which asks the server to provide a list of diagnostic images which are available on that server and which have been created in the image directory on the server.

Example:

```
# connect to the server
connect(…)

# switch to the server runtime
serverRuntime()

getAvailableCapturedImages()
```

Or call it using the interactive mode

```
wls:/testdomain/serverRuntime> getAvailableCapturedImages()
Connecting to http://localhost:12001 with userid weblogic ...
array(java.lang.String,['diagnostic_image_AdminServer_2014_05_30_17_13_07.zi
p', 'diagnostic_image_AdminServer_2014_05_30_17_25_08.zip',
'diagnostic_image_AdminServer_2014_05_30_17_26_19.zip'])
```

saveDiagnosticImageCaptureFile

This method does not trigger a "capture" activity. It just downloads an existing diagnostic image from the server.

saveDiagnosticImageCaptureFile(imageName, outputFile=None)

- imageName = name of the diagnostic Image

- outputFile = path to store retrieved image file to. (defaults to imageName in the current folder)

Example:

```
# connect to the server
connect(…)

# switch to the server runtime
serverRuntime()

saveDiagnosticImageCaptureFile(imageName, '<localFileName>.zip')
```

Or call it using the interactive mode:

```
# Get the list of images
wls:/mydomain/serverRuntime>images=getAvailableCapturedImages()
Connecting to http://localhost:7001 with userid weblogic ...

# Retrieve the first image in the returned array
wls:/mydomain/serverConfig> saveDiagnosticImageCaptureFile(images[0])
Retrieving diagnostic_image_myserver_2009_06_25_12_12_50.zip to local path
diagnostic_image_myserver_2009_06_25_12_12_50.zip
Connecting to http://localhost:7001 with userid weblogic ...
```

saveDiagnosticImageCaptureEntryFile

Diagnostic images can grow large. As already discussed, an image consists of multiple files. This command does not download the complete image but just a part of this images. This feature is especially useful to download flight recorder information.

saveDiagnosticImageCaptureEntryFile(imageName,   imageEntryName, outputFile=None)

- imageName = diagnostic image name file containing the desired entry.

- imageEntryName = entry name in image entry to download; the following are supported

    image.summary
    JTA.img
    JRockitFlightRecorder.jfr
    WatchSource.img
    configuration.img
    WORK_MANAGER.img
    JNDI_IMAGE_SOURCE.img
    APPLICATION.img
    InstrumentationImageSource.img
    SAF.img
    Logging.img
    PERSISTENT_STORE.img
    JDBC.img
    PathService.img
    JMS.img
    Deployment.img
    JVM.img
    CONNECTOR.img

- outputFile = local path to store the retrieved image entry

Example:

```
# connect to the server
connect(…)

# switch to the server runtime
serverRuntime()

saveDiagnosticImageCaptureEntryFile("diag…", 'image.summary', 'testWLD.sum')
```

exportDiagnosticDataFromServer

Executes a query on the server and downloads the data. The downloaded data is saved in an XML file

exportDiagnosticDataFromServer(logicalName="", exportFileName="", query="")

- beginTimestamp = Timestamp (inclusive) of the earliest record to be added

- endTimestamp = Timestamp (exclusive) of the latest record to be added

- exportFileName = file name for the exported data

- logicalName = logical name of the log file (e.g. HarvestedDataArchive, EventsDataArchive, ServerLog, DomainLog, HTTPAccessLog, WebAppLog, ConnectorLog, and JMSMessageLog)

- query = filter condition expression

Example:

```
# connect to the server
connect(…)

# switch to the server runtime
serverRuntime()

exportDiagnosticDataFromServer(logicalName="HTTPAccessLog",
exportFileName="myExport.xml")
```

The resulting file will look similar to this:

```
<?xml version='1.0' encoding='utf-8'?>
<DiagnosticData xmlns:xsi="http://www.w3.org/2001/XMLSchema-instance"
xsi:schemaLocation="http://www.bea.com/ns/weblogic/90/diagn
ostics/accessor/export.xsd export.xsd"
xmlns="http://www.bea.com/ns/weblogic/90/diagnostics/accessor/Export">
  <DataInfo>
    <ColumnInfo><Name>RECORDID</Name><Type>java.lang.Long</Type></ColumnInfo>
    <ColumnInfo><Name>DATE</Name><Type>java.lang.String</Type></ColumnInfo>
    <ColumnInfo><Name>SEVERITY</Name><Type>java.lang.String</Type></ColumnInfo>
    <ColumnInfo><Name>SUBSYSTEM</Name><Type>java.lang.String</Type></ColumnInfo>
    <ColumnInfo><Name>MACHINE</Name><Type>java.lang.String</Type></ColumnInfo>
    <ColumnInfo><Name>SERVER</Name><Type>java.lang.String</Type></ColumnInfo>
    <ColumnInfo><Name>THREAD</Name><Type>java.lang.String</Type></ColumnInfo>
    <ColumnInfo><Name>USERID</Name><Type>java.lang.String</Type></ColumnInfo>
    <ColumnInfo><Name>TXID</Name><Type>java.lang.String</Type></ColumnInfo>
    <ColumnInfo><Name>CONTEXTID</Name><Type>java.lang.String</Type></ColumnInfo>
    <ColumnInfo><Name>TIMESTAMP</Name><Type>java.lang.Long</Type></ColumnInfo>
    <ColumnInfo><Name>MSGID</Name><Type>java.lang.String</Type></ColumnInfo>
    <ColumnInfo><Name>MESSAGE</Name><Type>java.lang.String</Type></ColumnInfo>
  </DataInfo>
  <DataRecord><ColumnData>1</ColumnData><ColumnData>Apr 14, 2014 12:19:58 AM
CEST</ColumnData><ColumnData>Info</ColumnData><Colum
nData>Security</ColumnData><ColumnData>martin-
middleware</ColumnData><ColumnData></ColumnData><ColumnData>[ACTIVE] ExecuteThread:
 '0' for queue: 'weblogic.kernel.Default (self-
tuning)'</ColumnData><ColumnData></ColumnData><ColumnData></ColumnData><ColumnData
></ColumnData><ColumnData>1397427598729</ColumnData><ColumnData>BEA-
000000</ColumnData><ColumnData>Disabling the CryptoJ JCE Prov
ider self-integrity check for better startup performance. To enable this check, specify -
Dweblogic.security.allowCryptoJDefaultJC
EVerification=true.</ColumnData></DataRecord>
  <DataRecord><ColumnData>2</ColumnData><ColumnData>Apr 14, 2014 12:19:58 AM
CEST</ColumnData><ColumnData>Info</ColumnData><Colum
nData>Security</ColumnData><ColumnData>martin-
middleware</ColumnData><ColumnData></ColumnData><ColumnData>[ACTIVE] ExecuteThread:
 '0' for queue: 'weblogic.kernel.Default (self-
tuning)'</ColumnData><ColumnData></ColumnData><ColumnData></ColumnData><ColumnData
></ColumnData><ColumnData>1397427598880</ColumnData><ColumnData>BEA-
000000</ColumnData><ColumnData>Changing the default Random Nu
mber Generator in RSA CryptoJ from ECDRBG to FIPS186PRNG. To disable this change, specify -
Dweblogic.security.allowCryptoJDefault
PRNG=true.</ColumnData></DataRecord>
```

Summary

The Diagnostic Image features in WLDF provides a useful feature which captures the most important pieces of data of many different runtime MBeans. These images will be saved in a zip archive to a predefined folder. Different events can trigger WebLogic to capture and save an image. This includes events, WLST scripts, JMX programs and notification events.

Watch out for diagnostic conditions

Watches

Monitoring is an exhausting and tedious task which is nearly impossible for humans. Can you imagine sitting down for hours and hours (or even days or weeks) looking continuously at a screen and watching dozens or even hundreds of state values for specific conditions to happen? Beside the fact that it is impossible for humans to concentrate that long and to remember all the different conditions to consider we would not be able to react fast enough, especially if multiple conditions happen at the same time. This is definitely not a task for humans but for automated processes. WLDF defines a special component for this task which is called "Watch".

Data created by different sources can be filtered and analyzed for specific events. This filtering and analyzing in WLDF is done by the WLDF watch subcomponents.

Introduction to Diagnostics

Collecting metrics and images are always the first step as this creates the foundation for analysis and actions. In WLDF actions are configured using the WLDF component Watches and Notifications. Both WLDF components watches and notifications are depending on each other even though they are configured separately. In diagnostics, it is necessary to associate a watch with a notification. Watches and notifications actually have a many-to-many relationship with each other, which means that it is possible to associate different notifications to a watch. On the other hand, one notification can work together with multiple watches.

Watches consume the data collected by metric, images or log files and - based on rules - filter out the data which you are interested in. If a watch find an interesting piece of information, all associated notifications will be invoked in order to process their tasks. Therefore instead of waiting and searching for special events or conditions to happen, the system will inform you whenever this is the case. This is based on the different rules which can be configured for each watch.

Note that watches and notifications will always be configured as part of an existing diagnostic module.

Here are the differences between watches and notifications

Watch:

- Based on the collected data and the configured rule set identifies events/conditions which are of interest
- Watch rules contain a rule expression, conditions when to raise an alarm and one or many notifications which should be informed

Notification

- Notification is not the data analysis but an action which must be executed whenever a watch condition was raised
- Different types of notifications are supported, e.g. JMX, JMS,SNMP, SMTP
- Also images can be created as a result of a notification

Data can be generated from three different sources (metrics, log files and instrumentation). The different watch rules defined in the different watches will analyze and filter that data. These are managed by the watch manager

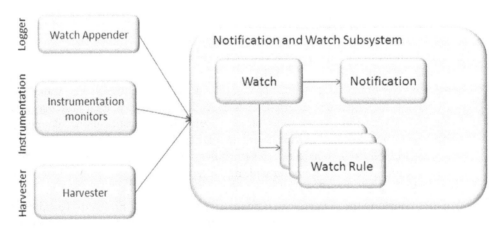

Figure 10.1: *Relationship between data sources, watches, notifications and watch rules*

Types of Watches

Due to the different sources of the information WLDF supports three different kind of watches. Each type has also different watch rules and rule execution times. Rules which have to be evaluated against metrics will only be applied after the harvester execution has been completed. All of the other rules are executed in real time when the data events arrive.

- **Harvester watches:** Watches which contains rules which will be applied to the metric data collected by the configured harvesters (Note: harvesters from the same diagnostic module!)

- **Log watches:** Watches which contains rules which will be applied to log events in the current server log. Note that this can be further restricted by log severity

- **Instrumentation:** Watches which contains rules which will be applied to events created by instrumentation components

General configuration

Watches are sub-configurations of a diagnostic module. Therefore, they are also configured as part of a diagnostic module.

Figure 10.2: *Main configuration screen for watches*

There are three main configuration items which can be configured for all watches.
- It is possible to enable or disable the complete WLDF subsystem.
- It is possible to define the default severity category

- It is possible to define which level of log events should be considered for the watch manager to pass on to the watch evaluation.

In order to configure a watch module which contains only watches and notifications for critical errors (like stuck threads, out-of-memory or similar) the following settings can be used.

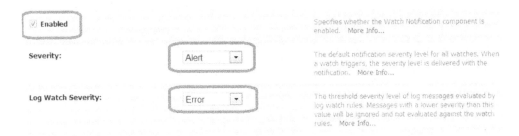

Figure 10.3: *Watch subsystem configuration for critical content*

This can also be done using WLST:

```
# connect to the admin server
connect(...)

# start the edit mode
edit()
startEdit()

# change to the watch mbean of your diagnostic module  -  in this case
'TestModule'
cd
('/WLDFSystemResources/TestModule/WLDFResource/TestModule/WatchNotification/
TestModule')

# enable the module
cmo.setEnabled(true)

# set the level of log entries you are interested in getting (in this case
to 'Error')
cmo.setLogWatchSeverity('Error')

# set the default severity which will be passed to the notifications
cmo.setSeverity('Alert')

save()
activate()
```

As this is a change which does not require a restart and will be effective immediately, this means that this change can be done at any time. Especially the log severity is very useful. So it is possible for an administrator to run the log file watch with "Error" for normal operation but in case of an issue he can lower this down to "Info" or even "Debug".

This can also be done using JMX. The following code shows how to enable the watch subsystem using JMX:

```
private void setWatchAndNotificationEnabledFlag(ObjectName myDiagnosticModule, boolean enabled)
         throws WLDFAutomationException
{
  try {
     // get WLDF resource
     ObjectName myWLDFresourceMBean =
            (ObjectName)myJMXEditWrapper.getAttribute(myDiagnosticModule, "WLDFResource");

     // from the resource get the watch subsystem
     ObjectName myWatchNotificationMBean =
            (ObjectName)myJMXEditWrapper.getAttribute(myWLDFresourceMBean, "WatchNotification");

     // set harvester flag to true
     myJMXEditWrapper.setAttribute(myWatchNotificationMBean,
                   new Attribute("Enabled",new Boolean(enabled)));
  }
  catch(Exception ex) {
     ex.printStackTrace();
     throw new WLDFAutomationException(ex);
  }
}
```

Watches can be created by adding them using "New" to the watch manager.

Figure 10.4: *Create a new watch*

Creation of a watch will depend on the type of the watch. The most common watch will most likely be a harvester watch but WebLogic also supports other types as explained in the next sections of this chapter.

Creating a Harvester watch

A watch which is based on data collected by metrics is called a harvester watch. When a watch is created, the type must be selected and the watch must get a unique name.

The following screenshots shows how to select the watch type using the WLS admin console.

Figure 10.5: *Creating a harvester watch*

In the generic form to create watches you need to specify a unique name and the watch type (in this case "collected metrics").

After the watch framework has been created, the next screen will allow you to define the watch rule

Create Watch

Back   Next   Finish   Cancel

Configure Watch Rule Expressions

Add expressions to create the rule for your watch

Current Watch Rule:

Edit

Expressions :

Add Expressions   Combine   Uncombine   Move Up   Move Down   Remove   Negate

No Rule Specified

Add Expressions   Combine   Uncombine   Move Up   Move Down   Remove   Negate

Figure 10.6: *By default the watch rule is empty*

Watches are only as good as the rules defined for a watch. We need to note that WebLogic uses a rather unusual convention for rule definitions. The "${}" syntax is used to describe an MBean attribute. Such an attribute consist of the MBean and the attribute name. Within "${}" the MBean type is defined with a "[]" boundary. WebLogic uses the "//" combination in order to separate MBean type and attribute name.

So a simplified complete definition is ${[<MBean type name>]//<attribute-name>}.

For this example we are using a rule which fires as soon as the free memory heap falls below 10% of the complete heap. The following rule will be used:

```
${[weblogic.management.runtime.JVMRuntimeMBean]//HeapFreePercent} < 10
```

The rule above has a number of shortcuts. The main shortcut is, that it defines an MBean type. This means that the rule will fire for all instances of this type, which in some occasions is exactly what we want.

It is possible to further define and restrict the MBean definition by also specifying the real MBean instance name and also the MBean environment.

So a more complete definition is ${environment>//[<MBean type name>]<MBean-instance-name>//<attribute-name>}.

By clicking on the "Edit" button, a new form will show up which allows the experienced user to enter the watch rule as free text. This form will also be used later to fine tune generated watch rules, because the expression generator has its limitations.

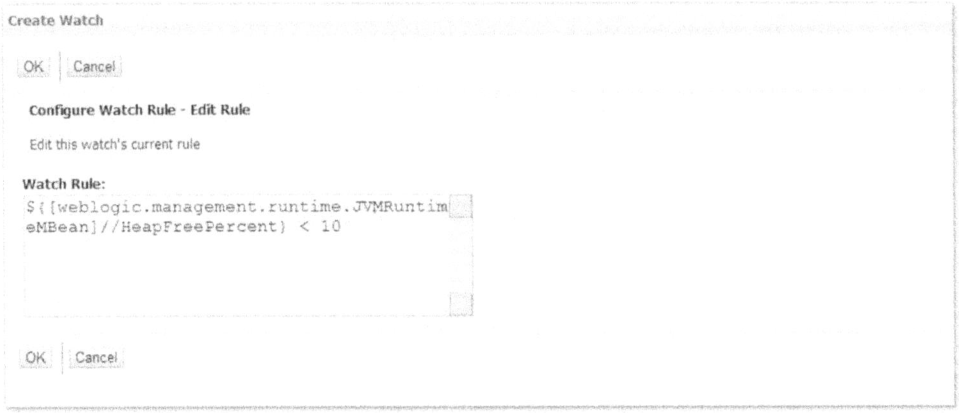

Figure 10.7: *Edit form in order to enter the watch rule as free text*

After confirming this rule (using "Ok") the rule will show up on the watch definition.

Figure 10.8: *Watch containing one expression*

It is possible to add more rules to a watch and to combine them using the Boolean operators "and" or "or". Additional expressions can either entered directly as text (as we have done with the first expression) or can be added by using the expression wizard. For demonstration purpose, the following steps will depict how to define the same rule using the expression wizard.

In the first step the user can chose which MBean runtime server should be used. Two different options are available: ServerRuntime and DomainRuntime

Figure 10.9: *Selection of Runtime-MBeantree*

Depending on the selected runtime, the user can now either chose an MBean type from the dropdown list or enter (-> custom type) an MBean type name.

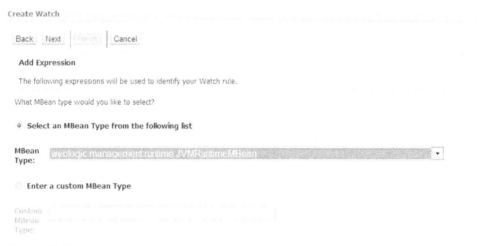

Figure 10.10: *Select or enter the MBean type name*

After the type has been selected, the user will advance to the next step in the wizard. This step enables the user select an available server instance. The content of the drop down list depends on the runtime type and on the list of actual running server in the domain. Note that this list does not allow you to select servers which are not running. In order to use a server which is actually not running, you need to edit the rule afterwards.

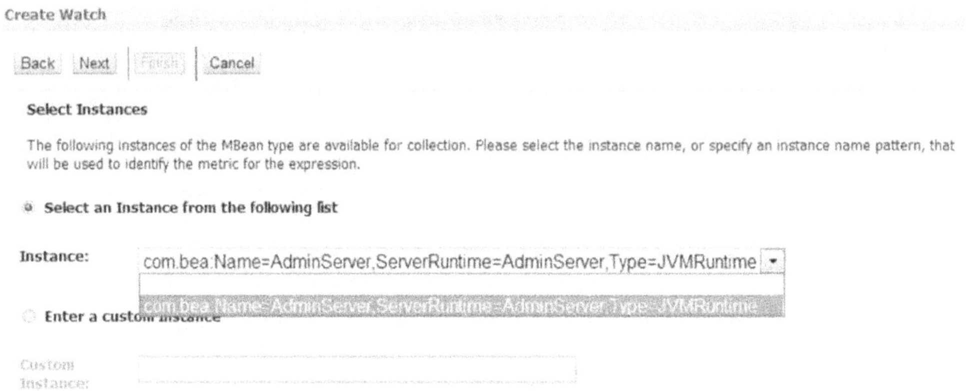

Figure 10.11: *Selection of MBean instance*

Finally the last step allows the user to define the watch expression based on the MBean type and/or instance defined during the steps of this wizard.

Similar to other steps, if is either possible to select an attribute from a drop down list in case the MBean type is known to the wizard or it is possible to enter a full attribute expression.

In addition to the attribute the user needs to specify a Boolean operator and a value against which the attribute should be evaluated.

Add Expression

The following expressions will be used to identify your Watch rule.

You need to identify the MBean attribute(s) that will identify which values you would like to watch. You can select a single attribute to watch, or enter an attribute expression.

An attribute expression can be used to identify a single attribute, a single nested attribute, or even a collection of attributes that is deeply nested within an MBean instance. If an attribute expression results in more than one value, the Watch expression will be evaluated against each value returned. See the WebLogic Diagnostics Framework documentation for more details on attribute expressions.

How would you like to identify this Watch expression attribute?

○ **Select an attribute from the following list**

Message Attribute: HeapFreePercent ▾

○ **Enter an Attribute Expression**

Attribute Expression:

What operator would you like to select?

Operator: <   ▾

What is the value of your expression?

Value: 10

Figure 10.12: *Define attribute and expression*

WLDF watch rule expressions support a number of operators which can be used for evaluation.

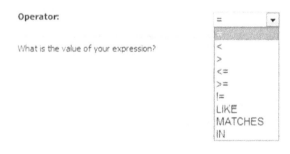

Figure 10.13: *Supported operators*

Finally – after committing the changes - the rule will show up in the watch definition.

Configure Watch Rule Expressions

Add expressions to create the rule for your watch

Current Watch Rule:

```
(${ServerRuntime//
[weblogic.management.runtime.JVMRuntimeM
Bean]
com.bea:Name=AdminServer,ServerRuntime=A
dminServer,Type=JVMRuntime//HeapFreePerc
ent} < 10)
```

Edit

Expressions :

Add Expressions | Combine | Uncombine | Move Up | Move Down | Remove | Negate

☐ **${ServerRuntime//[weblogic.management.runtime.JVMRuntimeMBean]
com.bea:Name=AdminServer,ServerRuntime=AdminServer,Type=JVMRuntime//HeapFreePercent} <
10**

Figure 10.14: *Rule defined with expression editor*

Note that this rule looks slightly different to the rule we had entered directly at the first step. In addition to the first rule the reader can see the runtime MBean environment and the MBean instance name.

The new rule is:

```
(${ServerRuntime//[weblogic.management.runtime.JVMRuntimeMBean]com.bea:Name=
AdminServer,ServerRuntime=AdminServer,Type=JVMRuntime//HeapFreePercent} <
10)
```

Of course this rule can then be edited directly and the parts which might be unwanted can be removed or changed.

Create the same watch using WLST:

It is of course possible to create the same watch and rule using WLST or JMX. The following code script shows how to create the same configuration using WLST.

```
# start the edit mode  (must be already connected to the admin server !)
edit()
startEdit()

cd ('/')
# create the watch MBean
cmo.createWatch('JVM-HeapWatch')

#change to the new MBean (note the deep path)
cd('/WLDFSystemResources/TestModule/WLDFResource/TestModule/WatchNotification/TestModule/Watches/JVM-
HeapWatch')
# set to type "Harvester"
cmo.setRuleType('Harvester')
# enable the watch
cmo.setEnabled(true)
# create the rule expression
```

```
cmo.setRuleExpression('(${ServerRuntime//[weblogic.management.runtime.JVMRuntimeMBean]com.bea:Name=Ad
minServer,ServerRuntime=AdminServer,Type=JVMRuntime//HeapFreePercent} < 10)')
cmo.setAlarmType(None)

# save work and activate changes
save()
activate()
```

Create the same using JMX:

The following method shows how a watch can be created using JMX.

```
public void createWatch( ObjectName myDiagnosticModule, String watchName,
                         String ruleType, String ruleExpressions,
                         String alarmType, int alarmRestPeriod,
                         boolean enabled, ObjectName[] notifications)  throws WLDFAutomationException
{
   if (doesWatchExist(myDiagnosticModule, watchName))
      throw new WLDFAutomationException("Watch "+watchName+" already exist !");

   try {
      // get WLDF resource
      ObjectName myWLDFresourceMBean =
               (ObjectName)myJMXEditWrapper.getAttribute(myDiagnosticModule, "WLDFResource");

      // from the resource => get the harvester
      ObjectName myWatchNotificationMBean = (ObjectName)
               myJMXEditWrapper.getAttribute(myWLDFresourceMBean, "WatchNotification");

      // create new type
      ObjectName myNewWatchMBean = (ObjectName)myJMXEditWrapper.invoke(myWatchNotificationMBean,
                         "createWatch",
                         new Object[]{new String(watchName)},
                         new String [] {String.class.getName()});

      // set values
      myJMXEditWrapper.setAttribute(myNewWatchMBean, new Attribute("Enabled",new Boolean(enabled)));
      myJMXEditWrapper.setAttribute(myNewWatchMBean, new Attribute("RuleType",ruleType));
      myJMXEditWrapper.setAttribute(myNewWatchMBean,
                         new Attribute("RuleExpression",ruleExpressions));
      myJMXEditWrapper.setAttribute(myNewWatchMBean, new Attribute("AlarmType",alarmType));
      myJMXEditWrapper.setAttribute(myNewWatchMBean,
                         new Attribute("AlarmResetPeriod",new Integer(alarmRestPeriod)));

      // set attributes
      if (notifications==null)
              notifications = new ObjectName[0];
      myJMXEditWrapper.setAttribute(myNewWatchMBean, new Attribute("Notifications",notifications));
   }
   catch(Exception ex) {
      ex.printStackTrace();
      throw new WLDFAutomationException(ex);
   }
}
```

Creating a Log watch

A watch which is based on log file data is called a log watch. When a watch is created, the type must be selected and the watch must get a unique name.

The following screenshots shows how to select the watch type using the WLS admin console.

Figure 10.15: *Creating a log watch*

In the generic form to create watches you need to specify a unique name and the watch type (in this case "collected metrics").

After the watch framework has been created, the next screen will allow you to define the watch rule. This screen is very similar to the watch view of the harvester watch.

Create Watch

Back   Next   Finish   Cancel

Configure Watch Rule Expressions

Add expressions to create the rule for your watch

Current Watch Rule:

Edit

Expressions :

Add Expressions   Combine   Uncombine   Move Up   Move Down   Remove   Negate

No Rule Specified

Add Expressions   Combine   Uncombine   Move Up   Move Down   Remove   Negate

Figure 10.16: *Empty log watch view*

The possibility to enter a log watch rule is basically the identical input form as we have seen for the harvester expression rule. Therefore we will only examine the expression wizard in this section.

By clicking on "Add Expression" the console will bring up the wizard to define a log watch rule.

Figure 10.17: *Definition of the log watch rule*

This wizard has three parts, the message attribute, the operator and the values. It is possible to choose from a list of attributes WebLogic may have in its log messages.

Figure 10.18: *Create a log watch expression*

In the above case we have defined a rule which will watch out for "ERROR" log file entries. It is also possible by using the "IN" parameter to define a list of possible values.

The corresponding watch rule would look like:

```
SEVERITY IN ('CRITICAL', 'ERROR', 'WARNING')
```

In the next step it is optionally possible to define alarm settings.

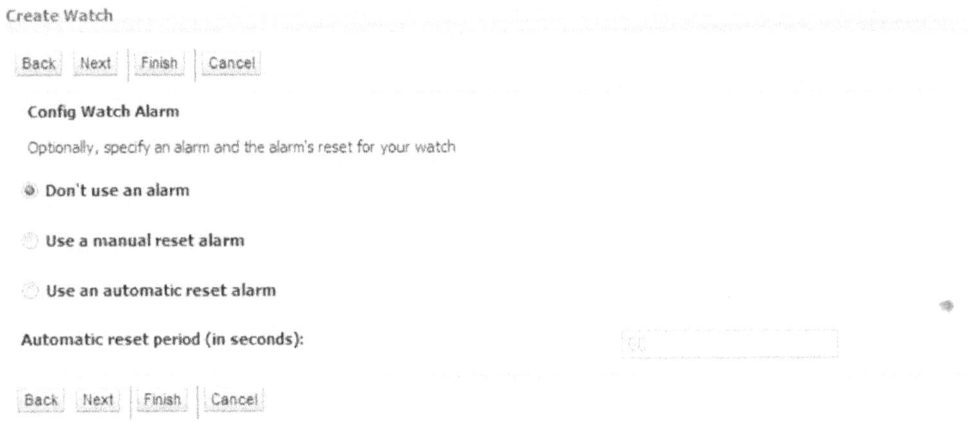

Figure 10.19: *Alarm settings for log watch rule*

In the last step it is possible to select one or more notification modules which should be used in case this rule results positive.

Figure 10.20: *Notification selection for log watch rules*

Are more complex example can include nested boolean combinations of expressions. For example a more complex rule might be:

```
((SERVER = 'MS1') AND (MACHINE = 'testsystem.test.com')) OR (SEVERITY IN
('CRITICAL', 'ERROR', 'WARNING'))
```

In the WebLogic console this would look like:

Figure 10.21: *Complex watch rule*

Create the same watch using WLST:

It is of course possible to create the same watch and rule using WLST or JMX. The following code script shows how to create the same configuration using WLST.

```
# start the edit mode  (must be already connected to the admin server !)
edit()
startEdit()

# switch to the diagnostic module and create the watch MBean
cd('/WLDFSystemResources/TestModule/WLDFResource/TestModule/WatchNotificatio
n/TestModule')

# create watch
cmo.createWatch('TestServerLog')

# switch to the watch mbean
```

```
cd('/WLDFSystemResources/TestModule/WLDFResource/TestModule/WatchNotificatio
n/TestModule/Watches/TestServerLog')

# configure the watch mbean
cmo.setRuleType('Log')
cmo.setEnabled(true)

# set the expression
cmo.setRuleExpression('(SEVERITY = \'ERROR\')')

# set the alarm
cmo.setAlarmType('None')

# set the notification
set('Notifications',jarray.array([ObjectName('com.bea:Name=SERVER.PROFILE,Ty
pe=weblogic.diagnostics.descriptor.WLDFJMXNotificationBean,Parent=[martinTes
t_1]/WLDFSystemResources[TestModule],Path=WLDFResource[TestModule]/WatchNoti
fication[TestModule]/JMXNotifications[SERVER.PROFILE]')], ObjectName))

# save work and activate changes
save()
activate()
```

The next WLST script shows how to create the complex rule describes above which
contains three expressions and partly nested logical combinations.

```
# start the edit mode  (must be already connected to the admin server !)
edit()
startEdit()

# switch to the diagnostic module and create the watch MBean
cd('/WLDFSystemResources/TestModule/WLDFResource/TestModule/WatchNotificatio
n/TestModule')

# create watch
cmo.createWatch(ComplexLogfileWatch)

# switch to the watch mbean
cd('/WLDFSystemResources/TestModule/WLDFResource/TestModule/WatchNotificatio
n/TestModule/Watches/TestServerLog')

# configure the watch mbean
cmo.setRuleType('Log')
cmo.setEnabled(true)

# set the expression
cmo.setRuleExpression('((SERVER = \'MS1\') AND (MACHINE =
\'testsystem.test.com\')) OR (SEVERITY IN (\'CRITICAL\', \'ERROR\',
\'WARNING\'))')

# set the alarm
cmo.setAlarmType('None')

# set the notification
set('Notifications',jarray.array([ObjectName('com.bea:Name=SERVER.PROFILE,Ty
pe=weblogic.diagnostics.descriptor.WLDFJMXNotificationBean,Parent=[martinTes
```

```
t_1]/WLDFSystemResources[TestModule],Path=WLDFResource[TestModule]/WatchNoti
fication[TestModule]/JMXNotifications[SERVER.PROFILE]')], ObjectName))

# save work and activate changes
save()
activate()
```

Creating an instrumentation watch

A watch which is based on an instrumentation event is called an "Event Data" watch. When a watch is created, the type must be selected and the watch must get a unique name.

The following screenshots shows how to select the watch type using the WLS admin console.

Figure 10.22: *Creating an event watch*

In the generic form to create watches you need to specify a unique name and the watch type (in this case "Event Data").

After the watch framework has been created, the next screen will allow you to define the watch rule. This screen is very similar to the watch view of the harvester watch.

The following steps describe how to create an event watch rule.

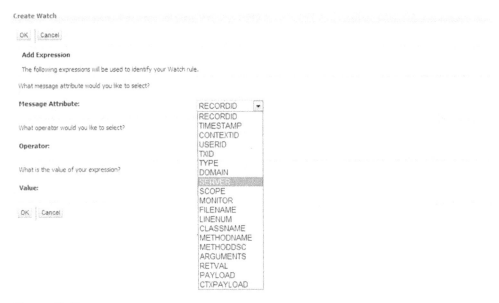

Figure 10.23: *Expression wizard for event watch rules*

An event expression consists of an attribute which can be selected from a drop-down list, a Boolean operator and a value to validate against. All three items can be defined using this expression wizard view.

The other steps like alarm and notifications are equal to the other two watch types.

Create the same watch using WLST:

It is of course possible to create the same watch and rule using WLST or JMX. The following code script shows how to create the same configuration using WLST.

```
# start the edit mode   (must be already connected to the admin server !)
edit()
startEdit()

# switch to the diagnostic module and create the watch MBean
cd('/WLDFSystemResources/TestModule/WLDFResource/TestModule/WatchNotificatio
n/TestModule')

# create watch
cmo.createWatch('EventTestWatch')

# switch to the watch mbean
cd('/WLDFSystemResources/TestModule/WLDFResource/TestModule/WatchNotificatio
n/TestModule/Watches/EventTestWatch')

# configure the watch mbean
```

```
cmo.setRuleType('EventData')
cmo.setEnabled(true)

# set the expression
cmo.setRuleExpression('(SERVER = \'martinTest.testdomain.com\') AND (USERID
= \'martin\')')

# set the alarm
cmo.setAlarmType('None')

# set the notification
set('Notifications',jarray.array([ObjectName('com.bea:Name=SERVER.PROFILE,Ty
pe=weblogic.diagnostics.descriptor.WLDFJMXNotificationBean,Parent=[martinTes
t_1]/WLDFSystemResources[TestModule],Path=WLDFResource[TestModule]/WatchNoti
fication[TestModule]/JMXNotifications[SERVER.PROFILE]')], ObjectName))

# save work and activate changes
save()
activate()
```

Removing a watch from a diagnostic module

It is of course always also possible to remove a watch definition from a module. This
can be necessary if a diagnostic module should be changed, e.g. a change in the
profiles (see later chapters of this book regarding component profiles).

Delete a watch using WLST:

```
# start the edit mode   (must be already connected to the admin server !)
edit()
startEdit()

# switch to the diagnostic module and create the watch MBean
cd('/WLDFSystemResources/TestModule/WLDFResource/TestModule/WatchNotification/TestModule')

# destroy the watch
cmo.destroyWatch('TestServerLog')

# save work and activate changes
save()
activate()
```

Delete a watch using JMX:

```
public void deleteWatch(ObjectName myDiagnosticModule, String watchName)
        throws WLDFAutomationException
{
   if (doesWatchExist(myDiagnosticModule, watchName))
   {
      try {
         // get WLDF resource
         ObjectName myWLDFresourceMBean = (ObjectName)
                myJMXEditWrapper.getAttribute(myDiagnosticModule, "WLDFResource");

         // from the resource => get the harvester
         ObjectName myWatchNotificationMBean = (ObjectName)
                myJMXEditWrapper.getAttribute(myWLDFresourceMBean, "WatchNotification");

         // delete
         myJMXEditWrapper.invoke(myWatchNotificationMBean,
                     "destroyWatch",
```

```
                        new Object[]{getWatch(myDiagnosticModule, watchName)},
                        new String [] {ObjectName.class.getName()});
        }
    catch(Exception ex) {
        ex.printStackTrace();
        throw new WLDFAutomationException(ex);
    }
  }
 }
}
```

Summary

Watches consume the data collected by metric, images or log files and - based on rules - filter out the data which you are interested in. If a watch find an interesting piece of information, all associated notifications will be invoked in order to process their tasks. Therefore instead of waiting and searching for special events or conditions to happen, the system will inform you whenever this is the case.

This is based on the different rules which can be configured for each watch. WLDF supports three different types of watches: harvester, log and event watches. The difference is the source of the data. For all watches WLDF supports simple and complex rule expressions. Watches can be created using the admin console, WLST or JMX.

Getting notified and alarmed for certain system states

Notifications and WLDF

After special system states or conditions have been reached – as discussed in the previous chapter – some stakeholder must be informed. Without notifications, monitoring the systems is useless, and the notification must be done immediately. Furthermore, in our complex world, many different methods and protocols for sending out notifications are used.

This chapter discusses the notification component of WLDF. Whenever a watch found something which is of interest, it will trigger one or more notifications in order to inform certain stakeholders about this event. Different technologies for notifications are supported.

Introduction to Notifications

Notifications are configured actions within a diagnostic module which can be called whenever a watch rule expression has been evaluated to "true". Please note that notifications are defined in the scope of a diagnostic module but may need additional resource configurations from the underlying WebLogic. One example is the email notification which requires a JavaMail provider to be configured on WebLogic level. Up to WebLogic 12.1.3 WebLogic supports 5 different kinds of notifications. Please be aware that Oracle will add a more generic notification type in WebLogic 12.2.1 which allows the execution of a WLST command or script.

The following types of notifications are available up to WebLogic 12.1.2 and 12.1.3:

- **Java Management Extensions (JMX):** Send a JMX notification

- **Java Message Service (JMS):** Send a JMS message.

- **Simple Mail Transfer Protocol (SMTP):** Send an email based on the Java Mail API. This requires that a mail provider is configured in WebLogic and registered into the JNDI of the managed-server where the watch expression has been evaluated to true

---

- **Simple Network Management Protocol (SNMP):** Send an SNMP trap

- **Diagnostic image creation:** Create a diagnostic image.

Please note that watches and notifications are in a unidirectional many-to-,any (n:m) relationship, which means that one watch can trigger multiple notifiers, and one notifier can be triggered by multiple watches.

Figure 11.1: *Watch / Notification relationship*

All notifications are defined in the scope of a diagnostic module. Notifications are created independent from watches. You can define the notifications first and then assign them to watches during the definitions of watches. Or you can define the watches first, define the notifications afterwards and finally modify the watches and assign notifications to them.

Figure 11.2: *Define notifications in the scope of a diagnostic module*

The notification creation depends on the type of notification. Each type requires different settings and may even require the creation of resources outside of the diagnostic module.

WLDF Notifications and the WebLogic API

Due to the fact that WebLogic supports a number of different notification types, WebLogic offers different "create", "lookup" and "destroy" methods for the different notification types. In order to simplify the work with WLDF notifications when used from Java the following generalized methods can be used. Subsequent discussions show how to use the functions in your own code.

The following "enum" definition in Java will help us to generalize the method and still use type checking. Enums are almost always a better alternative than just using strings.

```
public enum NotificationType {
    JMX,
    JMS,
    SNMP,
    SMTP,
    Image
}
```

The following method can be used to create a notification. Note that this function will only create the empty notification without doing any configuration as this is then type dependent. Pay attention to the WebLogic MBean call **create"+notificationType.toString()+"Notification** as this will call the real – type specific – create method

```
public ObjectName createNotification( ObjectName myDiagnosticModule,
                                      NotificationType notificationType,
                                      String notificationName)  throws WLDFAutomationException
{
    if (doesWatchExist(myDiagnosticModule, notificationName))
        throw new WLDFAutomationException("Notification "+notificationName+" already exist !");

    try {
        // get WLDF resource
        ObjectName myWLDFresourceMBean = (ObjectName)
                myJMXEditWrapper.getAttribute(myDiagnosticModule, "WLDFResource");

        // from the resource => get the watch&notifaction container MBean
        ObjectName myWatchNotificationMBean = (ObjectName)
                myJMXEditWrapper.getAttribute(myWLDFresourceMBean, "WatchNotification");

        // create new type and return.  Configuration must be done elsewhere
        return (ObjectName)myJMXEditWrapper.invoke(myWatchNotificationMBean,
                        "create"+notificationType.toString()+"Notification",
                        new Object[]{new String(notificationName)},
                        new String [] {String.class.getName()});
    }
    catch(Exception ex) {
        ex.printStackTrace();
        throw new WLDFAutomationException(ex);
    }
}
```

In a very similar matter notifications can be destroyed. In order to clean up the system or — as discussed in the next part of the book - working with profiles it is often necessary to cleanup old configurations.

```
public void deleteNotification(ObjectName myDiagnosticModule, NotificationType notificationType,
                          String notificationName) throws WLDFAutomationException
{
   if (doesNotificationExist(myDiagnosticModule, notificationType, notificationName)) {
      try {
         // get WLDF resource
         ObjectName myWLDFresourceMBean = (ObjectName)
                  myJMXEditWrapper.getAttribute(myDiagnosticModule, "WLDFResource");

         // from the resource => get the harvester
         ObjectName myWatchNotificationMBean = (ObjectName)
                  myJMXEditWrapper.getAttribute(myWLDFresourceMBean, "WatchNotification");

         // delete
         myJMXEditWrapper.invoke(myWatchNotificationMBean,
                          "destroy"+notificationType.toString()+"Notification",
                          new Object[]{getNotification(myDiagnosticModule, notificationName)},
                          new String [] {ObjectName.class.getName()});
      }
      catch(Exception ex) {
          ex.printStackTrace();
          throw new WLDFAutomationException(ex);
      }
   }
}
```

It is a good programming style to check if a specific notification already exists before the program tries to create it.

```
public boolean doesNotificationExist(ObjectName myDiagnosticModule,
                      NotificationType notificationType, String notificationName)
                      throws WLDFAutomationException
{
   try {
      // get WLDF resource
      ObjectName myWLDFresourceMBean = (ObjectName)
               myJMXEditWrapper.getAttribute(myDiagnosticModule, "WLDFResource");

      // from the resource => get the harvester
      ObjectName myWatchNotificationMBean = (ObjectName)
               myJMXEditWrapper.getAttribute(myWLDFresourceMBean, "WatchNotification");

      // check if type exist
      ObjectName mynotificationMBean = (ObjectName)myJMXEditWrapper.invoke(myWatchNotificationMBean,
                       "lookup"+notificationType.toString()+"Notification",
                       new Object[]{new String(notificationName)},
                       new String [] {String.class.getName()});

      return mynotificationMBean != null;
   }
   catch(Exception ex) {
      ex.printStackTrace();
      throw new WLDFAutomationException(ex);
   }
}
```

Only for this check WebLogic also offers a type neutral lookup method called *lookupNotification*.

```
public boolean doesNotificationExist(ObjectName myDiagnosticModule, String notificationName)
                          throws WLDFAutomationException
{
   try {
      // get WLDF resource
      ObjectName myWLDFresourceMBean = (ObjectName)
```

```
                myJMXEditWrapper.getAttribute(myDiagnosticModule, "WLDFResource");

        // from the resource => get the harvester
        ObjectName myWatchNotificationMBean = (ObjectName)
                myJMXEditWrapper.getAttribute(myWLDFresourceMBean, "WatchNotification");

        // check if type exist
        ObjectName mynotificationMBean = (ObjectName)myJMXEditWrapper.invoke(myWatchNotificationMBean,
                "lookupNotification",
                new Object[]{new String(notificationName)},
                new String [] {String.class.getName()});

        return mynotificationMBean!= null;
    }
    catch(Exception ex) {
        ex.printStackTrace();
        throw new WLDFAutomationException(ex);
    }
}
```

JMX Notifications

The first notification types we will look at are JMX notifications. During the creation of the notification it is important to choose the correct type. The WLDF runtime component of WebLogic creates a JMX event for every enabled JMX notification as soon as a watch rule is evaluated to true. Consumer applications have to create a JMX listener application and have to register this listener with the WebLogic instance WLDFWatchJMXNotificationRuntimeMBeans in order to receive these notifications. The application clients are responsible of doing their own filtering.

Defining a JMX notification using the WebLogic Console

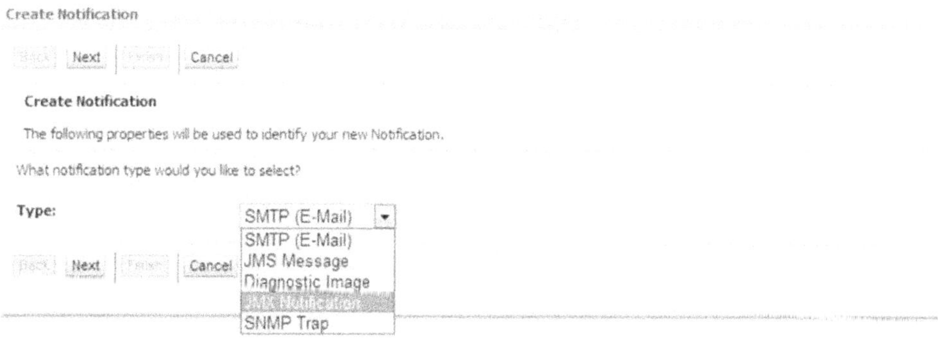

Figure 11.3: *Create a JMX notification*

After you have chosen the notification type, you need to provide a unique name for this notification and define if it is enabled or not.

Figure 11.4: *Define the notification name*

After the name has been defined, an empty notification with this name is created and appear in the notification list.

Figure 11.5: *Notification list with the new notification*

So far we have only create an empty notification which does not yet do much. IN the next step we need to select the newly created notification and specify appropriate properties. For a JMX notification type the only thing we can specify is the type of the notification event which will be issued by the WLDF subsystem. If there no custom types implemented, the only choice which can be selected is the default type with the name weblogic.diagnostics.watch.defaultNotificationType.

Figure 11.6: *Select weblogic.diagnostics.watch.defaultNotificationType*

Now the new JMX notification is ready to be used.

Defining a JMX notification using WLST

The same notification module can of course be created using WLST. The following script demonstrates how to create the same notification using WLST

```
# change to the diagnostic module
cd('/WLDFSystemResources/TestModule/WLDFResource/TestModule/WatchNotificatio
n/TestModule')

# create the new notification
cmo.createJMXNotification('TestJMXNotification')

# switch to the new notification
cd('/WLDFSystemResources/TestModule/WLDFResource/TestModule/WatchNotificatio
n/TestModule/JMXNotifications/TestJMXNotification')

# enable the notification
cmo.setEnabled(true)

# define the type of the notification
cmo.setNotificationType('weblogic.diagnostics.watch.defaultNotificationType'
)
```

It is of course also possible to create the same configuration items using JMX.

```
public void createJMXNotification(JMXWrapper myJMXEditWrapper,
                                  ObjectName myDiagnosticModule, String name)
                                  throws WLDFAutomationException
{
   ObjectName notificationRef = null;
   try {
      WatchNotificationUtils myUtils = new WatchNotificationUtils(myJMXEditWrapper);

      if (myUtils.doesNotificationExist(myDiagnosticModule,name))
      {
         notificationRef = myUtils.getNotification(myDiagnosticModule, name);
      }
      else // create
      {
         notificationRef = myUtils.createNotification(myDiagnosticModule,
                     NotificationType.JMX, name);
      }

      // do the configurations
```

```
    myJMXEditWrapper.setAttribute(notificationRef, new Attribute("Enabled",true));
    // set type
    myJMXEditWrapper.setAttribute(myJMXNotification,
                new Attribute("NotificationType",
                            "weblogic.diagnostics.watch.defaultNotificationType"));
  }
  catch(Exception ex) {
    ex.printStackTrace();
    throw new WLDFAutomationException(ex.getMessage());
  }
}
```

Receiving and using the notification events

These notifications are of course only useful if clients will register with the WebLogic MBeans in order to receive these events. This can be done by implementing a JMX client which registers with the WLS MBean server. The next chapter will show an example of such a listener. This client could also be an application component running inside WebLogic (if the code has the appropriate rights).

JMS Notifications

The second notification types we will look at are JMS notifications. During the creation of the notification it is important to choose the correct type.

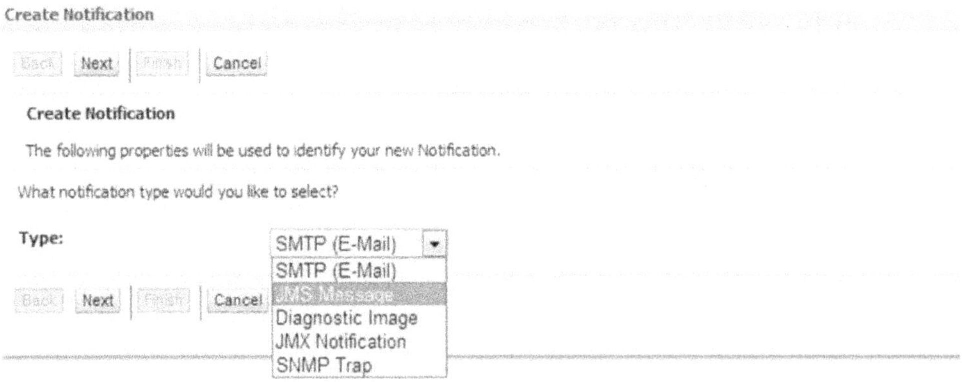

Figure 11.7: *Create a JMS notification*

After you have chosen the notification type, you need to provide a unique name for the new JMS notification and define if it is enabled or not.

Figure 11.8: *Provide a name for the JMS notification*

As a last step it is required to provide the JNDI name of a JMS destination (queue or topic) which should be used by WLDF to send the notification messages to. And of course the JNDI name of the connection factory for the JMS server is required.

Note that the actual creation of the JMS server configuration (if the WebLogic internal JMS server is used) and the definition of the JMS destination is outside of the diagnostic module configuration. These must already exist.

Figure 11.9: *JMS destination details for notifications*

So as you can see JMS notifications rely on external resource configurations which must be already defined on WebLogic level.

Note: This really means that there are resource configurations on WebLogic Level outside of the WLDF subsystem which are required for WLDF to work. This dependency must be understood, documented and communicated.

Defining a JMS notification using WLST

The same notification module can of course be created using WLST. The following script demonstrates how to create the same notification using WLST

```
# change to the diagnostic module
cd('/WLDFSystemResources/TestModule/WLDFResource/TestModule/WatchNotificatio
n/TestModule')

# create the new notification
cmo.createJMSNotification('JMSTestNotification')

# switch to the new configuration
cd('/WLDFSystemResources/TestModule/WLDFResource/TestModule/WatchNotificatio
n/TestModule/JMSNotifications/JMSTestNotification')

# enable it
cmo.setEnabled(true)

# define the JMS connection and destination details
cmo.setDestinationJNDIName('/jms/notifications')
cmo.setConnectionFactoryJNDIName('/jms/conneectionfactories/NotificationConn
factory')
```

Very similar can this also be implemented using JMX from within a Java program.

```
public void createJMSNotification(JMXWrapper myJMXEditWrapper, ObjectName myDiagnosticModule,
                  String connectionFactoryJNDIName, String destinationJNDIName,
                  String name) throws WLDFAutomationException
{
    ObjectName notificationRef = null;
    try {
        WatchNotificationUtils myUtils = new WatchNotificationUtils(myJMXEditWrapper);

        if (myUtils.doesNotificationExist(myDiagnosticModule, name)) {
            notificationRef = myUtils.getNotification(myDiagnosticModule,name);
        }
        else { // create
            notificationRef = myUtils.createNotification(myDiagnosticModule,
                        NotificationType.JMS, name);
        }

        // do the configurations
        myJMXEditWrapper.setAttribute(notificationRef, new Attribute("Enabled",true));

        // ConnectionFactoryJNDIName
        myJMXEditWrapper.setAttribute(notificationRef, new Attribute("ConnectionFactoryJNDIName",
                            connectionFactoryJNDIName));

        // DestinationJNDIName
        myJMXEditWrapper.setAttribute(notificationRef, new Attribute("DestinationJNDIName",
                            destinationJNDIName));
    }
    catch(Exception ex) {
        ex.printStackTrace();
        throw new WLDFAutomationException(ex.getMessage());
    }
}
```

Receiving and using the JMS notification events

These notifications are of course only useful if clients will register with the WebLogic MBeans in order to receive these events. This can be done by implementing a JMS client which registers with the JMS server and listens on the appropriate queue which was configured in WLDF setup. Whenever WLDF will fire a notification which will result in a JMS message to be send, this client will receive it. The next chapter will show an example of such a listener. This client could also be an application component running inside WebLogic (if the code has the appropriate rights).

Email Notifications

The third notification types we will look at are email notifications using SMTP. During the creation of the notification it is important to choose the correct type.

Figure 11.10: *Create an SMTP email notification*

EMail notifications are notifications based on the SMTP (Simple Mail Transfer Protocol) protocol. This is the second type of notifications which rely on a resource configuration defined on WebLogic level. In this case, an email session must have been defined for WebLogic and must be targeted to the server where this diagnostic module is running. The definition of the email session must have been done before an email notification is defined.

Inside the diagnostic module it is now necessary to create an email notification with a defined name (TestEMailNotification in our case) and link this to the email session defined on WebLogic level. It is important to define one or more recipient. All other fields like topic and body have predefined default values. It is possible - but optional - to overwrite these default values as part of the email notification definition.

As a second step, either defaults can be confirmed or customized values can be provided for the email template:

Figure 11.11: *Define email template details*

Also note that this page of the notification definition requires from the administrator to select which mail session should be used. Alternatively one can be created. The second option only means that the WebLogic wizard for creating mail sessions will be called. This example assumes that a mail session named "WldfTestMailSession" was already created.

Create the same EMail notification using WLST:

```
# switch to the diagnostic module
cd('/WLDFSystemResources/TestModule/WLDFResource/TestModule/WatchNotificatio
n/TestModule')

# create a smtp session
cmo.createSMTPNotification('TestEMailNotification')

# switch to your new notification MBean
cd('/WLDFSystemResources/TestModule/WLDFResource/TestModule/WatchNotificatio
n/TestModule/SMTPNotifications/TestEMailNotification')

# enable it
cmo.setEnabled(true)

# define which mail session should be used
cmo.setMailSessionJNDIName('mail/WldfTestMailSession')

# define the list of recipients who should get this email
set('Recipients',jarray.array([String('wldf_book@mh-
enterpriseconsulting.de')], String))

# define custom values for
cmo.setSubject('This is a notification from WLDF')
cmo.setBody('Invent some text here which describes the current issue (based
on the watch rules)')
```

The big benefit of this notification is that no special client is needed. The emails will be delivered directly to the administrator mailbox or can even be send to an automatic ticket system.

It is a good practice to every now and then examine the mbeans which have been created as this improves the understanding of the WebLogic internal configuration structure.

```
wls:/testdomain/serverConfig> cd ('WLDFSystemResources')
wls:/testdomain/serverConfig/WLDFSystemResources> ls()
dr--    TestModule

wls:/testdomain/serverConfig/WLDFSystemResources> cd ('TestModule')
wls:/testdomain/serverConfig/WLDFSystemResources/TestModule> ls()
dr--    Resource
dr--    SubDeployments
dr--    Targets
dr--    WLDFResource

-r--    CompatibilityName                   null
-r--    DeploymentOrder                     100
-r--    DeploymentPrincipalName             null
-r--    Description
-r--    DescriptorFileName                  diagnostics/TestModule.xml
-r--    DynamicallyCreated                  false
-r--    Id                                  0
-r--    ModuleType                          null
-r--    Name                                TestModule
-r--    Notes                               null
-r--    SourcePath                          ./config/diagnostics/TestModule.xml
-r--    Type                                WLDFSystemResource
```

```
-r-x    freezeCurrentValue                          Void : String(attributeName)
-r-x    getInheritedProperties                      String[] : String[](propertyNames)
-r-x    isInherited                                 Boolean : String(propertyName)
-r-x    isSet                                       Boolean : String(propertyName)
-r-x    unSet                                       Void : String(propertyName)

wls:/testdomain/serverConfig/WLDFSystemResources/TestModule> cd
('WLDFResource/TestModule/WatchNotification/TestModule')
wls:/testdomain/serverConfig/WLDFSystemResources/TestModule/WLDFResource/TestModule/WatchNotification
/TestModule> ls()
dr--    ImageNotifications
dr--    JMSNotifications
dr--    JMXNotifications
dr--    Notifications
dr--    SMTPNotifications
dr--    SNMPNotifications
dr--    Watches

-r--    Enabled                                     false
-r--    Id                                          0
-r--    LogWatchSeverity                            Warning
-r--    Name                                        TestModule
-r--    Severity                                    Notice


wls:/testdomain/serverConfig/WLDFSystemResources/TestModule/WLDFResource/TestModule/WatchNotification
/TestModule> ls('Notifications')
dr--    MailNotification
dr--    SERVER.PROFILE

wls:/testdomain/serverConfig/WLDFSystemResources/TestModule/WLDFResource/TestModule/WatchNotification
/TestModule> ls('SMTPNotifications')
dr--    MailNotification

wls:/testdomain/serverConfig/WLDFSystemResources/TestModule/WLDFResource/TestModule/WatchNotification
/TestModule> cd ('Notifications/MailNotification')
wls:/testdomain/serverConfig/WLDFSystemResources/TestModule/WLDFResource/TestModule/WatchNotification
/TestModule/Notifications/MailNotification> ls()

-r--    Body                                        This is your desired notification
-r--    Enabled                                     true
-r--    Id                                          0
-r--    MailSessionJNDIName                         mail/TestMailSession
-r--    Name                                        MailNotification
-r--    Recipients                                  java.lang.String[wldf@mh-enterpriseconsulting.de]
-r--    Subject                                     WLDF Test Notification

wls:/testdomain/serverConfig/WLDFSystemResources/TestModule/WLDFResource/TestModule/WatchNotification
/TestModule/Notifications/MailNotification> ls()

-r--    Body                                        This is your desired notification
-r--    Enabled                                     true
-r--    Id                                          0
-r--    MailSessionJNDIName                         mail/TestMailSession
-r--    Name                                        MailNotification
-r--    Recipients                                  java.lang.String[wldf@mh-enterpriseconsulting.de]
-r--    Subject                                     WLDF Test Notification
```

This can also be created using JMX. Note that the following code assumes that an email session configuration already exists in WebLogic.

```
public void createEMailNotification(JMXWrapper myJMXEditWrapper, ObjectName myDiagnosticModule,
                        String name, boolean enabled, String emailBody,
                        String eMailSessionJNDIName, String[] emailRecipients,
                        String emailSubject) throws WLDFAutomationException
{
    ObjectName notificationRef = null;
    try {
        WatchNotificationUtils myUtils = new WatchNotificationUtils(myJMXEditWrapper);

        if (myUtils.doesNotificationExist(myDiagnosticModule, name)) {
            notificationRef = myUtils.getNotification(myDiagnosticModule, name);
        }
```

```
        else { // create
            notificationRef = myUtils.createNotification(myDiagnosticModule, Notification.SMTP, name);
        }

        // do the configurations
        myJMXEditWrapper.setAttribute(notificationRef, new Attribute("Enabled",enabled));

        // Recipients
        myJMXEditWrapper.setAttribute(notificationRef, new Attribute("Recipients",emailRecipients));

        // mail session
        myJMXEditWrapper.setAttribute(notificationRef,
                            new Attribute("MailSessionJNDIName",eMailSessionJNDIName));

        // Optional settings
        if (profileBody != null)
            myJMXEditWrapper.setAttribute(notificationRef, new Attribute("Body",emailBody));

        if (profileSubject != null)
            myJMXEditWrapper.setAttribute(notificationRef, new Attribute("Subject",emailSubject));
    }
    catch(Exception ex) {
        ex.printStackTrace();
        throw new WLDFAutomationException(ex.getMessage());
    }
}
```

In order for this setup to work, an email session must be setup in this WLS domain and must be targeted in the same way as the diagnostic module. Furthermore the SMTP provider settings must be correct.

Diagnostic Image Notifications

The fourth type of notifications we will look at are diagnostic image creation notifications. During the creation of the notification it is important to choose the correct type.

Figure 11.12: *Create a diagnostic image notification*

This kind of notification will create a diagnostic image. The next part of the wizard allows the administrator to define the directory where the image should be created and a so called lockout period which defines a minimum delay time between the same notification can create another image. This is very important so that in case of even storms the amount of files created can be limited. This restrict resource usages on WebLogic and of course also file system space consumption.

Create Notification

Back   Next   Finish   Cancel

Config Notification - Diagnostic Image Properties

Config Diagnostic Image Properties

Enter Image Directory

Image Directory: logs/diagnostic_images

Please specify image lockout time

Lockout Time (in minutes):   0

Back   Next   Finish   Cancel

Figure 11.13: *Options for diagnostic image notifications*

The names of the image files which will be created will contain a timestamp. This ensures that a notification can create multiple images into the same location without overwriting older image creations.

Create a diagnostic image notification using WLST

```
cd('/WLDFSystemResources/TestModule/WLDFResource/TestModule/WatchNotificatio
n/TestModule')
cmo.createImageNotification('TestDiagnosticImageNotification')

cd('/WLDFSystemResources/TestModule/WLDFResource/TestModule/WatchNotificatio
n/TestModule/ImageNotifications/TestDiagnosticImageNotification')
cmo.setEnabled(true)
cmo.setImageDirectory('logs/diagnostic_images')
cmo.setImageLockout(0)
```

As this notification just writes out an image to the local file system there is no external integration necessary.

An image notification can also be created using JMX.

```
public void createImageNotification(JMXWrapper myJMXEditWrapper, ObjectName myDiagnosticModule,
                        String name, boolean enabled, String imageDirectory,
                        int lockoutTime) throws WLDFAutomationException
{
   ObjectName notificationRef = null;
   try {
     WatchNotificationUtils myUtils = new WatchNotificationUtils(myJMXEditWrapper);

     if (myUtils.doesNotificationExist(myDiagnosticModule, name)) {
      notificationRef = myUtils.getNotification(myDiagnosticModule, name);
     }
     else { // create
```

```
            notificationRef = myUtils.createNotification(myDiagnosticModule, Notification.Image, name);
        }

        // do the configurations
        myJMXEditWrapper.setAttribute(notificationRef, new Attribute("Enabled",enabled));

        // image dir
        myJMXEditWrapper.setAttribute(notificationRef, new Attribute("ImageDirectory",imageDirectory));

        // timeout
        myJMXEditWrapper.setAttribute(notificationRef,
                                new Attribute("ImageLockout",new Integer(lockoutTime)));
    }
    catch(Exception ex) {
        ex.printStackTrace();
        throw new WLDFAutomationException(ex.getMessage());
    }
}
```

SNMP Notifications

The last type of notification we will look at are SNMP notifications. During the creation of the notification it is important to choose the correct type.

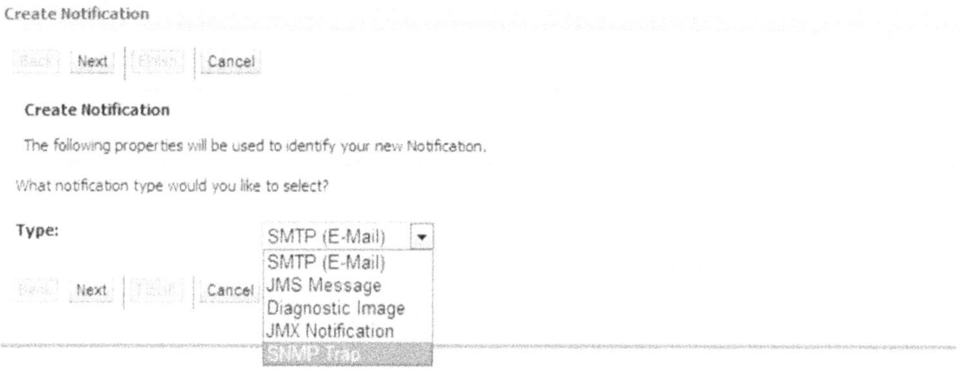

Figure 11.14: *Create a SNMP notification*

In order to configure a SNMP notification the only configuration item available is the name. There are no other values you can specify. The reason is that this implementation relies on a proper SNMP setup on WebLogic level. Furthermore the TRAP details are documented and standardized.

Here, we use WLST to create a SNMP notification:

```
cd('/WLDFSystemResources/TestModule/WLDFResource/TestModule/WatchNotificatio
n/TestModule')
cmo.createSNMPNotification('WldfSNMPTestNotification')

cd('/WLDFSystemResources/TestModule/WLDFResource/TestModule/WatchNotificatio
n/TestModule/SNMPNotifications/WldfSNMPTestNotification')
cmo.setEnabled(true)
```

Whenever a watch evaluates to true, the notification defined above will fire a SNMP trap of type 85. This trap contains the following values, whereas "<...>" means that this values will be replaced by actual information.

```
.1.3.6.1.4.1.140.625.100.5 timestamp (e.g. Dec 9, 2004 6:46:37 PM EST
.1.3.6.1.4.1.140.625.100.145 domainName (e.g. mydomain")
Configuring SMTP Notifications
11-4 Configuring and Using the Diagnostics Framework for Oracle WebLogic Server
.1.3.6.1.4.1.140.625.100.10 serverName (e.g. myserver)
.1.3.6.1.4.1.140.625.100.120 <severity> (e.g. Notice)
.1.3.6.1.4.1.140.625.100.105 <name> [of watch] (e.g.
simpleWebLogicMBeanWatchRepeatingAfterWait)
.1.3.6.1.4.1.140.625.100.110 <rule-type> (e.g. HarvesterRule)
.1.3.6.1.4.1.140.625.100.115 <rule-expression>
.1.3.6.1.4.1.140.625.100.125 values which caused rule to
fire (e.g..State =
null,weblogic.management.runtime.WLDFHarvesterRuntimeMBean.
TotalSamplingTime = 886,.Enabled =
null,weblogic.management.runtime.ServerRuntimeMBean.
OpenSocketsCurrentCount = 1,)
.1.3.6.1.4.1.140.625.100.130 <alarm-type> (e.g. None)
.1.3.6.1.4.1.140.625.100.135 <alarm-reset-period> (e.g. 10000)
.1.3.6.1.4.1.140.625.100.140 <name>
```
(© Oracle Documentation)

It is of course also possible to create the same configuration items using JMX.

```
public void createSNMPNotification(JMXWrapper myJMXEditWrapper,
                                   ObjectName myDiagnosticModule, String name)
                                   throws WLDFAutomationException
{
    ObjectName notificationRef = null;
    try {
        WatchNotificationUtils myUtils = new WatchNotificationUtils(myJMXEditWrapper);

        if (myUtils.doesNotificationExist(myDiagnosticModule,name))
        {
            notificationRef = myUtils.getNotification(myDiagnosticModule, name);
        }
        else // create
        {
            notificationRef = myUtils.createNotification(myDiagnosticModule,
                         NotificationType.SNMP, name);
        }

        // do the configurations
        myJMXEditWrapper.setAttribute(notificationRef, new Attribute("Enabled",true));
    }
    catch(Exception ex) {
        ex.printStackTrace();
        throw new WLDFAutomationException(ex.getMessage());
    }
}
```

Future developments

Up to WebLogic 12.1.3 WLDF notifications are limited to the 5 different types explained above. WebLogic 12.2.1 will bring another additional type which will really provide a much richer usage of notifications.

Starting with WebLogic 12.2.1 it will be possible to perform WLST commands or even complete scripts in response to a watch rule event.

In combination with WLST extensions to the dynamic cluster feature, this will bring a very powerful control mechanism and allows the configuration of self-organizing domains. This means that domains can react to events and handle automatically (like e.g. add/remove managed-server due to resource issues. Many uses-cases could be imagined for this.

Summary

WLDF supports a number of different types of notifications. This enables the administrator or user to define different ways to either get notified when a specific event happens or a way to do automatic actions. Some of these notifications require other WebLogic resources (outside of the diagnostic module) to be defined, like JMS destinations, email resources or SNMP agents.

Notifications are THE means in WLDF to get other parties notified. This is a kind of pushing events. The alternative in WLDF the data accessor which will be discussed later in the book provides a way to pull out information.

Complete Examples

Complete Examples

The previous chapters have introduced the basic and most important building blocks for WLDF. Before we will be looking into specific usage patterns, profiles and advanced topics, this chapter will provide some complete examples with the WLDF components that we have discussed so far.

Introduction

In the previous we have discussed the fundamental building blocks (except instrumentation) of WLDF. All these chapter were written with real live examples in mind. Nevertheless questions may arise like "So how does all this fit together?" or "What can I really do with it ?"

The answer cannot be given in a simple chapter, therefore this chapter will introduce a few complete examples using all WLDF parts already discussed.

Whenever looking at WLDF examples – especially if they appear to be complex, please keep the following view in mind which was discussed at the beginning of the book.

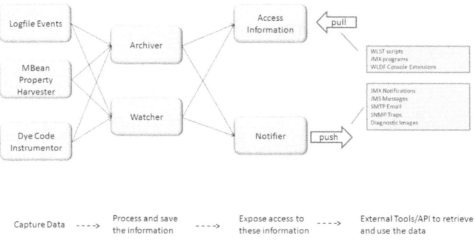

| Capture Data | - - - -> | Process and save the information | - - - -> | Expose access to these information | - - - -> | External Tools/API to retrieve and use the data |

Figure 12.1: *Simplified view on WLDF*

WLDF is not really so complex as it often looks like. WLDF just offer a number of different components in order to be flexible enough.

The following examples will provide a few more advanced usages of WLDF but all will be build using the basic building blocks which we have discussed in the previous chapters.

Utilize WLDF to monitor custom MBeans with machine data

The first example will show a possible solution for extended monitoring, where it is possible to monitor system information from the underlying operating system. This is actually a pretty often asked question, especially in combination with an internal or even external hosting provider. Whenever the deployer or operator do not have access to the physical machines they are usually asking for information like machine load, processes running on the machine, memory utilization and more. WebLogic does not provide this out of the box but with a little extension this is nicely possible.

The solution discussed here will install a module which will offer system information through custom MBeans. Then this information can be queried using standard WLST/JMX methods and therefore also via WLDF. So in this example we will use harvesting to collect this system data, and also JMX notification to get notified when specific thresholds are reached.

The extension module

In the open source community space two projects can be found which provide us with exactly the implementation we need in order to get all the data from the underlying operating system. The base project is called "sigar" – see http://sourceforge.net/projects/sigar/ - which implements the raw data gathering using external libraries and provide access to them via JNI (Java Native Interface). On top of it the project wlhostmachinestats – see http://sourceforge.net/projects/wlhostmchnstats/ - is an implementation which provide access to these data through a WebLogic custom MBean. This is exactly what we need for this implementation.

Please follow the information provided on the Wiki page of the project wlhostmchnstats to download and install the application. It is necessary to copy some files to <domain>/lib and deploy a web application.

Access to the system data

After the libs are copied and the application is deployed and running, it is possible to check if the MBean has been created and which attributes are available. This project has installed a new custom MBean.

The MBean name is:

```
mbean name:  wlhostmachinestats:name=WLHostMachineStats
```

Before defining the WLDF module it is possible to test the custom MBean. This can either be done by using interactive WLST or with a WLST script.

The following example shows how to use interactive WLST to access the data.

```
wls:/offline> connect('weblogic','test1234','t3://localhost:12001')
Connecting to t3://localhost:12001 with userid weblogic ...

wls:/base_domain/serverConfig> custom()
Location changed to custom tree. This is a writable tree with No root.
For more help, use help('custom')

wls:/base_domain/custom> ls()
drw-    JMImplementation
drw-    com.sun.management
drw-    java.lang
drw-    java.nio
drw-    java.util.logging
drw-    wlhostmachinestats

wls:/base_domain/custom> cd ('wlhostmachinestats')
wls:/base_domain/custom/wlhostmachinestats> ls()
drw-    wlhostmachinestats:name=WLHostMachineStats

wls:/base_domain/custom/wlhostmachinestats> cd ('wlhostmachinestats:name=WLHostMachineStats')
wls:/base_domain/custom/wlhostmachinestats/wlhostmachinestats:name=WLHostMachineStats> ls()
-r--    JVMInstanceCoresUsed                        0.0
```

```
-r--    JVMInstancePhysicalMemoryUsedMegabytes      4104
-r--    MBeanVersion                                0.3.0
-r--    MonitoredNetworkInferfaceName               eth0
-r--    NativeProcessesCount                        258
-r--    NetworkRxDropped                            0
-r--    NetworkRxErrors                             0
-r--    NetworkRxFrame                              0
-r--    NetworkRxMegabytes                          12
-r--    NetworkRxMillionPackets                     0
-r--    NetworkRxOverruns                           0
-r--    NetworkTxCarrier                            0
-r--    NetworkTxCollisions                         0
-r--    NetworkTxDropped                            0
-r--    NetworkTxErrors                             0
-r--    NetworkTxMegabytes                          3
-r--    NetworkTxMillionPackets                     0
-r--    NetworkTxOverruns                           0
-r--    PhysicalMemoryUsedPercent                   37
-r--    PhysicalSwapUsedPercent                     0
-r--    ProcessorLastMinuteWorkloadAverage          0.0
-r--    ProcessorUsagePercent                       8
-r--    RootFilesystemUsedPercent                   25
-r--    TcpCloseWaitCount                           1
-r--    TcpEstablishedCount                         7
-r--    TcpListenCount                              21
-r--    TcpTimeWaitCount                            0

wls:/base_domain/custom/wlhostmachinestats/wlhostmachinestats:name=WLHostMachineStats>
```

You can also run the following WLST script instead of using the interactive mode:

```
connect('weblogic','test1234','t3://localhost:12001')
custom()
cd ('wlhostmachinestats/wlhostmachinestats:name=WLHostMachineStats')
print 'PhysicalMemoryUsedPercent : ' + str(get('PhysicalMemoryUsedPercent'))
```

 Important note:
You need to decide on which WLS server (admin server and or managed server(s)) you want to use this data. The data copied to the lib folder and the targeting of the web application define on which machine this custom MBean is available. This is very important for the next steps.

Setting up the WLDF diagnostic module and artifacts

After the custom MBeans are installed and working the next step is to define the diagnostic module with the appropriate watches and notifications. In this example we will define 2 different watches. Note that this time we will not define harvesters as we do not need them for this example. This does not mean that this is not possible or might not be useful.

The script implements the following steps:

1. Creates a diagnostic module

2. Create two watches (examples) which are observing attributes of the custom MBean described above

3. Create two notifications – one for each MBean and assign these notifications to the watches

```
connect('weblogic','welcome1','t3://localhost:12001')

edit()
startEdit()

cd ('/')

# create the diagnostic module
# ------------------------------------

# create the diagnostic module
cmo.createWLDFSystemResource('HostMonitorDiagnosticModule')

# switch to the new module and set the description text
cd('/WLDFSystemResources/HostMonitorDiagnosticModule')
cmo.setDescription('This is a new WLDF module in order to monitor OS level parameters')

# create the first watch
# ------------------------------------

# create the watch MBean
cd('/WLDFSystemResources/HostMonitorDiagnosticModule/WLDFResource/HostMonitorDiagnosticModule/WatchNo
tification/HostMonitorDiagnosticModule')
cmo.createWatch('PhysicalMemoryUsedPercent-Watch')

#change to the new MBean (note the deep path)
cd('/WLDFSystemResources/HostMonitorDiagnosticModule/WLDFResource/HostMonitorDiagnosticModule/WatchNo
tification/HostMonitorDiagnosticModule/Watches/PhysicalMemoryUsedPercent-Watch')
# set to type â€œHarvesterâ€
cmo.setRuleType('Harvester')
# enable the watch
cmo.setEnabled(true)
# create the rule expression
cmo.setRuleExpression('(${ServerRuntime//[wlhostmachinestats.mbeans.WLHostMachineStats]wlhostmachines
tats:name=WLHostMachineStats//PhysicalMemoryUsedPercent} > 80)')
cmo.setAlarmType(None)


# create the second watch
# ------------------------------------

# create the watch MBean
cd('/WLDFSystemResources/HostMonitorDiagnosticModule/WLDFResource/HostMonitorDiagnosticModule/WatchNo
tification/HostMonitorDiagnosticModule')
cmo.createWatch('ProcessorUsagePercent-Watch')

#change to the new MBean (note the deep path)
cd('/WLDFSystemResources/HostMonitorDiagnosticModule/WLDFResource/HostMonitorDiagnosticModule/WatchNo
tification/HostMonitorDiagnosticModule/Watches/ProcessorUsagePercent-Watch')
# set to type â€œHarvesterâ€
cmo.setRuleType('Harvester')
# enable the watch
cmo.setEnabled(true)
# create the rule expression
cmo.setRuleExpression('(${ServerRuntime//[wlhostmachinestats.mbeans.WLHostMachineStats]wlhostmachines
tats:name=WLHostMachineStats//ProcessorUsagePercent} > 80)')
cmo.setAlarmType(None)


# create the notifications and attach them to the watches
# ----------------------------------------------------------
cd('/WLDFSystemResources/HostMonitorDiagnosticModule/WLDFResource/HostMonitorDiagnosticModule/WatchNo
tification/HostMonitorDiagnosticModule')
cmo.createJMXNotification('PhysicalMemoryUsedPercent-Notification')
```

```
cd('/WLDFSystemResources/HostMonitorDiagnosticModule/WLDFResource/HostMonitorDiagnosticModule/WatchNo
tification/HostMonitorDiagnosticModule/JMXNotifications/PhysicalMemoryUsedPercent-Notification')
cmo.setEnabled(true)

cd('/WLDFSystemResources/HostMonitorDiagnosticModule/WLDFResource/HostMonitorDiagnosticModule/WatchNo
tification/HostMonitorDiagnosticModule')
cmo.createJMXNotification('ProcessorUsagePercent-Notification')

cd('/WLDFSystemResources/HostMonitorDiagnosticModule/WLDFResource/HostMonitorDiagnosticModule/WatchNo
tification/HostMonitorDiagnosticModule/JMXNotifications/ProcessorUsagePercent-Notification')
cmo.setEnabled(true)

cd('/WLDFSystemResources/HostMonitorDiagnosticModule/WLDFResource/HostMonitorDiagnosticModule/WatchNo
tification/HostMonitorDiagnosticModule/Watches/PhysicalMemoryUsedPercent-Watch')

set('Notifications',jarray.array([ObjectName('com.bea:Name=PhysicalMemoryUsedPercent-
Notification,Type=weblogic.diagnostics.descriptor.WLDFJMXNotificationBean,Parent=[base_domain]/WLDFSy
stemResources[HostMonitorDiagnosticModule],Path=WLDFResource[HostMonitorDiagnosticModule]/WatchNotifi
cation[HostMonitorDiagnosticModule]/JMXNotifications[PhysicalMemoryUsedPercent-Notification]')],
ObjectName))

cd('/WLDFSystemResources/HostMonitorDiagnosticModule/WLDFResource/HostMonitorDiagnosticModule/WatchNo
tification/HostMonitorDiagnosticModule/Watches/ProcessorUsagePercent-Watch')

set('Notifications',jarray.array([ObjectName('com.bea:Name=ProcessorUsagePercent-
Notification,Type=weblogic.diagnostics.descriptor.WLDFJMXNotificationBean,Parent=[base_domain]/WLDFSy
stemResources[HostMonitorDiagnosticModule],Path=WLDFResource[HostMonitorDiagnosticModule]/WatchNotifi
cation[HostMonitorDiagnosticModule]/JMXNotifications[ProcessorUsagePercent-Notification]')],
ObjectName))

# activate the module and target it
# -----------------------------------------
cd('/WLDFSystemResources/HostMonitorDiagnosticModule')

set('Targets',jarray.array([ObjectName('com.bea:Name=AdminServer,Type=Server'),
ObjectName('com.bea:Name=TestCluster,Type=Cluster')], ObjectName))

# save work and activate changes
save()
activate()
```

After this setup is completed, the complete diagnostic module is finished. You can check this by looking at the WebConsole or at the configuration files created by WebLogic. The configuration files should look like:

Definition in the config.xml:

```
...
  <wldf-system-resource>
    <name>HostMonitorDiagnosticModule</name>
    <target>AdminServer,TestCluster</target>
    <descriptor-file-name>diagnostics/HostMonitorDiagnosticModule-2075.xml</descriptor-file-name>
    <description>This is a new WLDF module in order to monitor OS level parameters</description>
  </wldf-system-resource>
...
```

Definition of the file HostMonitorDiagnosticModule-2075.xml (name can be different if you try it):

```
<?xml version='1.0' encoding='UTF-8'?>
<wldf-resource ...>
  <name>HostMonitorDiagnosticModule</name>
  <watch-notification>
    <watch>
      <name>PhysicalMemoryUsedPercent-Watch</name>
      <enabled>true</enabled>
      <rule-type>Harvester</rule-type>
```

```
        <rule-
expression>(${ServerRuntime//[wlhostmachinestats.mbeans.WLHostMachineStats]wlhostmachinestats:name=WL
HostMachineStats//PhysicalMemoryUsedPercent} &gt; 50)</rule-expression>
        <alarm-type>AutomaticReset</alarm-type>
        <alarm-reset-period>30000</alarm-reset-period>
        <notification>PhysicalMemoryUsedPercent-Notification</notification>
    </watch>
    <watch>
        <name>ProcessorUsagePercent-Watch</name>
        <enabled>true</enabled>
        <rule-type>Harvester</rule-type>
        <rule-
expression>(${ServerRuntime//[wlhostmachinestats.mbeans.WLHostMachineStats]wlhostmachinestats:name=WL
HostMachineStats//ProcessorUsagePercent} &gt; 50)</rule-expression>
        <alarm-type xsi:nil="true"></alarm-type>
        <notification>ProcessorUsagePercent-Notification</notification>
    </watch>
    <jmx-notification>
        <name>PhysicalMemoryUsedPercent-Notification</name>
        <enabled>true</enabled>
    </jmx-notification>
    <jmx-notification>
        <name>ProcessorUsagePercent-Notification</name>
        <enabled>true</enabled>
    </jmx-notification>
  </watch-notification>
</wldf-resource>
```

Defining the JMX notification listener

These notifications are of course only useful if clients will register with the WebLogic
MBeans in order to receive these events. The following JAVA code discusses how to
write a simple JMX client to consume these notifications.

```
import javax.management.*;
import com.wldfexamples.utils.*;

// used for type check and type cast in handleNotification
import weblogic.diagnostics.watch.WatchNotification;
import weblogic.diagnostics.watch.JMXWatchNotification;

public class HostJMXNotificationExample implements NotificationListener
{
    private JMXWrapper myServerConnection = null;
    private String myWLSServerName = null;

    public HostJMXNotificationExample(JMXWrapper myWrapper) throws Exception
    {
        myServerConnection = myWrapper;
        myWLSServerName = myServerConnection.getMainServerDomainValues().get("serverName");

      // register the callback

      // get own server runtime
      myServerConnection.getServerRuntime(myWLSServerName);

      // add notification handler

      ObjectName myWatchruntime =
          new ObjectName(
                "com.bea:Name=DiagnosticsJMXNotificationSource,ServerRuntime=" + myWLSServerName +
                ",Type=WLDFWatchJMXNotificationRuntime,WLDFRuntime=WLDFRuntime,"+
                "WLDFWatchNotificationRuntime=WatchNotification"
            );

      System.out.println("Register local client jmx notification listener for: " +
                        myWatchruntime.toString());

      myServerConnection.getConnection().addNotificationListener(myWatchruntime, this, null, null);
    }
```

```
/**
 * This is the callback implementation which will be called as soon
 * as the WDF module has fired a notification
 *
 * In this example case it only prints out some details about the notfication
 */
public void handleNotification(Notification myNotification, Object callback)
{
    try {
      if (myNotification instanceof JMXWatchNotification)
      {
          WatchNotification notificationContent =
                      ((JMXWatchNotification)myNotification).getExtendedInfo();

          System.out.println("Name:             " + notificationContent.getWatchName());
          System.out.println("DomainName:       " + notificationContent.getWatchDomainName());
          System.out.println("ServerName:       " + notificationContent.getWatchServerName());
          System.out.println("Time:             " + notificationContent.getWatchTime());
          System.out.println("Severity:         " + notificationContent.getWatchSeverityLevel());
          System.out.println("RuleType:         " + notificationContent.getWatchRuleType());
          System.out.println("Rule:             " + notificationContent.getWatchRule());
          System.out.println("AlarmType:        " + notificationContent.getWatchAlarmType());
          System.out.println("AlarmResetPeriod: " + notificationContent.getWatchAlarmResetPeriod());
          System.out.println("Message:          " + notificationContent.getMessage());
          System.out.println("Data:             " + notificationContent.getWatchDataToString());
          System.out.println("\n");
      }
    }
    catch (Exception ex)
    {
      ex.printStackTrace();
    }

}

public static void  main(String[] args)
{
    try {
    JMXWrapperRemote myJMX = new JMXWrapperRemote();
    myJMX.connectToAdminServer(false, false, "weblogic", "test1234", "t3://localhost:12001");

    HostJMXNotificationExample myNotifyExample = new HostJMXNotificationExample(myJMX);

    // Sleep as long as possible.
    // Note that this is an example only, therefore we just put the main thread to sleep.
    Thread.sleep(Long.MAX_VALUE);
    }
    catch (Exception ex)
    {
      ex.printStackTrace();
    }
  }
}
```

Running the example

Now we are ready to run the example. First of all we need to start the WebLogic
server(s). Then we need to run the notification client(s) as described above. Now we
have to start some load or resource intensive applications so that we reach the defined
threshold. If the values exceed their threshold values, then we should see
notifications being created.

```
Register local client jmx notification listener for:
com.bea:Name=DiagnosticsJMXNotificationSource,ServerRuntime=AdminServer,Type=WLDFWatchJMXNotification
Runtime,WLDFRuntime=WLDFRuntime,WLDFWatchNotificationRuntime=WatchNotification
Name:              PhysicalMemoryUsedPercent-Watch
DomainName:        base_domain
ServerName:        AdminServer
Time:              Jun 29, 2014 1:08:58 AM CEST
Severity:          Notice
```

```
RuleType:          Harvester
Rule:
(${ServerRuntime//[wlhostmachinestats.mbeans.WLHostMachineStats]wlhostmachinestats:name=WLHostMachine
Stats//PhysicalMemoryUsedPercent} > 50)
AlarmType:         AutomaticReset
AlarmResetPeriod: 30000
Message:           WatchName: PhysicalMemoryUsedPercent-Watch WatchSeverityLevel: Notice
Data:              wlhostmachinestats:name=WLHostMachineStats//PhysicalMemoryUsedPercent = 61
```

Important note: The frequency of the notifications really rely on your alarm settings you have done on the watch. E.g. with manual alarm reset you won't get any further notification until you have reset the alarm via console or WLST.

Use WLDF for automatic scaling of an application

This example is based on the blog from René van Wijk. Thanks a lot to Rene for his permission to use the material in this chapter. Please see the blog at http://middlewaresnippets.blogspot.de/2014/01/automatic-scaling-application-using.html for further details like test application, screen shots and example outputs.

Say we want to add (or start) managed server instances when running an application, for example, when the number of open sessions reach a certain value. For this value we have calculated that the memory consumption is beyond a level, such that the garbage collection is affected. By adding (or starting) a new server we balance the load (the number of sessions with its corresponding memory consumption) across multiple servers. By using the WebLogic Diagnostic Framework, we can collect the metrics we need and create a watch for that metric with a corresponding notification. By using this notification we can then create the logic needed in order to add (or start) a managed server. For example, by using the notification service that comes with the WebLogic Diagnostic Framework, we can send a JMS message or a JMX notification. In this example we are going to use the JMS notification approach.

The WebLogic environment consists of a cluster, spanning two machines, and consisting of four managed servers.

In the diagnostic module we create a harvester that collects the OpenSessionCurrentCount attribute from the WebAppComponentRuntimeMBean. The watch checks if the OpenSessionCurrentCount attribute is greater than 1000. If this occurs than a JMS message (notification) is send. Note that the sample time of the harvester is set at 30 seconds. When we need a more instant notification the sample time, this value can be lowered.

The Diagnostic Module can be created by using the following WLST script:

```
import socket;

wldf_module_name='DiagnosticModule';
target_name='cluster';
```

```
servers_to_monitor=['all'];
applications_to_monitor=['SessionTest'];

namespace='ServerRuntime';

harvester_type='weblogic.management.runtime.WebAppComponentRuntimeMBean';
harvester_attribute_names = ['OpenSessionsCurrentCount'];
harvester_instances=[];

watch_name='OpenSessionWatch';
watch_trigger_attribute_name='OpenSessionsCurrentCount';
watch_trigger_operator='>';
watch_trigger_value='1000';
watch_trigger_rules=[];

notification_name='JMSNotification';
destination_jndi_name='jms/CompanyQueue';
connection_factory_jndi_name='jms/ConnectionFactory';

def connect_to_admin_server():
    print 'CONNECT TO ADMIN SERVER';
    admin_server_listen_address = socket.gethostname();
    admin_server_url = 't3://' + admin_server_listen_address + ':' + admin_server_listen_port;
    connect(admin_username, admin_password, admin_server_url);

# Create instances for the harvester, and watch rules for the watch/notification
# Note that instances are JMX ObjectNames, by using the domainRuntimeService we obtain the
# A watch rule is of the following form
# (${<NAMESPACE>//[<RUNTIME_MBEAN_TYPE>]<INSTANCE_OBJECT_NAME>//<INSTANCE_ATTRIBUTE_NAME}
# <OPERATOR> <VALUE>)
def create_harvester_instances_and_watch_rule(servers_to_monitor, applications_to_monitor):
    print 'CREATE HARVESTER INSTANCES AND WATCH RULE';
    server_runtimes = [];
    servers = domainRuntimeService.getServerRuntimes();
    if 'all' in servers_to_monitor:
        server_runtimes = servers;
    else:
        for server in servers:
            if server.getName() in servers_to_monitor:
                server_runtimes.append(server);

    for server_runtime in server_runtimes:
        application_runtimes = server_runtime.getApplicationRuntimes();
        for application_runtime in application_runtimes:
            if ('all' in applications_to_monitor) or
                (application_runtime.getName() in applications_to_monitor):
                component_runtimes = application_runtime.getComponentRuntimes();
                for component_runtime in component_runtimes:
                    objectname_parts = repr(component_runtime.getObjectName()).split(',');
                    # lose the location part of the objectname as the harvester is in the ServerRuntime
                    # namespace (location is only applicable for the DomainRuntime)
                    objectname = objectname_parts[0] + ',' + objectname_parts[1] + ','
                                + objectname_parts[2] + ',' + objectname_parts[4];
                    harvester_instances.append(objectname);

    watch_trigger_rules.append('(${' + namespace + '//[' + harvester_type + ']' +
                                harvester_instances[0] + '//' + watch_trigger_attribute_name + '} ' +
                                watch_trigger_operator + ' ' + watch_trigger_value + ')');


def create_diagnostic_module():
    print 'CREATE DIAGNOSTIC MODULE';
    wldf_module = cmo.createWLDFSystemResource(wldf_module_name);
    wldf_module.setDescription('a useful description');

    targets = [];
    target_path = getPath('com.bea:Name=' + target_name + ',Type=Cluster');
    target = getMBean(target_path);
    targets.append(ObjectName(repr(target.getObjectName())));

    cd('/WLDFSystemResources/'+ wldf_module_name);
    set('Targets', jarray.array(targets, ObjectName));
    cd('/');

    wldf_resource = wldf_module.getWLDFResource();
    harvester = wldf_resource.getHarvester();
    harvester.setSamplePeriod(30000);
```

```
    harvester.setEnabled(java.lang.Boolean('true'));
    harvester.createHarvestedType(harvester_type);
    harvested_type = harvester.lookupHarvestedType(harvester_type);
    harvested_type.setNamespace(namespace);
    harvested_type.setHarvestedAttributes(jarray.array(harvester_attribute_names, String));
    harvested_type.setHarvestedInstances(jarray.array(harvester_instances, String));

    watch_notification = wldf_resource.getWatchNotification();
    watch_notification.createJMSNotification(notification_name);
    jms_notification = watch_notification.lookupJMSNotification(notification_name);
    jms_notification.setEnabled(java.lang.Boolean('true'));
    jms_notification.setDestinationJNDIName(destination_jndi_name);
    jms_notification.setConnectionFactoryJNDIName(connection_factory_jndi_name);

    watch_notification.createWatch(watch_name);
    watch = watch_notification.lookupWatch(watch_name);
    watch.setEnabled(java.lang.Boolean('true'));
    watch.setRuleType('Harvester');
    watch.setRuleExpression(watch_trigger_rules[0]);
    watch.setAlarmType('AutomaticReset');
    watch.setAlarmResetPeriod(120000);

    notifications = watch.getNotifications();
    notifications.append(jms_notification);
    watch.setNotifications(notifications);

def start_edit_mode():
    print 'START EDIT MODE';
    edit();
    startEdit();

def save_and_active_changes():
    print 'SAVE AND ACTIVATE CHANGES';
    save();
    activate(block='true');


connect_to_admin_server();

create_harvester_instances_and_watch_rule(servers_to_monitor, applications_to_monitor);

start_edit_mode();

create_diagnostic_module();

save_and_active_changes();

print 'DISCONNECT FROM THE ADMIN SERVER';
disconnect();
```

This WLST script will create a WLDF diagnostic module with the following configuration defined in the configuration files:

```
# From config.xml
<wldf-system-resource>
    <name>DiagnosticModule</name>
    <target>cluster</target>
    <descriptor-file-name>diagnostics/DiagnosticModule-5133.xml</descriptor-file-name>
    <description></description>
</wldf-system-resource>

# From diagnostics/DiagnosticModule-5133.xml
<wldf-resource ...>
    <name>DiagnosticModule</name>
    <harvester>
        <enabled>true</enabled>
        <sample-period>30000</sample-period>
        <harvested-type>
            <name>weblogic.management.runtime.WebAppComponentRuntimeMBean</name>
            <harvested-attribute>OpenSessionsCurrentCount</harvested-attribute>
            <harvested-instance>com.bea:ApplicationRuntime=SessionTest,Name=server_0_0_/SessionTest,
                    ServerRuntime=server_0_0,Type=WebAppComponentRuntime</harvested-instance>
            <harvested-instance>com.bea:ApplicationRuntime=SessionTest,Name=server_1_0_/SessionTest,
                    ServerRuntime=server_1_0,Type=WebAppComponentRuntime</harvested-instance>
```

Data Archives

151

```
            <harvested-instance>com.bea:ApplicationRuntime=SessionTest,Name=server_0_1_/SessionTest,
                    ServerRuntime=server_0_1,Type=WebAppComponentRuntime</harvested-instance>
            <harvested-instance>com.bea:ApplicationRuntime=SessionTest,Name=server_1_1_/SessionTest,
                    ServerRuntime=server_1_1,Type=WebAppComponentRuntime</harvested-instance>
            <namespace>ServerRuntime</namespace>
        </harvested-type>
    </harvester>
    <watch-notification>
        <watch>
            <name>OpenSessionWatch</name>
            <enabled>true</enabled>
            <rule-type>Harvester</rule-type>
            <rule-expression>
                    (${ServerRuntime//[weblogic.management.runtime.WebAppComponentRuntimeMBean]
                        com.bea:ApplicationRuntime=SessionTest,Name=server_0_0_/SessionTest,
                        ServerRuntime=server_0_0,Type=WebAppComponentRuntime//
                        OpenSessionsCurrentCount} > 1000)</rule-expression>
            <alarm-type>AutomaticReset</alarm-type>
            <alarm-reset-period>120000</alarm-reset-period>
            <notification>OpenSessionNotification</notification>
        </watch>
        <jms-notification>
            <name>OpenSessionNotification</name>
            <enabled>true</enabled>
            <destination-jndi-name>jms/CompanyQueue</destination-jndi-name>
            <connection-factory-jndi-name>jms/ConnectionFactory</connection-factory-jndi-name>
        </jms-notification>
    </watch-notification>
</wldf-resource>
```

Starting servers

The logic in order to start a server when the JMS notification is send can be put in message-driven bean. The following code shows an example implementation

```java
package model.logic;

import javax.ejb.ActivationConfigProperty;
import javax.ejb.MessageDriven;
import javax.jms.*;
import javax.management.*;
import javax.management.remote.JMXConnector;
import javax.management.remote.JMXConnectorFactory;
import javax.management.remote.JMXServiceURL;
import javax.naming.Context;
import java.io.IOException;
import java.util.Hashtable;


@MessageDriven(mappedName = "jms/CompanyQueue", activationConfig = {
    @ActivationConfigProperty(propertyName = "destinationName", propertyValue = "jms/CompanyQueue"),
    @ActivationConfigProperty(propertyName = "destinationType", propertyValue = "javax.jms.Queue")
})
public class CheckMDB implements MessageListener
{
    public static final String HOSTNAME = "machine1.com";
    public static final Integer PORT = 7001;
    public static final String USERNAME = "weblogic";
    public static final String PASSWORD = "snippets12c";

    public static final String PROTOCOL = "t3";
    public static final String JNDI_ROOT = "/jndi/";

    public static final String MBEAN_SERVER = "weblogic.management.mbeanservers.domainruntime";
    public static final String SERVICE_NAME =
"com.bea:Name=DomainRuntimeService,Type=weblogic.management.mbeanservers.domainruntime.DomainRuntimeS
erviceMBean";

    private JMXConnector connector;

    public void onMessage(Message message) {
        try {
            MBeanServerConnection connection = getMBeanServerConnection();
```

```
        ObjectName service = new ObjectName(SERVICE_NAME);
        ObjectName domainRunTime = (ObjectName) connection.getAttribute(service, "DomainRuntime");
        ObjectName[] serverLifeCycleRunTimes = (ObjectName[])
                    connection.getAttribute(domainRunTime, "ServerLifeCycleRuntimes");

        String serverName = null;
        String serverState = null;

        for (int i = 0; i < serverLifeCycleRunTimes.length; i++) {
            serverName = (String) connection.getAttribute(serverLifeCycleRunTimes[i], "Name");
            serverState = (String) connection.getAttribute(serverLifeCycleRunTimes[i], "State");

            System.out.println("INFO " + serverName + ", " + serverState);

            if (!serverName.equals("AdminServer") && serverState.equals("SHUTDOWN")) {
                System.out.println("STARTING " + serverName);
                connection.invoke(serverLifeCycleRunTimes[i], "start", null, null);
                break;
            }
        }

        closeJmxConnector();
    }
    catch (Exception e) {
        e.printStackTrace();
    }
}

private MBeanServerConnection getMBeanServerConnection() throws IOException {
    return getJmxConnector().getMBeanServerConnection();
}

private JMXConnector getJmxConnector() throws IOException {
    JMXServiceURL serviceURL =
                new JMXServiceURL(PROTOCOL, HOSTNAME, PORT, JNDI_ROOT + MBEAN_SERVER);

    Hashtable hashtable = new Hashtable();
    hashtable.put(Context.SECURITY_PRINCIPAL, USERNAME);
    hashtable.put(Context.SECURITY_CREDENTIALS, PASSWORD);
    hashtable.put(JMXConnectorFactory.PROTOCOL_PROVIDER_PACKAGES, "weblogic.management.remote");

    connector = JMXConnectorFactory.connect(serviceURL, hashtable);
    return connector;
}

private void closeJmxConnector() throws IOException {
    connector.close();
}
}
```

Here, we obtain an array of ServerLifeCycleRuntimeMBean instances. By using the ServerLifeCyleRuntimeMBean we check if a server is shutdown, and if so, we can start the server. Note that this can also be done the other way around, i.e., when we notice that the number of sessions falls below a certain value, we can also stop servers (being sure to keep at least one server running in the cluster). In order to check if the number of sessions fall below a certain number, we create a new watch rule and corresponding notification (that sends its JMS message to a different queue).

Starting and adding servers

We can extend this (starting servers) by adding new servers if the need arises, for example, the message-driven can be rewritten as

```
package model.logic;
```

```
import javax.ejb.ActivationConfigProperty;
import javax.ejb.MessageDriven;
import javax.jms.*;
import javax.management.*;
import javax.management.remote.JMXConnector;
import javax.management.remote.JMXConnectorFactory;
import javax.management.remote.JMXServiceURL;
import javax.naming.Context;
import java.io.IOException;
import java.util.Hashtable;
import java.util.Random;


@MessageDriven(mappedName = "jms/CompanyQueue", activationConfig = {
    @ActivationConfigProperty(propertyName = "destinationName", propertyValue = "jms/CompanyQueue"),
    @ActivationConfigProperty(propertyName = "destinationType", propertyValue = "javax.jms.Queue")
    })
public class CheckMDB implements MessageListener
{
    public static final String HOSTNAME = "machine1.com";
    public static final Integer PORT = 7001;
    public static final String USERNAME = "weblogic";
    public static final String PASSWORD = "snippets12c";

    public static final String PROTOCOL = "t3";
    public static final String JNDI_ROOT = "/jndi/";

    public static final String RUNTIME_MBEAN_SERVER =
                        "weblogic.management.mbeanservers.domainruntime";
    public static final String RUNTIME_SERVICE_NAME = "com.bea:Name=DomainRuntimeService, "+
                "Type=weblogic.management.mbeanservers. domainruntime.DomainRuntimeServiceMBean";

    public static final String EDIT_MBEAN_SERVER = "weblogic.management.mbeanservers.edit";
    public static final String EDIT_SERVICE_NAME = "com.bea:Name=EditService, "+
                "Type=weblogic.management.mbeanservers.edit.EditServiceMBean";

    private JMXConnector runtimeConnector = null;
    private JMXConnector editConnector = null;

    public void onMessage(Message message) {
      try {
        MBeanServerConnection runtimeConnection = getRuntimeMBeanServerConnection();
        ObjectName runtimeService = new ObjectName(RUNTIME_SERVICE_NAME);
        ObjectName domainRunTime = (ObjectName)
                        runtimeConnection.getAttribute(runtimeService, "DomainRuntime");
        ObjectName[] serverLifeCycleRunTimes = (ObjectName[])
                        runtimeConnection.getAttribute(domainRunTime, "ServerLifeCycleRuntimes");

        for (int i = 0; i < serverLifeCycleRunTimes.length; i++) {
            String serverName = (String)
                        runtimeConnection.getAttribute(serverLifeCycleRunTimes[i], "Name");
            String serverState = (String)
                        runtimeConnection.getAttribute(serverLifeCycleRunTimes[i], "State");

        System.out.println("INFO " + serverName + ", " + serverState);

        if (!serverName.equals("AdminServer") && serverState.equals("SHUTDOWN")) {
            System.out.println("STARTING " + serverName);
            runtimeConnection.invoke(serverLifeCycleRunTimes[i], "start", null, null);
            break;
        } else {
            if (i == serverLifeCycleRunTimes.length - 1 && serverLifeCycleRunTimes.length < 5) {
                System.out.println("NO MORE SERVER LEFT TO START, CREATING A NEW ONE");
                MBeanServerConnection editConnection = getEditMBeanServerConnection();
                ObjectName editService = new ObjectName(EDIT_SERVICE_NAME);
                ObjectName configManager = (ObjectName)
                        editConnection.getAttribute(editService, "ConfigurationManager");

                ObjectName edit = (ObjectName) editConnection.invoke(configManager, "startEdit",
                            new Object[] {new Integer(60000), new Integer(120000)},
                            new String[] {"java.lang.Integer", "java.lang.Integer"});

                System.out.println("OBTAIN INFORMATION FROM EXISTING SERVER");
                Random random = new Random();
                int machineChoice = random.nextInt(2);

                ObjectName server = (ObjectName) editConnection.invoke(edit, "lookupServer",
                            new Object[] {"server_" + machineChoice + "_0"},
```

```
                            new String[] {"java.lang.String"});
                    Integer listenport = (Integer) editConnection.getAttribute(server, "ListenPort");
                    ObjectName cluster = (ObjectName) editConnection.getAttribute(server, "Cluster");
                    ObjectName machine = (ObjectName) editConnection.getAttribute(server, "Machine");
                    ObjectName nodemanager = (ObjectName)
                                    editConnection.getAttribute(machine, "NodeManager");
                    String listenaddress = (String)
                                    editConnection.getAttribute(nodemanager, "ListenAddress");

                    System.out.println("CREATE NEW SERVER");
                    editConnection.invoke(edit, "createServer",
                        new Object[] {"server_" + machineChoice + "_" + serverLifeCycleRunTimes.length},
                        new String[] {"java.lang.String"});
                    ObjectName newserver = (ObjectName) editConnection.invoke(edit, "lookupServer",
                        new Object[] {"server_" + machineChoice + "_" + serverLifeCycleRunTimes.length},
                        new String[] {"java.lang.String"});

                    Attribute listenPortAttribute = new Attribute("ListenPort", listenport +
                                                serverLifeCycleRunTimes.length);
                    Attribute clusterAttribute = new Attribute("Cluster", cluster);
                    Attribute machineAttribute = new Attribute("Machine", machine);
                    Attribute listenAddressAttribute = new Attribute("ListenAddress", listenaddress);

                    editConnection.setAttribute(newserver, clusterAttribute);
                    editConnection.setAttribute(newserver, machineAttribute);
                    editConnection.setAttribute(newserver, listenPortAttribute);
                    editConnection.setAttribute(newserver, listenAddressAttribute);

                    System.out.println("SAVE CHANGES");
                    editConnection.invoke(configManager, "save", null, null);

                    Object[] unactivatedChanges = (Object[])
                            editConnection.getAttribute(configManager, "UnactivatedChanges");
                    if (unactivatedChanges.length > 0) {
                        System.out.println("ACTIVATING CHANGES");
                        editConnection.invoke(configManager, "activate",
                            new Object[] { new Long(120000) }, new String[] { "java.lang.Long" });
                    } else {
                        System.out.println("CANCEL EDIT SESSION");
                        editConnection.invoke(configManager, "cancelEdit", null, null);
                    }
                }
            }
        }
    }
    catch (MalformedObjectNameException e) {
        e.printStackTrace();
    }
    finally {
        try {
            closeConnectors();
        } catch (IOException e) {
            e.printStackTrace();
        }
    }
}

private MBeanServerConnection getRuntimeMBeanServerConnection() throws IOException {
    System.out.println("RUNTIME MBEAN SERVER CONNECTION");
    return getRuntimeJmxConnector().getMBeanServerConnection();
}

private JMXConnector getRuntimeJmxConnector() throws IOException {
    JMXServiceURL serviceURL =
            new JMXServiceURL(PROTOCOL, HOSTNAME, PORT, JNDI_ROOT + RUNTIME_MBEAN_SERVER);

    Hashtable hashtable = new Hashtable();
    hashtable.put(Context.SECURITY_PRINCIPAL, USERNAME);
    hashtable.put(Context.SECURITY_CREDENTIALS, PASSWORD);
    hashtable.put(JMXConnectorFactory.PROTOCOL_PROVIDER_PACKAGES, "weblogic.management.remote");

    runtimeConnector = JMXConnectorFactory.connect(serviceURL, hashtable);
    return runtimeConnector;
}

private MBeanServerConnection getEditMBeanServerConnection() throws IOException {
    System.out.println("EDIT MBEAN SERVER CONNECTION");
    return getEditJmxConnector().getMBeanServerConnection();
```

```
    }

    private JMXConnector getEditJmxConnector() throws IOException {
        JMXServiceURL serviceURL =
                    new JMXServiceURL(PROTOCOL, HOSTNAME, PORT, JNDI_ROOT + EDIT_MBEAN_SERVER);

        Hashtable hashtable = new Hashtable();
        hashtable.put(Context.SECURITY_PRINCIPAL, USERNAME);
        hashtable.put(Context.SECURITY_CREDENTIALS, PASSWORD);
        hashtable.put(JMXConnectorFactory.PROTOCOL_PROVIDER_PACKAGES, "weblogic.management.remote");

        editConnector = JMXConnectorFactory.connect(serviceURL, hashtable);
        return editConnector;
    }

    private void closeConnectors() throws IOException {
        if (runtimeConnector != null) {
            System.out.println("CLOSE RUNTIME MBEAN SERVER CONNECTION");
            runtimeConnector.close();
        }

        if (editConnector != null) {
            System.out.println("CLOSE EDIT MBEAN SERVER CONNECTION");
            editConnector.close();
        }
    }
}
```

Dynamic clusters

When working with WebLogic 12.1.2 it is much easier to use dynamic clusters, when
we want to scale automatically. To create a dynamic cluster (that initially has two
servers), we use the following WLST script

```
def create_dynamic_cluster():
    print 'CREATE DYNAMIC CLUSTER';

    cluster = cmo.createCluster(cluster_name);
    cluster.setClusterMessagingMode('unicast');

    cmo.createServerTemplate('server_template');
    server_template = cmo.lookupServerTemplate('server_template');
    server_template.setListenPort(managed_server_listen_port_start);
    server_template.setCluster(cluster);
    cluster.getDynamicServers().setServerTemplate(server_template);
    cluster.getDynamicServers().setMaximumDynamicServerCount(2);
    cluster.getDynamicServers().setMachineNameMatchExpression('machine*');
    cluster.getDynamicServers().setServerNamePrefix('server_');
    cluster.getDynamicServers().setCalculatedListenPorts(java.lang.Boolean('true'));
    cluster.getDynamicServers().setCalculatedMachineNames(java.lang.Boolean('true'));
    cluster.getDynamicServers().setCalculatedListenPorts(java.lang.Boolean('true'));

    return cluster;
```

The message-driven bean can altered as follows

```
package model.logic;

import javax.ejb.ActivationConfigProperty;
import javax.ejb.MessageDriven;
import javax.jms.*;
import javax.management.*;
import javax.management.remote.JMXConnector;
import javax.management.remote.JMXConnectorFactory;
import javax.management.remote.JMXServiceURL;
import javax.naming.Context;
import java.io.IOException;
import java.util.Hashtable;
import java.util.Random;
```

```java
@MessageDriven(mappedName = "jms/CompanyQueue", activationConfig = {
    @ActivationConfigProperty(propertyName = "destinationName", propertyValue = "jms/CompanyQueue"),
    @ActivationConfigProperty(propertyName = "destinationType", propertyValue = "javax.jms.Queue")
    })
public class CheckMDB implements MessageListener {

    public static final String HOSTNAME = "machine1.com";
    public static final Integer PORT = 7001;
    public static final String USERNAME = "weblogic";
    public static final String PASSWORD = "snippets12c";

    public static final String PROTOCOL = "t3";
    public static final String JNDI_ROOT = "/jndi/";

    public static final String RUNTIME_MBEAN_SERVER =
                        "weblogic.management.mbeanservers.domainruntime";
    public static final String RUNTIME_SERVICE_NAME =
"com.bea:Name=DomainRuntimeService,Type=weblogic.management.mbeanservers.domainruntime.DomainRuntimeS
erviceMBean";

    public static final String EDIT_MBEAN_SERVER = "weblogic.management.mbeanservers.edit";
    public static final String EDIT_SERVICE_NAME =
"com.bea:Name=EditService,Type=weblogic.management.mbeanservers.edit.EditServiceMBean";

    private JMXConnector runtimeConnector = null;
    private JMXConnector editConnector = null;

    public void onMessage(Message message) {
        try {
            MBeanServerConnection runtimeConnection = getRuntimeMBeanServerConnection();
            ObjectName runtimeService = new ObjectName(RUNTIME_SERVICE_NAME);
            ObjectName domainRunTime = (ObjectName)
                        runtimeConnection.getAttribute(runtimeService, "DomainRuntime");
            ObjectName[] serverLifeCycleRunTimes = (ObjectName[])
                        runtimeConnection.getAttribute(domainRunTime, "ServerLifeCycleRuntimes");

            for (int i = 0; i < serverLifeCycleRunTimes.length; i++) {
                String serverName = (String)
                        runtimeConnection.getAttribute(serverLifeCycleRunTimes[i], "Name");
                String serverState = (String)
                        runtimeConnection.getAttribute(serverLifeCycleRunTimes[i], "State");

                System.out.println("INFO " + serverName + ", " + serverState);

                if (!serverName.equals("AdminServer") && serverState.equals("SHUTDOWN")) {
                    System.out.println("STARTING " + serverName);
                    runtimeConnection.invoke(serverLifeCycleRunTimes[i], "start", null, null);
                    break;
                } else {
                    if (i == serverLifeCycleRunTimes.length - 1 && serverLifeCycleRunTimes.length < 7) {
                        System.out.println("NO MORE SERVER LEFT TO START, "+
                                    "INCREASING THE NUMBER OF DYNAMIC SERVERS");
                        MBeanServerConnection editConnection = getEditMBeanServerConnection();
                        ObjectName editService = new ObjectName(EDIT_SERVICE_NAME);
                        ObjectName configManager = (ObjectName)
                                editConnection.getAttribute(editService, "ConfigurationManager");

                        ObjectName edit = (ObjectName) editConnection.invoke(configManager, "startEdit",
                                    new Object[] {new Integer(60000), new Integer(120000)},
                                    new String[] {"java.lang.Integer", "java.lang.Integer"});

                        ObjectName cluster = (ObjectName) editConnection.invoke(edit, "lookupCluster",
                                    new Object[] {"cluster"}, new String[] {"java.lang.String"});
                        ObjectName dynamicservers = (ObjectName)
                                editConnection.getAttribute(cluster, "DynamicServers");
                        Integer maximumDynamicServerCount = (Integer)
                                editConnection.getAttribute(dynamicservers, "MaximumDynamicServerCount");

                        Attribute maximumDynamicServerCountAttribute =
                                new Attribute("MaximumDynamicServerCount", maximumDynamicServerCount + 2);
                        editConnection.setAttribute(dynamicservers, maximumDynamicServerCountAttribute);

                        System.out.println("SAVE CHANGES");
                        editConnection.invoke(configManager, "save", null, null);

                        Object[] unactivatedChanges = (Object[])
                                editConnection.getAttribute(configManager, "UnactivatedChanges");
```

```
                    if (unactivatedChanges.length > 0) {
                        System.out.println("ACTIVATING CHANGES");
                        editConnection.invoke(configManager, "activate",
                                              new Object[] { new Long(120000) },
                                              new String[] { "java.lang.Long" });
                    } else {
                        System.out.println("CANCEL EDIT SESSION");
                        editConnection.invoke(configManager, "cancelEdit", null, null);
                    }
                }
            }
        }
    } catch (Exception e) {
        e.printStackTrace();
    }
    finally {
        try {
            closeConnectors();
        }
        catch (IOException e) {
            e.printStackTrace();
        }
    }
}

private MBeanServerConnection getRuntimeMBeanServerConnection() throws IOException {
    System.out.println("RUNTIME MBEAN SERVER CONNECTION");
    return getRuntimeJmxConnector().getMBeanServerConnection();
}

private JMXConnector getRuntimeJmxConnector() throws IOException {
    JMXServiceURL serviceURL =
                new JMXServiceURL(PROTOCOL, HOSTNAME, PORT, JNDI_ROOT + RUNTIME_MBEAN_SERVER);

    Hashtable hashtable = new Hashtable();
    hashtable.put(Context.SECURITY_PRINCIPAL, USERNAME);
    hashtable.put(Context.SECURITY_CREDENTIALS, PASSWORD);
    hashtable.put(JMXConnectorFactory.PROTOCOL_PROVIDER_PACKAGES, "weblogic.management.remote");

    runtimeConnector = JMXConnectorFactory.connect(serviceURL, hashtable);
    return runtimeConnector;
}

private MBeanServerConnection getEditMBeanServerConnection() throws IOException {
    System.out.println("EDIT MBEAN SERVER CONNECTION");
    return getEditJmxConnector().getMBeanServerConnection();
}

private JMXConnector getEditJmxConnector() throws IOException {
    JMXServiceURL serviceURL =
                new JMXServiceURL(PROTOCOL, HOSTNAME, PORT, JNDI_ROOT + EDIT_MBEAN_SERVER);

    Hashtable hashtable = new Hashtable();
    hashtable.put(Context.SECURITY_PRINCIPAL, USERNAME);
    hashtable.put(Context.SECURITY_CREDENTIALS, PASSWORD);
    hashtable.put(JMXConnectorFactory.PROTOCOL_PROVIDER_PACKAGES, "weblogic.management.remote");

    editConnector = JMXConnectorFactory.connect(serviceURL, hashtable);
    return editConnector;
}

private void closeConnectors() throws IOException {
    if (runtimeConnector != null) {
        System.out.println("CLOSE RUNTIME MBEAN SERVER CONNECTION");
        runtimeConnector.close();
    }

    if (editConnector != null) {
        System.out.println("CLOSE EDIT MBEAN SERVER CONNECTION");
        editConnector.close();
    }
}
}
```

Here, we look if there are any servers left to start, if not we increase the value of the MaximumDynamicServerCount attribute by two. Note that the maximum number of servers in the domain is set to seven in the example above (this includes the admin server). As the names of the servers have been changed we need to configure the harvester and the watch such that the right instances are picked up.

Sending JMS notifications in case of stuck threads

The third example demonstrate the use of JMS notifications. The following real life example demonstrates the monitoring of a typical production issue. Hanging back ends, blocked resources or not responding partner systems causes thread in WebLogic to not respond for a long time. WebLogic will mark them after a given amount of time as "stuck" which normally always indicates a production issue.

The following example will define a WLDF watch which will monitor the stuck thread counter of the default work manager in WebLogic. If this counter goes above 0 then it will generate a JMS notification. A JMS client is provided to receive these JMS messages.

Setup the JMS server and a JMS destination for the WLDF notifications

The following WLST cod will setup all the JMS elements which are necessary so that WLDF can send out JMS notifications. Please note that the JMS configurations are NOT part of the WLDF subsystem in WebLogic. It can be either an own dedicated JMS server or a queue on a shared JMS server.

Step 1: Create the File Store:
```
cd('/')
cmo.createFileStore('WLDFFileStore')
cd('/FileStores/WLDFFileStore')
cmo.setDirectory('/tmp')
set('Targets',jarray.array([ObjectName('com.bea:Name=AdminServer,Type=Server')], ObjectName))
```

Step 2: Create the JMS Server for WLDF Notification:
```
cd('/')
print 'Creating JMS Server.'
cmo.createJMSServer('WLDFJMSServer')
cd('/JMSServers/WLDFJMSServer')
cmo.setPersistentStore(getMBean('/FileStores/WLDFFileStore'))
cmo.addTarget(getMBean('/Servers/AdminServer'))
```

Step 3: Create the JMS Module for WLDF notification:
```
cd('/')
cmo.createJMSSystemResource('WLDFJMSSystemResource')
cd('/JMSSystemResources/WLDFJMSSystemResource')
cmo.addTarget(getMBean('/Servers/AdminServer'))
cmo.createSubDeployment('WLDFSubdeDloyment')
```

Step 4: Create the Connection Factory:
```
cd('/JMSSystemResources/WLDFJMSSystemResource/JMSResource/WLDFJMSSystemResource')
```

```
cmo.createConnectionFactory('WLDFConnectionfactory')
cd('/JMSSystemResources/WLDFJMSSystemResource/JMSResource/WLDFJMSSystemResource/ConnectionFactories/W
LDFConnectionfactory')
cmo.setJNDIName('jms/myWLDFFactory')
cd('/JMSSystemResources/WLDFJMSSystemResource/JMSResource/WLDFJMSSystemResource/ConnectionFactories/W
LDFConnectionfactory/SecurityParams/WLDFConnectionfactory')
cmo.setAttachJMSXUserId(false)
cd('/JMSSystemResources/WLDFJMSSystemResource/JMSResource/WLDFJMSSystemResource/ConnectionFactories/W
LDFConnectionfactory/ClientParams/WLDFConnectionfactory')
cmo.setClientIdPolicy('Restricted')
cmo.setSubscriptionSharingPolicy('Exclusive')
cmo.setMessagesMaximum(1000)
cd('/JMSSystemResources/WLDFJMSSystemResource/JMSResource/WLDFJMSSystemResource/ConnectionFactories/W
LDFConnectionfactory')
cmo.setDefaultTargetingEnabled(true)
```

Final Step 5: Create the Queue for our WLDF notifications:

```
cd('/JMSSystemResources/WLDFJMSSystemResource/JMSResource/WLDFJMSSystemResource')
cmo.createQueue('WLDFMonitoringQueue')
cd('/JMSSystemResources/WLDFJMSSystemResource/JMSResource/WLDFJMSSystemResource/Queues/WLDFMonitoring
Queue')
set('JNDIName','jms/WLDFSTuckThreadNotificationQueue')
set('SubDeploymentName','WLDFSubdeDloyment')
cd('/JMSSystemResources/WLDFJMSSystemResource/SubDeployments/WLDFSubdeDloyment')
cmo.addTarget(getMBean('/JMSServers/WLDFJMSServer'))

print 'WLDF JMS Resources are created'
```

After the following steps have been completed, WebLogic has created a JMS configuration. JMS configurations in WebLogic are stored in own configuration files which are saved in the "jms" subfolder of the <domain>/config directory.

The following configuration was created:

```
<weblogic-jms ...>
  <connection-factory name="WLDFConnectionfactory">
    <default-targeting-enabled>true</default-targeting-enabled>
    <jndi-name>jms/myWLDFFactory</jndi-name>
    <client-params>
      <client-id-policy>Restricted</client-id-policy>
      <subscription-sharing-policy>Exclusive</subscription-sharing-policy>
      <messages-maximum>1000</messages-maximum>
    </client-params>
    <security-params>
      <attach-jmsx-user-id>false</attach-jmsx-user-id>
    </security-params>
  </connection-factory>
  <queue name="WLDFMonitoringQueue">
    <sub-deployment-name>WLDFSubdeDloyment</sub-deployment-name>
    <jndi-name>jms/WLDFSTuckThreadNotificationQueue</jndi-name>
  </queue>
</weblogic-jms>
```

Setup the WLDF module

Next we have to define and setup the WLDF diagnostic module. As stated above, the WLDF configuration will make use of the JMS configuration defined above and which is defined outside of the WLDF module.

```
edit()
startEdit()

cd('/')
cmo.createWLDFSystemResource('StuckThreadDetectionModule')

cd('/WLDFSystemResources/StuckThreadDetectionModule')
cmo.setDescription('Module to detect stuck threads')
```

```
cd('/WLDFSystemResources/StuckThreadDetectionModule/WLDFResource/StuckThreadDetectionModule/WatchNoti
fication/StuckThreadDetectionModule')
cmo.createJMSNotification('StuckThreadNotification')

cd('/WLDFSystemResources/StuckThreadDetectionModule/WLDFResource/StuckThreadDetectionModule/WatchNoti
fication/StuckThreadDetectionModule/JMSNotifications/StuckThreadNotification')
cmo.setEnabled(true)
cmo.setDestinationJNDIName('jms/WLDFSTuckThreadNotificationQueue')
cmo.setConnectionFactoryJNDIName('jms/myWLDFFactory')

cd('/WLDFSystemResources/StuckThreadDetectionModule')
set('Targets',jarray.array([ObjectName('com.bea:Name=AdminServer,Type=Server')], ObjectName))

cd('/WLDFSystemResources/StuckThreadDetectionModule/WLDFResource/StuckThreadDetectionModule/WatchNoti
fication/StuckThreadDetectionModule')
cmo.createWatch('StuckThreadWatch')

cd('/WLDFSystemResources/StuckThreadDetectionModule/WLDFResource/StuckThreadDetectionModule/WatchNoti
fication/StuckThreadDetectionModule/Watches/StuckThreadWatch')
cmo.setRuleType('Harvester')
cmo.setEnabled(true)
cmo.setRuleExpression('(${ServerRuntime//[weblogic.management.runtime.WorkManagerRuntimeMBean]//Stuck
ThreadCount} > 0)')
cmo.setAlarmType('AutomaticReset')
cmo.setAlarmResetPeriod(30000)
set('Notifications',jarray.array([ObjectName('com.bea:Name=StuckThreadNotification,Type=weblogic.diag
nostics.descriptor.WLDFJMSNotificationBean,Parent=[base_domain]/WLDFSystemResources[StuckThreadDetect
ionModule],Path=WLDFResource[StuckThreadDetectionModule]/WatchNotification[StuckThreadDetectionModule
]/JMSNotifications[StuckThreadNotification]')], ObjectName))

print 'WLDF diagnostic module is created'
activate()
```

WeLogic has created the following WLDF configuration in the "diagnostic" subfolder:

```
<wldf-resource ...>
  <name>StuckThreadDetectionModule</name>
  <watch-notification>
    <watch>
      <name>StuckThreadWatch</name>
      <enabled>true</enabled>
      <rule-type>Harvester</rule-type>
      <rule-
expression>(${ServerRuntime//[weblogic.management.runtime.WorkManagerRuntimeMBean]//StuckThreadCount}
&gt; 0)</rule-expression>
      <alarm-type>AutomaticReset</alarm-type>
      <alarm-reset-period>30000</alarm-reset-period>
      <notification>StuckThreadNotification</notification>
    </watch>
    <jms-notification>
      <name>StuckThreadNotification</name>
      <enabled>true</enabled>
      <destination-jndi-name>jms/WLDFSTuckThreadNotificationQueue</destination-jndi-name>
      <connection-factory-jndi-name>jms/myWLDFFactory</connection-factory-jndi-name>
    </jms-notification>
  </watch-notification>
</wldf-resource>
```

Define the JMS client

These notifications are only useful if clients will register with the WebLogic MBeans in order to receive these events. The following JAVA code discusses how to write a simple JMX client to consume these notifications.

```
public class ReceiveJMSNotificationExample implements MessageListener
{
  public final static String JMS_CONNECTION_FACTORY="jms/myWLDFFactory";
```

```java
public final static String WLDF_NOTIFICATION_QUEUE="WLDFSTuckThreadNotificationQueue";

private QueueConnectionFactory jmsConnectionFactory;
private QueueConnection jmsConnection;
private QueueSession jmsSession;
private QueueReceiver jmsQueueReceiver;

/**
 * Initialize the JMS layer and start listening
 * @param ctx
 * @throws Exception
 */
public void init(Context ctx) throws Exception
{
  jmsConnectionFactory = (QueueConnectionFactory) ctx.lookup(JMS_CONNECTION_FACTORY);
  jmsConnection = jmsConnectionFactory.createQueueConnection();
  jmsSession = jmsConnection.createQueueSession(false, Session.AUTO_ACKNOWLEDGE);
  jmsQueueReceiver = jmsSession.createReceiver((Queue) ctx.lookup(WLDF_NOTIFICATION_QUEUE));
  jmsQueueReceiver.setMessageListener(this);
  jmsConnection.start();
}

/**
 * Action to do whenever a message is received. In this case we just print it.
 * For this scenario a good idea could be to connect to the server where the message is comming
 * from and issue a thread dump.
 */
public void onMessage(Message myWLDFMessage)
{
  try
  {
    if (myWLDFMessage instanceof TextMessage)
    {
      System.out.println("Message Received: "+  ((TextMessage)myWLDFMessage).getText());
    }
    else if (myWLDFMessage instanceof MapMessage)
    {
      System.out.println("Message Received: "+ myWLDFMessage.toString());
      MapMessage map = (MapMessage)myWLDFMessage;
      Enumeration en = map.getMapNames();
      while (en.hasMoreElements()){
        String nE = (String)en.nextElement();
        System.out.println("    "+nE+" = "+ map.getObject(nE).toString());
      }
    }
    else
    {
      System.out.println("Message Received: "+ myWLDFMessage.toString());
    }
  }
  catch (JMSException ex) {
    ex.printStackTrace();
  }
}


/**
 * Cleanup the JMS layer and close resources
 * @throws JMSException
 */
public void cleanupJMSResources() throws JMSException
{
  jmsQueueReceiver.close();
  jmsSession.close();
  jmsConnection.close();
}


public static void main(String[] args) throws Exception
{
  Hashtable<String,String> envProperties = new Hashtable<String,String>();
  envProperties.put(Context.INITIAL_CONTEXT_FACTORY, "weblogic.jndi.WLInitialContextFactory");
  envProperties.put(Context.PROVIDER_URL, "t3://localhost:12001");
  InitialContext ctx = new InitialContext(envProperties);

  ReceiveJMSNotificationExample myReceiver = new ReceiveJMSNotificationExample();
  myReceiver.init(ctx);
```

```
        System.out.println("WLDF Notification Listener is now listening " +
                            "for WLDF notification JMS Messages");

        // very bad implementation - just to make example short !!!!!!!
        Thread.sleep(Long.MAX_VALUE);


        myReceiver.cleanupJMSResources();
    }
}
```

Please note that we are distinguishing between the different types JMS messages we might receive. Also note that, (for simplicity), most error handling and a better way of sleeping in the main method has been deleted.

Run the example

When we start the example, it is assumed that the AdminServer is running, the JMS server is active and that the WLDF module is active. Then we start the client which will connect to the JMS server of the AdminServer and waits for messages.

If we are running into a stuck thread situation then the following message will be received. Note that WLS is sending a MapMessage with a number of information. For a better understanding of what is send from WebLogic the complete received messages is printed below:

```
WLDF Notificatin Listener is now listening for WLDF notification JMS Messages
Message Received: MapMessage[ID:<261079.1404683786387.0>]
    WatchAlarmResetPeriod = 30000
    WatchSeverityLevel = Notice
    WatchRule =
(${ServerRuntime//[weblogic.management.runtime.WorkManagerRuntimeMBean]//StuckThreadCount} > 0)
    WatchDomainName = base_domain
    WatchModule = StuckThreadDetectionModule
    WatchData =
com.bea:Name=weblogic.kernel.System,ServerRuntime=AdminServer,Type=WorkManagerRuntime//StuckThreadCou
nt = 0
com.bea:ApplicationRuntime=bea_wls_management_internal2,Name=default,ServerRuntime=AdminServer,Type=W
orkManagerRuntime//StuckThreadCount = 0
com.bea:Name=OneWayJTACoordinatorWM,ServerRuntime=AdminServer,Type=WorkManagerRuntime//StuckThreadCou
nt = 0
com.bea:Name=weblogic.jms.WLDFJMSServer.System,ServerRuntime=AdminServer,Type=WorkManagerRuntime//Stu
ckThreadCount = 0
com.bea:ApplicationRuntime=StuckThreadDetectionModule,Name=default,ServerRuntime=AdminServer,Type=Wor
kManagerRuntime//StuckThreadCount = 0
com.bea:Name=weblogic.Rejector,ServerRuntime=AdminServer,Type=WorkManagerRuntime//StuckThreadCount =
0
com.bea:ApplicationRuntime=bea_wls_diagnostics,Name=default,ServerRuntime=AdminServer,Type=WorkManage
rRuntime//StuckThreadCount = 0
com.bea:Name=wl_oldBootStrap,ServerRuntime=AdminServer,Type=WorkManagerRuntime//StuckThreadCount = 0
com.bea:Name=HARVESTER_WM,ServerRuntime=AdminServer,Type=WorkManagerRuntime//StuckThreadCount = 0
com.bea:Name=direct,ServerRuntime=AdminServer,Type=WorkManagerRuntime//StuckThreadCount = 0
com.bea:Name=JmsDispatcher,ServerRuntime=AdminServer,Type=WorkManagerRuntime//StuckThreadCount = 0
com.bea:Name=weblogic.kernel.WTC,ServerRuntime=AdminServer,Type=WorkManagerRuntime//StuckThreadCount
= 0 com.bea:Name=weblogic.kernel.Non-
Blocking,ServerRuntime=AdminServer,Type=WorkManagerRuntime//StuckThreadCount = 0
com.bea:Name=weblogic.admin.RMI,ServerRuntime=AdminServer,Type=WorkManagerRuntime//StuckThreadCount =
0
com.bea:ApplicationRuntime=bea_wls_deployment_internal,Name=default,ServerRuntime=AdminServer,Type=Wo
rkManagerRuntime//StuckThreadCount = 0 com.bea:ApplicationRuntime=wlhostmachinestats-
030,Name=default,ServerRuntime=AdminServer,Type=WorkManagerRuntime//StuckThreadCount = 0
com.bea:ApplicationRuntime=DAPInfoWebLogic,Name=default,ServerRuntime=AdminServer,Type=WorkManagerRun
time//StuckThreadCount = 0
com.bea:Name=WatchManagerEvents,ServerRuntime=AdminServer,Type=WorkManagerRuntime//StuckThreadCount =
0
```

```
com.bea:Name=weblogic.jms.WLDFJMSServer.AsyncPush,ServerRuntime=AdminServer,Type=WorkManagerRuntime//
StuckThreadCount = 0
com.bea:Name=ImageWorkManager,ServerRuntime=AdminServer,Type=WorkManagerRuntime//StuckThreadCount = 0
com.bea:Name=JmsAsyncQueue,ServerRuntime=AdminServer,Type=WorkManagerRuntime//StuckThreadCount = 0
com.bea:ApplicationRuntime=WLDFJMSSystemResource,Name=default,ServerRuntime=AdminServer,Type=WorkMana
gerRuntime//StuckThreadCount = 0
com.bea:Name=weblogic.logging.DomainLogBroadcasterClient,ServerRuntime=AdminServer,Type=WorkManagerRu
ntime//StuckThreadCount = 0
com.bea:ApplicationRuntime=bea_wls_internal,Name=default,ServerRuntime=AdminServer,Type=WorkManagerRu
ntime//StuckThreadCount = 0
com.bea:Name=weblogic.jms.WLDFJMSServer.Limited,ServerRuntime=AdminServer,Type=WorkManagerRuntime//St
uckThreadCount = 0
com.bea:ApplicationRuntime=consoleapp,Name=consoleWorkManager,ServerRuntime=AdminServer,Type=WorkMana
gerRuntime//StuckThreadCount = 0
com.bea:Name=weblogic.logging.LogBroadcaster,ServerRuntime=AdminServer,Type=WorkManagerRuntime//Stuck
ThreadCount = 0
com.bea:Name=UserLockout,ServerRuntime=AdminServer,Type=WorkManagerRuntime//StuckThreadCount = 0
com.bea:ApplicationRuntime=bea_wls9_async_response,Name=default,ServerRuntime=AdminServer,Type=WorkMa
nagerRuntime//StuckThreadCount = 0 com.bea:ApplicationRuntime=wls-
wsat,Name=default,ServerRuntime=AdminServer,Type=WorkManagerRuntime//StuckThreadCount = 0
com.bea:Name=DataRetirementWorkManager,ServerRuntime=AdminServer,Type=WorkManagerRuntime//StuckThread
Count = 0
com.bea:Name=weblogic.kernel.Default,ServerRuntime=AdminServer,Type=WorkManagerRuntime//StuckThreadCo
unt = 0
com.bea:ApplicationRuntime=dummy,Name=default,ServerRuntime=AdminServer,Type=WorkManage
rRuntime//StuckThreadCount = 1
com.bea:ApplicationRuntime=consoleapp,Name=default,ServerRuntime=AdminServer,Type=WorkManagerRuntime/
/StuckThreadCount = 0
com.bea:Name=weblogic.nodemanager.ConfigPoler,ServerRuntime=AdminServer,Type=WorkManagerRuntime//Stuc
kThreadCount = 0
com.bea:Name=JTACoordinatorWM,ServerRuntime=AdminServer,Type=WorkManagerRuntime//StuckThreadCount = 0
com.bea:ApplicationRuntime=mejb,Name=default,ServerRuntime=AdminServer,Type=WorkManagerRuntime//Stuck
ThreadCount = 0
    JMSNotificationName = StuckThreadNotification
    WatchAlarmType = AutomaticReset
    WatchRuleType = Harvester
    WatchName = StuckThreadWatch
    WatchServerName = AdminServer
    WatchTime = Jul 6, 2014 11:56:26 PM CEST
```

The reason which the "WatchData" section is so big is that WebLogic by default has a large number of WorkManagers. In our setup we did not restrict the notification to s specific instance, otherwise this section would be much smaller.

If you look carefully at the "WatchData" section you can see the reason for the notification.

```
com.bea:ApplicationRuntime=dummy,Name=default,ServerRuntime=AdminServer,Type
=WorkManagerRuntime//StuckThreadCount = 1
```

This tell us that a thread in the "default" WorkManager and here in the application "dummy" got stuck. And this is true as the "dummy" application has enforced the situation (it was just a very simple servlet which did nothing but slept for 15 min). So you get a number of very valuable information like which application, which server, when, which domain and more. If you have a proper unique naming for your WLS domains then it would be easy now to automatically connect to this domain and this server and enforce a thread-dump in order to get more information.

Creating a diagnostic image if heap reaches critical value

The last example demonstrate the use of diagnostic images and image notifications. The following real life example monitors the heap usages of the WebLogic server virtual machine. If the heap usage reaches a critical value (e.g. 90 %), an image notification will be fired which will generate a diagnostic image.

WLST also includes – as discussed earlier – functions to list diagnostic images and download complete images or certain parts of an image. These features can be used in this example to get the image downloaded to your local machine.

Setup the WLDF module including all required components

This example does not involve other resource like JMS or SNMP therefore the only thing we need to do is to setup the diagnostic module.

The following WLST script will do the setup for us:

```
# First of all create the diagnostic module
cd('/')
cmo.createWLDFSystemResource('HeapOverservationModule')

cd('/WLDFSystemResources/HeapOverservationModule')
cmo.setDescription('This diagnostic module will watch the heap usage and creates a diagnostic images
if the heap reaches a defined limit')

# create a harvester in order to get long term analysis data
cd('/WLDFSystemResources/HeapOverservationModule/WLDFResource/HeapOverservationModule/Harvester/HeapO
verservationModule')
cmo.createHarvestedType('weblogic.management.runtime.JVMRuntimeMBean')

cd('/WLDFSystemResources/HeapOverservationModule/WLDFResource/HeapOverservationModule/Harvester/HeapO
verservationModule/HarvestedTypes/weblogic.management.runtime.JVMRuntimeMBean')
set('HarvestedAttributes',jarray.array([String('HeapFreePercent'), String('HeapFreeCurrent'),
String('HeapSizeCurrent'), String('HeapSizeMax')], String))
cmo.setHarvestedInstances(None)
cmo.setNamespace('ServerRuntime')

# now create our heap watch
cd('/WLDFSystemResources/HeapOverservationModule/WLDFResource/HeapOverservationModule/WatchNotificati
on/HeapOverservationModule')
cmo.createWatch('HeapFreePercentWatch')

# configure the heap watch
cd('/WLDFSystemResources/HeapOverservationModule/WLDFResource/HeapOverservationModule/WatchNotificati
on/HeapOverservationModule/Watches/HeapFreePercentWatch')
cmo.setRuleType('Harvester')
cmo.setEnabled(true)
cmo.setRuleExpression('(${ServerRuntime//[weblogic.management.runtime.JVMRuntimeMBean]com.bea:Name=Ad
minServer,ServerRuntime=AdminServer,Type=JVMRuntime//HeapFreePercent} < 20)')
cmo.setAlarmType('AutomaticReset')
cmo.setAlarmResetPeriod(30000)

# create our notification
cd('/WLDFSystemResources/HeapOverservationModule/WLDFResource/HeapOverservationModule/WatchNotificati
on/HeapOverservationModule')
cmo.createImageNotification('HeapUsageNotification')

# configure our notification
cd('/WLDFSystemResources/HeapOverservationModule/WLDFResource/HeapOverservationModule/WatchNotificati
on/HeapOverservationModule/ImageNotifications/HeapUsageNotification')
```

```
cmo.setEnabled(true)
cmo.setImageDirectory('logs/diagnostic_images')
cmo.setImageLockout(5)

# attach the notification to the watch
cd('/WLDFSystemResources/HeapOverservationModule/WLDFResource/HeapOverservationModule/WatchNotificati
on/HeapOverservationModule/Watches/HeapFreePercentWatch')
set('Notifications',jarray.array([ObjectName('com.bea:Name=HeapUsageNotification,Type=weblogic.diagno
stics.descriptor.WLDFImageNotificationBean,Parent=[base_domain]/WLDFSystemResources[HeapOverservation
Module],Path=WLDFResource[HeapOverservationModule]/WatchNotification[HeapOverservationModule]/ImageNo
tifications[HeapUsageNotification]')], ObjectName))
martin@martin-laptop:~$

# activate and target the diagnostic module
cd('/WLDFSystemResources/HeapOverservationModule')
set('Targets',jarray.array([ObjectName('com.bea:Name=AdminServer,Type=Server')], ObjectName))
```

Afterwards the complete setup is done for us. The diagnostic image has been created with all required artifacts like watch and notification. Please note that this example ONLY targets the WLDF module to the AdminServer which might not be a realistic example for real systems. This must be adapted to your setup accordingly.

The following configuration has been created in the WebLogic configuration section:

```
<wldf-resource …">
  <name>HeapOverservationModule</name>
  <harvester>
    <harvested-type>
      <name>weblogic.management.runtime.JVMRuntimeMBean</name>
      <harvested-attribute>HeapFreePercent</harvested-attribute>
      <harvested-attribute>HeapFreeCurrent</harvested-attribute>
      <harvested-attribute>HeapSizeCurrent</harvested-attribute>
      <harvested-attribute>HeapSizeMax</harvested-attribute>
      <harvested-
instance>com.bea:Name=AdminServer,ServerRuntime=AdminServer,Type=JVMRuntime</harvested-instance>
      <namespace>ServerRuntime</namespace>
    </harvested-type>
  </harvester>
  <watch-notification>
    <watch>
      <name>HeapFreePercentWatch</name>
      <enabled>true</enabled>
      <rule-type>Harvester</rule-type>
      <rule-
expression>(${ServerRuntime//[weblogic.management.runtime.JVMRuntimeMBean]com.bea:Name=AdminServer,Se
rverRuntime=AdminServer,Type=JVMRuntime//HeapFreePercent} &lt; 58)</rule-expression>
      <alarm-type>AutomaticReset</alarm-type>
      <alarm-reset-period>30000</alarm-reset-period>
      <notification>HeapUsageNotification</notification>
    </watch>
    <image-notification>
      <name>HeapUsageNotification</name>
      <enabled>true</enabled>
      <image-directory>logs/diagnostic_images</image-directory>
      <image-lockout>1</image-lockout>
    </image-notification>
  </watch-notification>
</wldf-resource>
```

Access to the generated images

Please refer to chapter 6 (Diagnostic Images) for a detailed list of commands and examples of how to list available images and download images or parts of images. This can be used here well in order to work with the generated image archives.

Summary

This chapter demonstrates some complete example usages of WLDF. The first example has demonstrated how custom MBeans and data can be used. JMX notifications can be retrieved by JMX clients, either embedded into WLS itself or external like for example external monitoring systems. The second examples has demonstrated an interesting way how WebLogic can react based on notifications.

As already mentioned in WLS 12.2.1 this will even be easier which WLST based notifications. The third example uses JMS notification to inform any interesting party of potential production issues if threads get stuck and the last example demonstrates how diagnostic images can be utilized.

WLDF has many different usages and can be used in all stages from development to production. WLDF has no limitations and can be used in any domain setup like multinode or multi cluster domain.

Part IV

WLDF Profiles

The fourth part of the book introduces the idea of WLDF profiles, which are very useful in structuring WLDF components and working in complex system environments.

Organize and structure WLDF through Profiles

WLDF Profiles

Monitoring, troubleshooting, root cause analysis and other activities rely on the collection of different sets of metric data. In real life, with real project requirements for this data we usually follow repeating patterns. This means that similar requirements can be seen for different projects. It also means that certain types of data collectors will be required again and again, a condition which empowers reusable diagnostic configurations. Administrators, (especially when they are responsible for a larger hosting environment), need to react quickly and usually do not have the time for development of custom code. Therefore, the reuse of existing modules and structured collection of building blocks really help to get things done quickly and more efficiently.

This chapter discusses an approach which recommends to combine metrics relevant for certain scenarios or application types into profiles.

The idea of profiles

Monitoring, troubleshooting, root cause analysis and other areas are important activities in every production system. However these tasks are hard to anticipate as error conditions are often not known upfront. Also, monitoring requirements changes dramatically depending on the nature of the application. All these different activities require us to collect a different set of metrics and different sets of alarms, watches or notifications.

Monitoring and troubleshooting activities also depend on the environment where they have to be performed and on the person who has to do the monitoring. If a developer has to do some monitoring or troubleshooting in his development environment, then this is rather straightforward because he exactly knows what to look for and where he needs to look. In this case, he also knows and controls the application. Usually in most organizations the higher level environments like integration testing, non-functional testing, production like environment, user acceptance testing (UAT) and especially production and training environment are owned and controlled by a group of administrators which implement a kind of hosting service for the organization.

In these types of systems, the individual developer does not (and should not!) have direct access to the application, application server or even machine. In these environments the situation is different. A group of people who do not have insights into the application (code) have to operate and maintain a large number of different applications. Usually (Murphy's law) the difficult problems only show up in the production or other higher level environments. Therefore this group has to constantly monitor the health of their applications and infrastructure (including the application servers!). They also have to be prepared to activate data collection in case of error conditions so that they can deliver sufficient data for the developers or support groups to analyze problem situations. In these environments application specific metric collection is required and it is also impossible to have all data collection running all the time (resource issues for CPU, disk and database usage!).

One solution which has been proven to be very successful is something we will call "monitoring profiles". This is not a standardized terminology and could be also named differently like "setup" or "constellations" or something else. The idea behind monitoring profiles is that many different combinations of metric collections and alarms/notifications will be prepared and made available for the administrator group. Each combination is called a "profile".

Speaking for WLDF, it is possible to even install all the different profiles in all WebLogic instances but leave them deactivated (WLS 12.1.2+) or untargeted so that theses configurations are not active and do not require and waste resources. The administrator group will get trained which profile has be to activated for which special error situations.

In case of WLDF different approaches are possible and should be considered:

1) Create one diagnostic module for each profile with all relevant components (harvester, watches, notifications or data accessor). These modules will we specified in WLST or JMX and installed in all relevant WebLogic domains. But none of the modules will be targeted to a specific server. The administrator group has scripts to activate (target) or deactivate (untarget) modules on demand.

2) Starting with WLS 12.1.2 it is possible to create one diagnostic module for each profile with all relevant components (harvester, watches, notifications or data accessor). These modules will we specified in WLST or JMX and installed in all relevant WebLogic domains and will also be targeted to the relevant server (not necessary but will save time afterwards). But none of the modules will be

activated. The administrator group has scripts to activate or deactivate modules on demand.

3) In case the WLDF metric collection is not needed very often and especially if the administrator group has no knowledge where it might be needed, a third option would be to create all modules in WLST or JMX but do NOT install them on the WebLogic domains. The administrator group will have scripts to install and activate (target) this modules on demand and to untarget and uninstall these modules.

These 3 different approaches have a number of advantages:

- Well-defined profiles
- Profiles can even be defined during development by the developers (and tested with the application) and then handed over to the administrator group
- Scoped metric collection. Not "collect-the-world" approach will be used but an approach which will save resources and performance.
- If the profiles are already developed from the application development teams then they know which data they will get in case the administrators have to run these modules. Benefit for all sides

There is only one little disadvantage for all three approaches. It is most likely the case that certain metric definitions are duplicated in potentially many modules. This might be wanted but this might also cause an overhead in maintaining the profiles. An alternative would be to define profile components like metric collections, watches, notifications and others. In addition the administrator group has scripts which define the real WLDF profiles. These scripts then contain the logic which profile components out of the components collection should be used to construct the profile.

I like to call this "dynamic WLDF profiles" or "component profiles". In real life, this is still an unusual approach because it requires quite a lot of WLST/JMX and WLDF skills on both sides the developer side and the administrator sides. Even though this approach will eliminate duplication, the script and profile setup is quite more complicated. The big benefit is that the administrator group can react much more flexibly to monitoring and/or troubleshooting requests.

The technology recommended for implementing the profiles is WLST. Based on experience, WLST is more flexible, better readable and especially for administrators who are used to use scripts the better choice anyway. It is quite rare to see administrators programming in Java. Of course JMX is from a technology perspective equally suited to be used to implement profiles but in real life has shown that WLST is the better choice.

There are few exceptions though. It is possible that applications (if they have the required access rights) can setup WLDF modules dynamically on demand (see the open source application domainhealth as an example). For these applications JMX is the better choice as these applications are written in Java anyway. Another example are monitoring and management frameworks which offer diagnostic facilities. For these tools also JMX is a very good choice as the implementation is part of these products and therefore closed source to the outside world.

Examples of useful profiles

This chapter discusses a list of potential profiles. Note that this list is based on general profiles. Every company, organization or project has its own project needs and special settings. Therefore the author's advice is to use the general profiles as a starting point and develop your custom profiles based on ideas and metrics discussed in the general profiles.

I will introduce the idea of profiles by providing four different categories of profiles. The first two categories will define specialized profiles. The third one is a special profile which is based on application code instrumentation, and the last category is most likely the most important category for most readers as this includes more general profiles. Profiles of the last category also include many aspects of the first three categories but this is on purpose.

Infrastructure profiles

Infrastructure profiles in this context means a number of WLDF profiles which defines metrics and watches for core WebLogic components. WebLogic here represents the "Infrastructure". These profiles are particularly useful if issues in the server core are expected

- **Virtual machine Profile:** Monitor virtual machine metrics, like free heap size, free % of heap and more. It might be useful to even distinguish profiles for the different virtual machine implementations like JRockit and Hotspot.

- **Server Core profile:** With server core profiles the administrator is able to monitor core behavior of WebLogic. This includes the state of the server the amount of running servers in a cluster. Starting with 12.2.1 this will include the state of the partitions. This also includes the core container of WebLogic.

- **Communication profile:** J2EE server like WebLogic heavily depend on communication. WebLogic has the notion of NetworkChannel for inbound communication. Every channel can be individually monitored with own MBeans.

This also includes virtual hosts, the internal WebLogic WebServer and other components.

- **Workmanager/Resource profile:** This includes especially threading which WebLogic implements with different so called WorkManager.

Service level profiles

Service level profiles in this context means a number of WLDF profiles which defines metrics and watches WebLogic services. WebLogic offers a number of services for communication and processing. This includes for example access to databases and backend systems.

- **Transaction Profile:** A transaction profile means monitoring the transaction service. This can include number heuristics, number of transaction rollbacks, long running transactions and other values which might indicate issues in transaction processing.

- **Data Access (JDBC) profile:** A database profile monitors access to a database via a WebLogic datasource. This can include number of connections, number of failed connections, failures to get a connection, request size or other values.

- **WTC Tuxedo Access Profile:** WTC stands for "WebLogic Tuxedo Connector" and implements a communication bridge to Oracle Tuxedo. It basically allows WebLogic to call Tuxedo service hosted in a remote Tuxedo domain or allows to import EJBs into a remote Tuxedo domain so that they can be called from Tuxedo.

- **JMS Messaging Profile:** A JMS profile monitors a JMS server hosted in WebLogic. Amount of messages and other values can be captured for diagnostic purposes.

- **Email Profile:** WebLogic also offers a email provider which can be sued to define email resources. These are also accessible via MBeans and therefore can be part of the monitoring.

- **SNMP Profile:** WebLogic has the ability to send out SNMP traps to monitoring systems. Even WLDF can utilize it send out notification traps. The SNMP subsystem itself can be part of a diagnostic investigation.

Application category profiles

Application category profiles in this sense means all aspects of the different categories mentioned above which are typically for a specific type of application. Note that in this context it does not mean application specific (business specific) profiles. All definitions in this category are still application independent.

- **WebApplication profile:** This includes typical values for web frontends. Especially web sessions, session creation rates, highest amount of sessions are of interest. Therefore this may include values of the WebLogic WebServer, the virtual host components and the http/s protocol NetworkChannel.

- **Enterprise (EJB) profile:** An Enterprise (EJB) profile is more concerned about transactions. Especially transaction times, transaction failures, pool sizes of EJBs, amount of sessions (Stateless Session Beans) are values included in this profile. Almost all EJB applications have database access, therefore datasources are also a hot topic in this area.

- **Integration profile:** Integration means talking to other systems. So this profile is mainly concerned about JCA (java connector architecture) components, JMS (Java Messaging System components), Tuxedo connectivity via WTC and similar values.

- **Messaging profile:** Messaging means using communication and notifications to other environments. This is a bit similar to the Integration profile but does more focus on JMS (Java Messaging System components), Email resources, SNMP (network management) and WebServices.

- **Backend profile:** A backend profile is also a bit similar to the integration type but with a clear focus on DataSources, JCA and WTC.

Application profiles

Every application is different and furthermore WebLogic cannot provide application specific MBeans. In case the application is providing custom MBeans then standard WLDF components like harvester can be used. Otherwise specific application profiles based on WLDF instrumentation must be defined. It is very hard – if at all possible – to define reusable profiles of this category.

Creating profiles in a WLS domain

It is recommended to not create comprehensive profiles. It is better to create multiple but specialized profiles. In almost all cases troubleshooting has to concentrate on certain server aspects and therefore specialized profiles have the benefit of creating less data but exactly the data needed for the analysis.

From experience it is absolutely recommended to provide profiles always with automated setup routines written in WLST or JMX. It is also advisable to provide scripts or programs which can create new profiles as a combination out of existing profiles. It is also advisable to create automations to activate (target) and deactivate (un-target) profiles. All of these activities will be discussed later in detail.

Activating / deactivating profiles

Please refer to the subsequent chapters which discussed the different profile types as activation is really different for the different types.

Summary

This chapter has discussed several ideas of profiles for WLDF. There are basically two major types of profiles which are either profile which contains the full diagnostic profile or component profiles which contain all WLDF artifacts needed for a specific subject area. The next two chapters will discuss these two different types with detailed examples.

Diagnostic component profiles using WLST

Diagnostic component profiles using WLST

This chapter discusses a recommended approach to WLDF profiles. Rather than defining entire diagnostic modules as profiles, it is also possible to define subject-matter profiles. In this case the profiles only contain all the necessary WLDF parts for a specific subject (e.g. transactions).

Introduction

Collections of profiles where each profile contains a full diagnostic module may lead to some disadvantages. It is most likely the case that certain metric definitions are duplicated into many modules. This might be desirable but this might also cause an overhead when maintaining the profiles. An alternative would be to define profile components like metric collections, watches, and notifications. In addition the administrator group has scripts which define the real WLDF profiles. These scripts then contain the logic which profile components out of the components collection should be used to construct the profile. The author like to call this "dynamic WLDF profiles". In real life this is (unfortunately) a rare approach as it requires quite a lot of WLST/JMX and WLDF skills on both sides - the developer side and the administrator sides. The big benefit is that the administrator group can react much more flexibly to monitoring and/or troubleshooting requests.

Artifact Profiles

There are different granularities of profiles possible. The finest grained category are profiles which just contain a certain WLDF component. Frankly this is more an academic approach rather than a real life project approach. But – if really done well – it can be a good foundation for the more coarse grained profiles types discussed after wards and in the next chapters.

A harvester watch for example can be packed into a profile which just contains the harvester and all its settings (like attribute rules).

Harvester Profile

Harvester

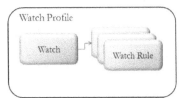

For example a watch profile will contain a watch description and all watch rules which belong to this watch.

A notification profile only contains a notification description. Example include a JMX notification profile, a personal email notification profile, an email notification profile which send emails to an alerting system or an SNMP notification.

Log profiles can be defined which contains log watch definitions.

And there are more possible types of profiles, like instrumentation.

The big benefit of these types of profiles is that they can be defined with no overlapping between different profiles. This guarantees a high level of flexibility and reuse.

The disadvantage of this approach is the large number of small profiles which are difficult to maintain and to overlook.

Subject Matter Profiles

Based on the artifact defined in the last section, this type of profile defines all WLDF components which together define all that is needed for a specific subject. For example a profile to monitor transactions will have a harvester for the JTARuntime, watches with rules for stuck transactions or long running transaction, and a notification system which may send an alert email. It can be seen as a combination of artifacts.

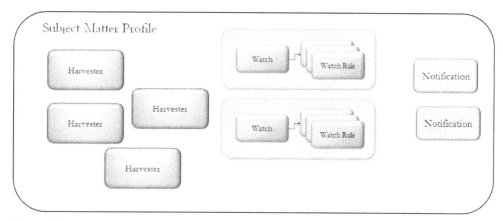

Figure 14.1: *Subject Matter Profile Example*

Of course there is no need to have all types of WLDF components in such a profile. It can be any combination which is needed for a specific topic or subtopic.

These profiles are more common as they define everything for a given subject. In addition they are easier to maintain as there are not so many profiles and all components needed are already combined.

The rest of this chapter will talk about subject matter profiles.

Combination into Diagnostic Modules

The previously discussed types of profiles cannot be used on their own. WLDF always needs a diagnostic module. The previously discussed types are meant to be building blocks in order to construct diagnostic modules as needed.

Examples

The first example shows a diagnostic module with an archive. This diagnostic module contains exactly one subject matter profile.

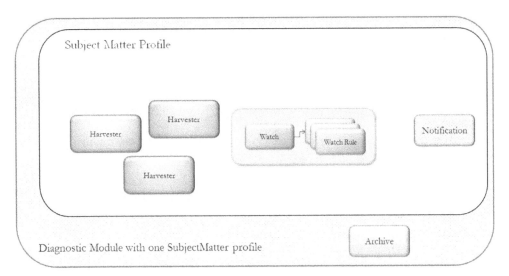

Figure 14.2: *Diagnostic module with one subject matter profile*

This is a typical case when WLDF diagnostic modules will be created for special purposes. In this case everything needed was defined in one subject matter profile.

The second example shows a more complicated scenario where more than one subject matter profiles are combined into one diagnostic module.

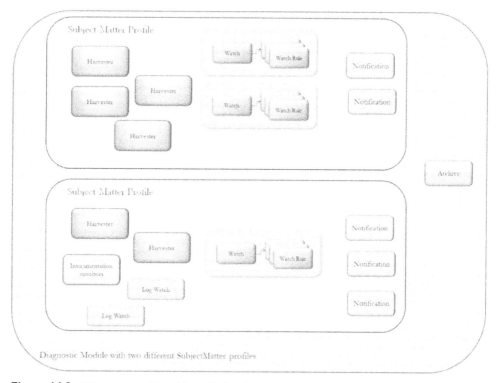

Figure 14.3: *Diagnostic module with multiple subject matter profiles*

This is a typical case when WLDF diagnostic modules will be created for a special diagnostic purpose but requires that multiple subjects needs to be monitored and evaluated. In this case the diagnostic profile will be constructed out of more than one subject matter profile.

Advantages and disadvantages

This granularity has a number of great advantages but also disadvantages which will be discussed in this section

Benefit of this approach:

- The subject matter profiles can concentrate on their subject area
- No replication of harvester, watches or other definitions in different profiles
- On demand the administrator can decide which subject areas are needed and combine them into one diagnostic module
- Very good tradeoff between granularity and reuse

- Administrator have full control which monitoring components are activated

Disadvantages of this approach:

- Administrator needs a good understanding of the monitoring needs or a good communication interface to the architects who request the monitoring
- The responsibility of maintaining the profiles and the WLDF scripts to combine them into diagnostic modules are now on the administrator side.

Example Implementation

The following section depicts and discusses a script library based on WLST which implements a number of subject matter profiles described in this chapter. This library does not use the new profiling features of WLS 12.1.2+. Different scripts are provided which define subject matter WLDF profiles for specific topics like transactions, EJB, core server, JMS and others. Rather than providing own scripts from the author, this chapter reprints and discusses a script library available from the Oracle website.

This section will look at the main parts of the library and explains the idea behind the implementation. Afterwards a number of usage scenarios are discussed which also show the script library in action.

Note: Unless specified otherwise, all source code shown in the example implementation and discussed in this chapter is copyright protected and owned by Oracle. Oracle has granted permission to use it in this chapter. It can be downloaded at: http://www.oracle.com/technetwork/indexes/samplecode/weblogic-sample-522121.html

---

Base class

This library is using object oriented concepts of Jython which also includes class definitions and also class inheritance. The following script shows the definition of the base class which defines the basic elements and methods for a component profile.

This definition is the foundation for all profiles discussed afterwards.

```
class WLDFProfileBase:
  packagePrefix="weblogic.management.runtime."

  attributes = {}
  watches = {}
  monitors = {}
  __wlsVer = None

  def getHarvestedAttributes(self):
```

```
    return self.attributes

def getWatchRules(self):
  return self.watches

def getInstrumentationMonitors(self):
  return self.monitors

"""
Used to determine the version of WLS we are running on; this is
necessary to avoid using syntax that is not available prior to
WLS 10.3 when running on earlier versions.
"""
def getWLSVersion(self):
  if self.__wlsVer is None:
    try:
      self.__wlsVer = float(version.split()[2])
    except:
      self.__wlsVer = 9.0
  return self.__wlsVer
```

Content of the base class are containers for attributes, watches and monitors and a number of access methods to them.

WebLogic Core Profile

The WebLogic core profile provides components which works with WebLogic core MBeans like workmanager, cluster, thread-pools and other core resources of WebLogic.

Whenever resource consumption is an issue, the core resources of WebLogic must be checked. Examples include too many threads in parallel, stuck threads due to hanging calls or resources, cluster members being down, out of memory issues and more.

Profile Class

The following WLST script implements the profile class for the core profile.

```
class WLSCoreProfile(WLDFProfileBase):

  def __init__(self, argsDict=None):
    workManagerType = self.packagePrefix + "WorkManagerRuntimeMBean"
    srtType = self.packagePrefix + "ServerRuntimeMBean"
    clusterType = self.packagePrefix + "ClusterRuntimeMBean"
    threadPoolType = self.packagePrefix + 'ThreadPoolRuntimeMBean'
    jvmType = self.packagePrefix + "JVMRuntimeMBean"
    jrockitType = self.packagePrefix + 'JRockitRuntimeMBean'

    self.attributes = {
      workManagerType : [ 'StuckThreadCount' , 'PendingRequests', 'CompletedRequests' ],
      srtType :         [ 'OpenSocketsCurrentCount' , 'SocketsOpenedTotalCount' ],
      clusterType :     [ 'AliveServerCount' ],
      threadPoolType :  [ 'CompletedRequestCount', 'PendingUserRequestCount', 'HoggingThreadCount',
                          'QueueLength', 'ExecuteThreadIdleCount', 'StandbyThreadCount',
                          'ExecuteThreadTotalCount', 'Throughput'],
      jvmType :         [ 'HeapSizeCurrent', 'HeapFreePercent', 'HeapFreeCurrent', 'HeapSizeMax' ],
      jrockitType :     [ 'HeapSizeCurrent', 'HeapFreePercent', 'HeapFreeCurrent',
                          'HeapSizeMax', 'JvmProcessorLoad', 'AllProcessorsAverageLoad']
    }

    print "core args: " + str(argsDict)
    dyeProps = getValue(argsDict, 'dyeProps', 'USER1=weblogic').replace(',','\n')
```

```
    print "dye properties: "  + dyeProps
    self.monitors = {
        "DyeInjection"  : { 'props' : dyeProps, 'actions' : None, 'desc' : "DyeInjection monitor",
                            'dyeMask' : None, 'dyeFiltering' : false }
    }

    self.watches = {
        'StuckThreadWatch' :
            { 'rule' : '${[' + workManagerType + ']//StuckThreadCount} > 0', 'ruleType' : 'Harvester',
'resetType' : 'AutomaticReset'},
        'ServerHealthStateWatch' :
            {'rule' : '${[' + srtType +']//State} IN
(\'FAILED\',\'FAILED_RESTARTING\',\'FAILED_NOT_RESTARTABLE\')', 'ruleType' : 'Harvester', 'resetType'
: 'AutomaticReset'},
        'ClusterServerWatch' :
            {'rule' : '${[' + clusterType +']//AliveServerCount} = 0', 'ruleType' : 'Harvester',
'resetType' : 'AutomaticReset'},
        'HeapWatch' :
            {'rule' : '${[' + jvmType +']//HeapFreePercent} < 10', 'ruleType' : 'Harvester', 'resetType'
: 'AutomaticReset'},
        'JRockitHeapWatch' :
            {'rule' : '${[' + jrockitType +']//HeapFreePercent} < 10', 'ruleType' : 'Harvester',
'resetType' : 'AutomaticReset'},
        'JRockitCPUWatch' :
            {'rule' : '${[' + jrockitType +']//AllProcessorsWatch} > 0.9', 'ruleType' : 'Harvester',
'resetType' : 'AutomaticReset'},
        'ServerLogWatch' :
            {'rule' : "SEVERITY IN ('CRITICAL', 'ERROR', 'WARNING')", 'ruleType' : 'Log', 'resetType' :
'AutomaticReset'},
    }

    if self.getWLSVersion() >= 10.3:
        slcType = self.packagePrefix + "ServerLifeCycleRuntimeMBean"
        self.watches['ServerLifeCycleWatch'] = {
        'rule' : '${DomainRuntime//[' + slcType +']//State} IN
(\'FAILED\',\'FAILED_RESTARTING\',\'FAILED_NOT_RESTARTABLE\')', 'ruleType' : 'Harvester', 'resetType'
: 'AutomaticReset'
        }
        self.watches['ClusterHealthWatch'] = {
        'rule' : '${[' + clusterType +']//HealthState.State} != 0', 'ruleType' : 'Harvester',
'resetType' : 'AutomaticReset'
        }
```

This example demonstrate one problem in WLDF. The notation and addressing of watches as well as other aspects looks quite complicated. The reason is that the addressing is based on the MBean names and the attribute names. These names can get rather complex. You will see the complex names in the attributes as well as in the rules which looks rather complex and difficult to understand if you are not familiar with the WebLogic MBeans.

Enable Profile

You can use the following WLST code in order to enable the profile.

```
execfile('WLDFProfiles.py')

argsDict = argsToDict(sys.argv)

connectIfNecessary(argsDict)

cd ("edit:/")
startEdit()

try:

    # obtain the WLDFSystemResourceMBean
    wldfResName = getValue(argsDict, 'wldfResource', 'mywldf')
```

```
wldfRes = WLDFResource(wldfResName)
profiles = [ WLSCoreProfile(argsDict) ]
profileMgr = WLDFProfileManager(wldfRes, argsDict, profiles)

profileMgr.apply()
wldfRes.dumpResource()

save()
activate()

finally:
  dumpStack()
  if cmgr.isEditor():
    stopEdit("y")
```

Enable a profile in this context means that a ProfileManager will be used in order to add all harvester, watched, notifications and monitors of this profile to the diagnostic module. If the diagnostic module does not exist, it will be created.

Disable Profile

You can use the following WLST code in order to disable the profile.

```
execfile('WLDFProfiles.py')

argsDict = argsToDict(sys.argv)

connectIfNecessary(argsDict)

cd ("edit:/")
startEdit()

try:

  # obtain the WLDFSystemResourceMBean
  wldfResName = getValue(argsDict, 'wldfResource', 'mywldf')

  wldfRes = WLDFResource(wldfResName)
  profiles = [ WLSCoreProfile() ]
  profileMgr = WLDFProfileManager(wldfRes, argsDict, profiles)

  profileMgr.unapply()
  wldfRes.dumpResource()

  save()
  activate()

except:
  dumpStack()
  if cmgr.isEditor():
    stopEdit("y")
```

To disable a profile in this context means that a ProfileManager will be used in order to remove all harvester, watches, notifications and monitors of this profile from the diagnostic module. As a diagnostic module can be a combination of multiple profiles, this script will not touch the diagnostic module.

EJB Profile

The WebLogic EJB profile focus on runtime values of EJBs. Depending on the 4 different types of EJBs (stateless sessions, stateful session, entities and message driven beans) WebLogic provides different values in its Runtime MBeans. This profile does include transactional information, locking and caching information and more.

Profile Class

The following WLST script shows an implementation of the EJB profile.

```
class WLSEJBProfile(WLDFProfileBase):

  def __init__(self):

    ejbCacheType = self.packagePrefix + 'EJBCacheRuntimeMBean'
    ejbCacheAttributes = [ 'CacheHitCount', 'CacheMissCount' ]

    # EJBLockingRuntimeMBean
    ejbLockType = self.packagePrefix + 'EJBLockingRuntimeMBean'
    ejbLockAttributes = [ 'LockEntriesCurrentCount', 'WaiterCurrentCount' ]

    # MDB
    mdbType = self.packagePrefix + 'MessageDrivenEJBRuntimeMBean'
    mdbAttributes = [ ]
    mdbWatchRules = {
      'MDBHealthWatch' :
        { 'rule' : '${[' + mdbType + ']//HealthState.State} != 0', 'ruleType' : 'Harvester',
          'resetType' : 'AutomaticReset'},
    }

    # EJBTimerRuntimeMBean
    ejbTimerType = self.packagePrefix + 'EJBTimerRuntimeMBean'
    ejbTimerAttributes = [ 'ActiveTimerCount', 'CancelledTimerCount', 'DisabledTimerCount',
                           'TimeoutCount' ]

    # EJBTransactionRuntimeMBean
    ejbTxType = self.packagePrefix + 'EJBTransactionRuntimeMBean'
    ejbTxAttributes = [ 'TransactionsCommittedTotalCount', 'TransactionsRolledBackTotalCount',
                        'TransactionsTimedOutTotalCount' ]

    # QueryCacheRuntimeMBean
    queryCacheType = self.packagePrefix + 'QueryCacheRuntimeMBean'
    queryCacheAttributes = [ 'CacheAccessCount', 'CacheHitCount', 'TotalCachedQueriesCount',
                             'TotalCacheMissCount' ]

    # EJBPoolRuntimeMBean
    ejbPoolType = self.packagePrefix + 'EJBPoolRuntimeMBean'
    ejbPoolAttributes = [ 'BeansInUseCurrentCount', 'IdleBeansCount', 'PooledBeansCurrentCount',
                          'WaiterCurrentCount' ]

    # KodoDataCacheRuntimeMBean
    kodoCacheType = self.packagePrefix + 'KodoDataCacheRuntimeMBean'
    kodoCacheAttributes = [ 'CacheHitRatio', 'TotalCurrentEntries' ]

    # KodoQueryCacheRuntimeMBean
    kodoQueryCacheType = self.packagePrefix + 'KodoQueryCacheRuntimeMBean'
    kodoQueryCacheAttributes = [ 'CacheHitRatio', 'TotalCurrentEntries' ]

    # KodoQueryCompilationCacheRuntimeMBean
    kodoCompileCacheType = self.packagePrefix + 'KodoQueryCompilationCacheRuntimeMBean'
    kodoCompileCacheAttributes = [ 'TotalCurrentEntries' ]

    self.attributes = {
      ejbCacheType          : ejbCacheAttributes,
      ejbLockType           : ejbLockAttributes,
      mdbType               : mdbAttributes,
      ejbTimerType          : ejbTimerAttributes,
      ejbTxType             : ejbTxAttributes,
      queryCacheType        : queryCacheAttributes,
      ejbPoolType           : ejbPoolAttributes,
      kodoCacheType         : kodoCacheAttributes,
      kodoQueryCacheType    : kodoQueryCacheAttributes,
      kodoCompileCacheType  : kodoCompileCacheAttributes
    }
```

```
    if self.getWLSVersion() >= 10.3 :
        self.watches = mdbWatchRules
```

As you can see in the code, this profile provides a number of subcategories. Not all of them are available for all EJB types. Some of them are EJB type specific and others are offered by all EJB types (like transactions).

Enable Profile

You can use the following WLST code to enable the profile:

```
execfile('WLDFProfiles.py')

argsDict = argsToDict(sys.argv)

connectIfNecessary(argsDict)

cd ("edit:/")
startEdit()

try:

    # obtain the WLDFSystemResourceMBean
    wldfResName = getValue(argsDict, 'wldfResource', 'mywldf')

    wldfRes = WLDFResource(wldfResName)
    profiles = [ WLSEJBProfile() ]
    profileMgr = WLDFProfileManager(wldfRes, argsDict, profiles)

    profileMgr.apply()

    save()
    activate()

    wldfRes.dumpResource()
except:
    dumpStack()
    if cmgr.isEditor():
        cd("edit:/")
        stopEdit("y")
```

The important line here is: "profiles = [WLSEJBProfile()]". This defines the selection of profiles which will be applied.

Disable a Profile

You can use the following WLST code in order to disable a profile.

```
execfile('WLDFProfiles.py')

argsDict = argsToDict(sys.argv)

connectIfNecessary(argsDict)

cd ("edit:/")
startEdit()

try:

    # obtain the WLDFSystemResourceMBean
    wldfResName = getValue(argsDict, 'wldfResource', 'mywldf')

    wldfRes = WLDFResource(wldfResName)
```

```
    profiles = [ WLSEJBProfile() ]
    profileMgr = WLDFProfileManager(wldfRes, argsDict, profiles)

    profileMgr.unapply()
    wldfRes.dumpResource()

    save()
    activate()
except:
  dumpStack()
  if cmgr.isEditor():
    cd("edit:/")
    stopEdit("y")
```

Disable a profile in this context means that a ProfileManager will be used in order to remove all harvester, watches, notifications and monitors of this profile from the diagnostic module. As a diagnostic module can be a combination of multiple profiles, this script will not touch the diagnostic module.

JDBC Profile

The WebLogic JDBC profile focuses on the connection to databases through datasources. WebLogic provides a long list of runtime attributes for each datasource like connections, poolsizes, statements, timeouts and much more.

Datasources are the most commonly used resource in WebLogic (after transaction) and the resource group which very often causes issues like database down, database slow, running out of connections or other issues. It is therefore very often necessary to monitor datasources.

Enable and disable the profile scripts are not shown as these are – except the profile selection – equal to the scripts discussed above.

Profile Class

The following WLST script implements the profile class for the JDBC profile.

```
class WLSJDBCProfile(WLDFProfileBase):

  def __init__(self):

    jdbcDSType = 'weblogic.management.runtime.JDBCDataSourceRuntimeMBean'
    jdbcDSAttributes = ['ActiveConnectionsAverageCount', 'ActiveConnectionsCurrentCount',
'CurrCapacity', 'LeakedConnectionCount', 'NumAvailable',
      'NumUnavailable', 'PrepStmtCacheHitCount', 'PrepStmtCacheMissCount', 'ConnectionDelayTime',
'FailuresToReconnectCount',
      'WaitingForConnectionFailureTotal', 'WaitingForConnectionCurrentCount']

    jdbcDSWatches = {
      'AvailableDSWatch' : { 'rule' : '${[' + jdbcDSType + ']//NumAvailable} = 0', 'ruleType' :
'Harvester', 'resetType' : 'AutomaticReset'},
      'ConnectionDelayWatch' : { 'rule' : '${[' + jdbcDSType + ']//ConnectionDelayTime} > 1000',
'ruleType' : 'Harvester', 'resetType' : 'AutomaticReset'},
      'ConnectFailures' : { 'rule' : '${[' + jdbcDSType + ']//FailuresToReconnectCount} > 0',
'ruleType' : 'Harvester', 'resetType' : 'ManualReset'}
      }
```

```
        self.attributes = { jdbcDSType : jdbcDSAttributes }
        self.watches = jdbcDSWatches

        if self.getWLSVersion() >= 10.3:
            self.watches['AvailableDSWatch'] = {
                'rule' : '${[' + self.packagePrefix + 'JDBCServiceRuntime]//HealthState.State} != 0',
'ruleType' : 'Harvester', 'resetType' : 'AutomaticReset'
                }

# JMS Profile
#
class WLSJMSProfile(WLDFProfileBase):

    def __init__(self):

        jmsConnectionType = self.packagePrefix + "JMSConnectionRuntimeMBean"
        jmsConnectionAttributes = [ 'SessionsCurrentCount' ]

        jmsDestType = self.packagePrefix + 'JMSDestinationRuntimeMBean'
        jmsDestAttributes = [
            'MessagesCurrentCount', 'MessagesPendingCount', 'ConsumersCurrentCount',
            'BytesCurrentCount', 'BytesPendingCount'
            ]

        jmsPoolType = self.packagePrefix + 'JMSPooledConnectionRuntimeMBean'
        jmsPoolAttributes = ['AverageReserved','NumAvailable','NumLeaked','NumReserved','NumWaiters']
        jmsPoolWatch = {
            'JMSPoolWatch' :
                { 'rule' : '${[' + jmsPoolType + ']//HealthState.State} != 0', 'ruleType' : 'Harvester',
'resetType' : 'AutomaticReset' }
            }

        jmsEndPointType = 'JMSRemoteEndpointRuntimeMBean'
        jmsEndPointAttributes = [
            'BytesCurrentCount', 'BytesPendingCount', 'MessagesCurrentCount',
            'MessagesPendingCount', 'MessagesReceivedCount'
            ]

        self.attributes = {
            jmsConnectionType : jmsConnectionAttributes,
            jmsDestType : jmsDestAttributes,
            jmsPoolType : jmsPoolAttributes,
            jmsEndPointType : jmsEndPointAttributes
            }

        if self.getWLSVersion() >= 10.3:
            self.watches = jmsPoolWatch
```

Please note that the above script implements only a fraction of the possible values. If other values are needed this profile needs to be extended or changed.

Transaction Profile

The WebLogic transaction profile provides metric collectors for transactional values. Especially values like "TransactionAbandonedTotalCount" or the different rollback values are important indicators which can reveal a potential problem with backends or resources (for example due to transactions which time out).

Profile Class

The following WLST script implements the profile class for the transaction profile.

```
class WLSJTAProfile(WLDFProfileBase):

    def __init__(self):
```

```
    jtaType = self.packagePrefix + 'JTARuntimeMBean'
    jtaAttributes = [
      'ActiveTransactionsTotalCount', 'TransactionAbandonedTotalCount',
      'TransactionCommittedTotalCount', 'TransactionRolledBackTotalCount',
      'TransactionTotalCount' ]
    jtaWatch = {
      'JTAWatch' :
        { 'rule' : '${[' + jtaType + ']//HealthState.State} != 0', 'ruleType' : 'Harvester',
'resetType' : 'AutomaticReset' }
      }

    self.attributes = { jtaType : jtaAttributes }
    if self.getWLSVersion() >= 10.3:
      self.watches = jtaWatch
```

Other profiles

The library contains more profiles like JMS or WebService profiles. And of course this list can be extended with more unusual resource profile like WTC (WebLogic Tuxedo Connector), Foreign JMS, Email, SNMP and other resources. These profiles are not displayed here in the book as they are very similar to the already shown example profiles.

Profile Manager

The implementation provides a WLST class called "Profile Manager". According to the inline documentation of this class, this manager is an implementation for applying and un-applying common WLDF profiles defined in this code collection.

```
class WLDFProfileManager(EditFunctions):
  __args = None
  __resource = None
  __profiles = None

  def __init__(self, wldfResource, args, profiles, auto=false):
    EditFunctions.__init__(self,auto)
    self.__args = args
    self.__resource = wldfResource
    self.__profiles = profiles

  def __applyProfile(self, profile, notifs, resetPeriod):
    monitors = profile.getInstrumentationMonitors()
    print "monitors: " + str(monitors)
    if monitors is not None and len(monitors) > 0:
      print "enabling instrumentation"
      self.__resource.getInstrumentation().setEnabled(true)
      self.__resource.enableDiagnosticContext(true)
      for monitorName, monProps in monitors.items():
        print "Adding monitor " + monitorName
        monitor = self.__resource.findOrCreateInstrumentationMonitor(monitorName)
        monitor.setActions(monProps['actions'])
        monitor.setProperties(monProps['props'])
        monitor.setDescription(monProps['desc'])
        monitor.setDyeMask(monProps['dyeMask'])
        monitor.setDyeFilteringEnabled(monProps['dyeFiltering'])

    for typeName, attributeList in profile.getHarvestedAttributes().items():
      self.__resource.setAttributeList(typeName, attributeList)

    for watchName, watchProps in profile.getWatchRules().items():
      #print "Properties for watch " + watchName + ": " + str(watchProps)
      watchReset = getValue(watchProps, 'resetPeriod', resetPeriod)
      if watchReset is None:
        watchReset = 60000
```

```
        try:
          print "Creating watch " + watchName + "..."
          watch = self.__resource.addWatch(
            watchName=watchName,
            watchRule=watchProps['rule'],
            watchType=watchProps['ruleType'],
            watchAlarmType=watchProps['resetType'],
            watchResetPeriod=watchReset,
            watchNotifs=notifs)
        except BeanAlreadyExistsException:
          print "Watch " + watchName + " already exists"

  def __unapplyProfile(self, profile):
    #
    # Destroy all monitors
    #
    monitors = profile.getInstrumentationMonitors()
    for monitorName, monProps  in monitors.items():
      self.__resource.destroyInstrumentationMonitorByName(monitorName)

    #
    # Remove all Harvested types for this profile
    #
    harvester = self.__resource.getHarvester()
    allHarvestedTypes = harvester.getHarvestedTypes()
    harvestedAttributes = {}
    profileTypes = profile.getHarvestedAttributes()
    for ht in allHarvestedTypes:
      # print "Checking harvested type in profile: " + ht.getName()
      if profileTypes.has_key(ht.getName()):
        print "Destroying harvested type " +  ht.getName()
        harvester.destroyHarvestedType(ht)
    #
    # Remove Watches assocated with this profile
    #
    watchManager = self.__resource.getWatch()
    watches = watchManager.getWatches()
    profileWatches = profile.getWatchRules()
    for watch in watches:
      if profileWatches.has_key(watch.getName()):
        print "Destroying watch " + watch.getName()
        watchManager.destroyWatch(watch)

  # returns the WLDFResource for this instance
  def getWLDFResource(self):
    return self.__resource

  # Returns the arguments dictionary used by this instance
  def getArgs(self):
    return self.__args

  # Checks the connection state of the WLST shell and attempts
  # a connection if necessary.
  #
  def connectIfNecessary(self):
    connectIfNecessary(self.__args)

  # Apply the profiles managed by this instance
  #
  def apply(self):
    self.connectIfNecessary()
    try:
      currentDrive=currentTree()
      cd("edit:/")

      self.beginEdit()

      # find or create the SystemResource
      self.getWLDFResource().findOrCreateResource()
      # save the auto-edit state of the WLDFResource object and
      # turn it off for the duration of this method
      saveAutoEdit = self.getWLDFResource().isAutoEdit()
      self.getWLDFResource().setAutoEdit(false)

      try:
        # set the harvester period if provided
        harvesterPeriod = long(getValue(self.__args, 'harvesterPeriod', 0))
        if harvesterPeriod > 0:
```

```
        print "Setting Harvester sample period to " + str(harvesterPeriod) + " millis"
        self.getWLDFResource().getHarvester().setSamplePeriod(harvesterPeriod)

      # get the watch reset period, default to 2*Harvester period
      defaultPeriod = 2*self.getWLDFResource().getHarvester().getSamplePeriod()
      resetPeriod = long(getValue(self.__args, 'resetPeriod', defaultPeriod))

      notifs = None
      notifNames = getValue(self.__args, 'notifications', None)
      if notifNames is not None:
        print 'notifications: ' + notifNames
        notifNameList = notifNames.split(',')
        print 'notification list: ' + str(notifNameList)
        notifs = self.getWLDFResource().findNotifications(notifNameList)
      else:
        notifJMX = self.getWLDFResource().findOrCreateJMXNotification('myJMXNotif')
        notifSNMP = self.getWLDFResource().findOrCreateSNMPNotification('mySNMPNotif')
        notifs = [ notifJMX, notifSNMP ]

      for profile in self.__profiles:
        self.__applyProfile(profile, notifs, resetPeriod)

      targets = getValue(self.__args, 'targets', None)
      if targets is not None:
        targetsList = targets.split(",")
        self.getWLDFResource().targetResource(targetsList)

      self.activate()
    finally:
      self.getWLDFResource().setAutoEdit(saveAutoEdit)

  finally:
    self.cancelEdit()
    currentDrive()

# Unapply the profiles managed by this instance
def unapply(self):
  self.connectIfNecessary()
  self.getWLDFResource().findResource()
  saveAutoEdit = self.getWLDFResource().isAutoEdit()
  self.getWLDFResource().setAutoEdit(false)
  try:
    currentDrive=currentTree()
    cd("edit:/")

    self.beginEdit()

    for profile in self.__profiles:
      self.__unapplyProfile(profile)
    self.activate()

  finally:
    self.cancelEdit()
    self.getWLDFResource().setAutoEdit(saveAutoEdit)
    currentDrive()
```

Please see the inline comments for detailed description of this functionality. As this manager supports component profiles, the manager basically adds the artifacts to an existing diagnostic module or removes only the artifacts from a diagnostic module. If the module does not exist it can create it.

Different profiles will be merged into one module. This code will not create separate diagnostic modules if multiple profiles are applied.

Working with Profiles

The following section will discuss a few examples how the profiles discussed above can be applied and use.

Enable All Profiles

This script combines all the different profiles into one as described in the first part of this chapter.

```
execfile('WLDFProfiles.py')

argsDict = argsToDict(sys.argv)

connectIfNecessary(argsDict)

cd ("edit:/")
startEdit()

try:

  # obtain the WLDFSystemResourceMBean
  wldfResName = getValue(argsDict, 'wldfResource', 'mywldf')

  wldfRes = WLDFResource(wldfResName)
  profiles = [ WLSCoreProfile(argsDict), WLSEJBProfile(), WLSJDBCProfile(),
               WLSJMSProfile(), WLSJTAProfile(), WLSWebAppProfile(),
               WLSWebServicesProfile() ]
  profileMgr = WLDFProfileManager(wldfRes, argsDict, profiles)

  profileMgr.apply()
  wldfRes.dumpResource()

  save()
  activate()

except:
  dumpStack()
  if cmgr.isEditor():
     cd("edit:/")
     stopEdit("y")
  raise
```

As you can see in the script code, this script will instance a ProfileManager with a list of all profile instances. Then during apply the profile manager will install all components

In order to execute this script to activate all profiles – which means to create a diagnostic module which contains all component profiles – the following command line can be used:

```
wlst.sh ./enableAllProfiles.py targets='TestCluster' wldfResource='allProfiles' harvesterPeriod=30000
user=weblogic pass=test1234 url=t3://localhost:12001
```

This script will switch into edit mode and create all the attributes, watches and monitors defined in all the profiles discussed above. The following out (reduced for printing) will be created:

```
WLDFResource name: allProfiles
connected, finding resourceallProfiles
Already in Edit Tree

core args: {'wldfResource': 'allProfiles', 'targets': 'TestCluster', 'user': 'weblogic',
'harvesterPeriod': '30000', 'url': 't3://localhost:12001', 'pass': 'test1234',
'./enableAllProfiles.py': ''}
dye properties: USER1=weblogic
Auto edit not enabled
Creating new WLDF System resource for allProfiles
Already in Edit Tree

Setting Harvester sample period to 30000 millis
monitors: {'DyeInjection': {'dyeFiltering': 0, 'props': 'USER1=weblogic', 'dyeMask': None, 'desc':
'DyeInjection monitor', 'actions': None}}
enabling instrumentation
Already in Edit Tree

Creating watch ServerLogWatch...
Adding watch 'ServerLogWatch', type 'Log', with rule 'SEVERITY IN ('CRITICAL', 'ERROR', 'WARNING')',
reset type: 'AutomaticReset', reset Period: 60000
notifs:
[[MBeanServerInvocationHandler]com.bea:Name=myJMXNotif,Type=weblogic.diagnostics.descriptor.WLDFJMXNo
tificationBean,Parent=[testdomain]/WLDFSystemResources[allProfiles],Path=WLDFResource[allProfiles]/Wa
tchNotification[allProfiles]/JMXNotifications[myJMXNotif],
[MBeanServerInvocationHandler]com.bea:Name=mySNMPNotif,Type=weblogic.diagnostics.descriptor.WLDFSNMPN
otificationBean,Parent=[testdomain]/WLDFSystemResources[allProfiles],Path=WLDFResource[allProfiles]/W
atchNotification[allProfiles]/SNMPNotifications[mySNMPNotif]]
Creating watch JRockitCPUWatch...
Adding watch 'JRockitCPUWatch', type 'Harvester', with rule
'${[weblogic.management.runtime.JRockitRuntimeMBean]//AllProcessorsWatch} > 0.9', reset type:
'AutomaticReset', reset Period: 60000

< .. other notifies … >

Adding weblogic.management.runtime.EJBLockingRuntimeMBean to harvestables collection for allProfiles
< .. adding other mbeans … >

Targets: ['TestCluster']
Looking up target TestCluster
Adding target TestCluster instance to list of targets...
Setting targets on allProfiles
Already in Edit Tree

Already in Edit Tree


Harvested types:

Type: weblogic.management.runtime.JVMRuntimeMBean
  Attributes: array(java.lang.String,['HeapSizeCurrent', 'HeapFreePercent', 'HeapFreeCurrent',
'HeapSizeMax'])
  Instances:  array(java.lang.String,[])

< … add other mbean attributes


Watches:

Watch: ServerLogWatch
  Type:    Log
  Rule:    SEVERITY IN ('CRITICAL', 'ERROR', 'WARNING')
  Alarm:   AutomaticReset
  Reset:   60000
  Enabled: 1
  Notifs:
  array(weblogic.diagnostics.descriptor.WLDFNotificationBean,[[MBeanServerInvocationHandler]com.bea:Nam
e=myJMXNotif,Type=weblogic.diagnostics.descriptor.WLDFJMXNotificationBean,Parent=[testdomain]/WLDFSys
temResources[allProfiles],Path=WLDFResource[allProfiles]/WatchNotification[allProfiles]/JMXNotificati
ons[myJMXNotif],
```

```
[MBeanServerInvocationHandler]com.bea:Name=mySNMPNotif,Type=weblogic.diagnostics.descriptor.WLDFSNMPN
otificationBean,Parent=[testdomain]/WLDFSystemResources[allProfiles],Path=WLDFResource[allProfiles]/W
atchNotification[allProfiles]/SNMPNotifications[mySNMPNotif]])

< .. add other watches … >

Saving all your changes ...
Saved all your changes successfully.
Activating all your changes, this may take a while ...
The edit lock associated with this edit session is released
once the activation is completed.
Activation completed
```

After this script has been completed the diagnostic module will contain all diagnostic components from all profiles.

For example by looking at the list for harvester metrics the user will see the complete list of different MBeans as a combination of all MBeans from the different profiles.

Figure 14.4: *List of combined MBeans*

Each harvester configuration has all the attributes activated which have been defined in the profiles.

Figure 14.5: *Example of a configured harvester*

And also the list of watches and notifications will include the combined list of all profiles

Figure 14.6: *List of combined watches*

Enable only one Profile

This script combine all the different profiles into one as described in the first part of this chapter. In this example the JDBC profile will be enabled.

```
execfile('WLDFProfiles.py')

argsDict = argsToDict(sys.argv)

connectIfNecessary(argsDict)

cd ("edit:/")
startEdit()

try:
```

```
    # obtain the WLDFSystemResourceMBean
    wldfResName = getValue(argsDict, 'wldfResource', 'mywldf')

    wldfRes = WLDFResource(wldfResName)
    profiles = [ WLSJDBCProfile() ]
    profileMgr = WLDFProfileManager(wldfRes, argsDict, profiles)

    profileMgr.apply()
    wldfRes.dumpResource()

    save()
    activate()

except:
  dumpStack()
  if cmgr.isEditor():
    stopEdit("y")
```

As you can see in the script code, this script will instance a ProfileManager with only one profile in the profile list.

The script in order to activate all profiles – which means to create a diagnostic module which contains all component profiles – the following script can be called:

```
wlst.sh ./enableJDBCProfile.py targets='TestCluster' wldfResource='allProfiles' harvesterPeriod=30000
user=weblogic pass=test1234 url=t3://localhost:12001
```

Script output:

```
Already in Edit Tree

Setting Harvester sample period to 30000 millis
monitors: {}
Adding weblogic.management.runtime.JDBCDataSourceRuntimeMBean to harvestables collection for
allProfiles
Creating watch ConnectFailures...
Adding watch 'ConnectFailures', type 'Harvester', with rule
'${[weblogic.management.runtime.JDBCDataSourceRuntimeMBean]//FailuresToReconnectCount} > 0', reset
type: 'ManualReset', reset Period: 60000
notifs:
[[MBeanServerInvocationHandler]com.bea:Name=myJMXNotif,Type=weblogic.diagnostics.descriptor.WLDFJMXNo
tificationBean,Parent=[testdomain]/WLDFSystemResources[allProfiles],Path=WLDFResource[allProfiles]/Wa
tchNotification[allProfiles]/JMXNotifications[myJMXNotif],
[MBeanServerInvocationHandler]com.bea:Name=mySNMPNotif,Type=weblogic.diagnostics.descriptor.WLDFSNMPN
otificationBean,Parent=[testdomain]/WLDFSystemResources[allProfiles],Path=WLDFResource[allProfiles]/W
atchNotification[allProfiles]/SNMPNotifications[mySNMPNotif]]
Creating watch ConnectionDelayWatch...
Adding watch 'ConnectionDelayWatch', type 'Harvester', with rule
'${[weblogic.management.runtime.JDBCDataSourceRuntimeMBean]//ConnectionDelayTime} > 1000', reset
type: 'AutomaticReset', reset Period: 60000
notifs:
[[MBeanServerInvocationHandler]com.bea:Name=myJMXNotif,Type=weblogic.diagnostics.descriptor.WLDFJMXNo
tificationBean,Parent=[testdomain]/WLDFSystemResources[allProfiles],Path=WLDFResource[allProfiles]/Wa
tchNotification[allProfiles]/JMXNotifications[myJMXNotif],
[MBeanServerInvocationHandler]com.bea:Name=mySNMPNotif,Type=weblogic.diagnostics.descriptor.WLDFSNMPN
otificationBean,Parent=[testdomain]/WLDFSystemResources[allProfiles],Path=WLDFResource[allProfiles]/W
atchNotification[allProfiles]/SNMPNotifications[mySNMPNotif]]
Creating watch AvailableDSWatch...
Adding watch 'AvailableDSWatch', type 'Harvester', with rule
'${[weblogic.management.runtime.JDBCDataSourceRuntimeMBean]//NumAvailable} = 0', reset type:
'AutomaticReset', reset Period: 60000
notifs:
[[MBeanServerInvocationHandler]com.bea:Name=myJMXNotif,Type=weblogic.diagnostics.descriptor.WLDFJMXNo
tificationBean,Parent=[testdomain]/WLDFSystemResources[allProfiles],Path=WLDFResource[allProfiles]/Wa
tchNotification[allProfiles]/JMXNotifications[myJMXNotif],
[MBeanServerInvocationHandler]com.bea:Name=mySNMPNotif,Type=weblogic.diagnostics.descriptor.WLDFSNMPN
otificationBean,Parent=[testdomain]/WLDFSystemResources[allProfiles],Path=WLDFResource[allProfiles]/W
atchNotification[allProfiles]/SNMPNotifications[mySNMPNotif]]
Targets: ['TestCluster']
Looking up target TestCluster
```

```
Adding target TestCluster instance to list of targets...
Setting targets on allProfiles
Already in Edit Tree

Saving all your changes ...
Saved all your changes successfully.
Activation completed
```

After the script has been completed, the diagnostic module will contain only the JDBC components (assumed that the module was empty before the script has been started).

Figure 14.7: *Only JDBC harvester*

And also the watch list will only contain the watches defined in the JDBC profile.

Figure 14.8: *JDBC profile watches*

Disable All Profiles

The following example shows a script available for the administrators to disable all profiles. This can be very handy in case all monitoring should be stopped in an automated way or to a certain point in time.

Example script to disable all WLDF components:

```
execfile('WLDFProfiles.py')
```

```
argsDict = argsToDict(sys.argv)

connectIfNecessary(argsDict)

cd ("edit:/")
startEdit()

try:

    # obtain the WLDFSystemResourceMBean
    wldfResName = getValue(argsDict, 'wldfResource', 'mywldf')

    wldfRes = WLDFResource(wldfResName)
    profiles = [ WLSCoreProfile(argsDict), WLSEJBProfile(), WLSJDBCProfile(),
                 WLSJMSProfile(), WLSJTAProfile(), WLSWebAppProfile(),
                 WLSWebServicesProfile() ]
    profileMgr = WLDFProfileManager(wldfRes, argsDict, profiles)

    profileMgr.unapply()
    wldfRes.dumpResource()

    save()
    activate()

except:
    dumpStack()
    if cmgr.isEditor():
        stopEdit("y")
```

As you can see in the script code, this script will instance a ProfileManager with a list of all profile instances. Then during the "unapply" call the profile manager will remove all components from the diagnostic module.

The following script can be called to disable all the profiles.

```
wlst.sh ./disableAllProfiles.py targets='TestCluster' wldfResource='allProfiles'
harvesterPeriod=30000 user=weblogic pass=test1234 url=t3://localhost:12001
```

This script will produce the following output.

```
Initializing WebLogic Scripting Tool (WLST) ...

Welcome to WebLogic Server Administration Scripting Shell

Type help() for help on available commands

Arguments: {'wldfResource': 'allProfiles', 'targets': 'TestCluster', 'user': 'weblogic',
'harvesterPeriod': '30000', './disableAllProfiles.py': '', 'url': 't3://localhost:12001', 'pass':
'test1234'}
Connecting with [weblogic,test1234,t3://localhost:12001]
Connecting to t3://localhost:12001 with userid weblogic ...
Successfully connected to Admin Server "AdminServer" that belongs to domain "testdomain".

Warning: An insecure protocol was used to connect to the
server. To ensure on-the-wire security, the SSL port or
Admin port should be used instead.

Location changed to edit tree. This is a writable tree with
DomainMBean as the root. To make changes you will need to start
an edit session via startEdit().

For more help, use help('edit')
You already have an edit session in progress and hence WLST will
continue with your edit session.
Starting an edit session ...
Started edit session, please be sure to save and activate your
changes once you are done.
Auto edit not enabled
WLDFResource name: allProfiles
```

```
connected, finding resourceallProfiles
Already in Edit Tree

core args: {'wldfResource': 'allProfiles', 'targets': 'TestCluster', 'user': 'weblogic',
'harvesterPeriod': '30000', './disableAllProfiles.py': '', 'url': 't3://localhost:12001', 'pass':
'test1234'}
dye properties: USER1=weblogic
Auto edit not enabled
Already in Edit Tree

Destroying harvested type weblogic.management.runtime.JVMRuntimeMBean
...
Destroying watch ServerLogWatch
...
Already in Edit Tree


Harvested types:


Watches:


Saving all your changes ...
Saved all your changes successfully.
Activating all your changes, this may take a while ...
The edit lock associated with this edit session is released
once the activation is completed.
Activation completed
```

Chain Profiles

As explained in the introduction in this chapter, different subject matter profiles (e.g. for Transactions and EJB) can be merged together in order to form a diagnostic profile which captures all values needed for a certain analysis.

Example of how to chain profile scripts together

```
execfile('enableCoreProfile.py')
execfile('enableJMSProfile.py')
execfile('enableEJBProfile.py')
execfile('enableWebAppProfile.py')
```

Each profile will be applied after each other.

The following script can be used in order to chain profiles.

```
wlst.sh ./chainedProfilesExample_2.py targets='TestCluster' wldfResource='allProfiles'
harvesterPeriod=30000 user=weblogic pass=test1234 url=t3://localhost:12001
```

The script will produce the following output. Please not the important difference to the "allProfiles" script. Each profile will be applied after each other.

```
Already in Edit Tree

core args: {'wldfResource': 'allProfiles', 'targets': 'TestCluster', 'user': 'weblogic',
'harvesterPeriod': '30000', './chainedProfilesExample_2.py': '', 'url': 't3://localhost:12001',
'pass': 'test1234'}
dye properties: USER1=weblogic
Auto edit not enabled
Already in Edit Tree
```

```
Setting Harvester sample period to 30000 millis
monitors: {'DyeInjection': {'dyeFiltering': 0, 'props': 'USER1=weblogic', 'dyeMask': None, 'desc':
'DyeInjection monitor', 'actions': None}}
enabling instrumentation
Already in Edit Tree

Adding monitor DyeInjection
Already in Edit Tree

Adding weblogic.management.runtime.JVMRuntimeMBean to harvestables collection for allProfiles
< ... >
Creating watch ServerLogWatch...
Adding watch 'ServerLogWatch', type 'Log', with rule 'SEVERITY IN ('CRITICAL', 'ERROR', 'WARNING')',
reset type: 'AutomaticReset', reset Period: 60000
notifs:
[[MBeanServerInvocationHandler]com.bea:Name=myJMXNotif,Type=weblogic.diagnostics.descriptor.WLDFJMXNo
tificationBean,Parent=[testdomain]/WLDFSystemResources[allProfiles],Path=WLDFResource[allProfiles]/Wa
tchNotification[allProfiles]/JMXNotifications[myJMXNotif],
[MBeanServerInvocationHandler]com.bea:Name=mySNMPNotif,Type=weblogic.diagnostics.descriptor.WLDFSNMPN
otificationBean,Parent=[testdomain]/WLDFSystemResources[allProfiles],Path=WLDFResource[allProfiles]/W
atchNotification[allProfiles]/SNMPNotifications[mySNMPNotif]]
Creating watch JRockitCPUWatch...
Adding watch 'JRockitCPUWatch', type 'Harvester', with rule
'${[weblogic.management.runtime.JRockitRuntimeMBean]//AllProcessorsWatch} > 0.9', reset type:
'AutomaticReset', reset Period: 60000
notifs:
[[MBeanServerInvocationHandler]com.bea:Name=myJMXNotif,Type=weblogic.diagnostics.descriptor.WLDFJMXNo
tificationBean,Parent=[testdomain]/WLDFSystemResources[allProfiles],Path=WLDFResource[allProfiles]/Wa
tchNotification[allProfiles]/JMXNotifications[myJMXNotif],
[MBeanServerInvocationHandler]com.bea:Name=mySNMPNotif,Type=weblogic.diagnostics.descriptor.WLDFSNMPN
otificationBean,Parent=[testdomain]/WLDFSystemResources[allProfiles],Path=WLDFResource[allProfiles]/W
atchNotification[allProfiles]/SNMPNotifications[mySNMPNotif]]
< ... >
Targets: ['TestCluster']
Looking up target TestCluster
Adding target TestCluster instance to list of targets...
Setting targets on allProfiles
Already in Edit Tree

<...>

Saving all your changes ...
Saved all your changes successfully.
Activating all your changes, this may take a while ...
The edit lock associated with this edit session is released
once the activation is completed.
Activation completed
No stack trace available.
Arguments: {'wldfResource': 'allProfiles', 'targets': 'TestCluster', 'user': 'weblogic',
'harvesterPeriod': '30000', './chainedProfilesExample_2.py': '', 'url': 't3://localhost:12001',
'pass': 'test1234'}
Starting an edit session ...
Started edit session, please be sure to save and activate your
changes once you are done.
Auto edit not enabled
WLDFResource name: allProfiles
connected, finding resourceallProfiles
Already in Edit Tree

Auto edit not enabled
Already in Edit Tree

Setting Harvester sample period to 30000 millis
monitors: {}
Adding weblogic.management.runtime.QueryCacheRuntimeMBean to harvestables collection for allProfiles
< ... >
Targets: ['TestCluster']
Looking up target TestCluster
Adding target TestCluster instance to list of targets...
Setting targets on allProfiles
Already in Edit Tree

Already in Edit Tree

Saving all your changes ...
Saved all your changes successfully.
Activating all your changes, this may take a while ...
The edit lock associated with this edit session is released
```

```
once the activation is completed.
Activation completed
<...>
```

Destroy the complete WLDF Resources

Capturing of data for analysis purposes is an important task which has be performed (unfortunately) pretty often directly in the production system. It is important to stop the capturing and do appropriate cleanup as soon as all necessary data has been captured.

Here is an example of a WLDF cleanup script:

```
execfile('WLDFResource.py')

argsDict = argsToDict(sys.argv)

connectIfNecessary(argsDict)

cd ("edit:/")
startEdit()

try:

    # obtain the WLDFSystemResourceMBean name, default to 'mywldf'
    srName = getValue(argsDict, 'wldfResource', 'mywldf')
    wldfSR = getMBean("WLDFSystemResources/" + srName)

    if wldfSR is not None:
        cmo.destroyWLDFSystemResource(wldfSR)

    save()
    activate()

except:
    dumpStack()
    if cmgr.isEditor():
        stopEdit('y')
```

This script will not disable one or a number of profiles. It will destroy the complete diagnostic module.

Summary

This chapter has discussed a possible approach to WLDF component profiles where profile only look at artifacts of a specific subject. Rather than defining whole diagnostic modules as profiles, it is also possible to define subject matter profiles. In this case the profiles only contain all the necessary WLDF parts for a specific subject (e.g. transactions).

Certainly it take quite some initial setup work and discipline to really get a lot of benefit from this approach and it may look pretty academic to many readers. But if defined carefully it allows administrators and troubleshooters to react quickly and gather exactly the information they need.

The next chapter will discuss full diagnostic module profiles as an alternative approach to the component profiles discussed in this chapter. For a comparison of both approaches with benefits and disadvantages please see the end of the next chapter.

Diagnostic module profiles using WLST

Diagnostic profiles using WLST

This chapter discusses another possible approach to WLDF profiles. Rather than defining components as profiles as discussed in the previous chapter, this chapter discusses the definition of whole diagnostic modules as profiles.

Introduction

Collections of profiles where each profile contains only a fraction of a diagnostic module - only the parts for a specific subject - may have some disadvantages. Profiles defined on diagnostic module scope can be defined and used independent of each other. These are complete diagnostic module definitions with all harvester, watches, monitors and notifications. These profiles are usually defined with a concrete application scope in mind as they can include components from different areas like web, EJB, resources and others.

Diagnostic Module Profiles

This type of profiles define each a complete diagnostic module. On the first glance this looks similar to the component profile discussed in the last chapter but it has a very important difference. This kind of profiles do define a complete diagnostic module. Whenever this profile is applied the complete diagnostic module will be activated.

It is not expected that different profiles will be combined. Prior to WLS 12.1.2 the activation of such a profile requires either the deletion of any other defined profile or the un-targeting of any other profile. Since WLS 12.1.2 it is possible to have multiple active profiles so that activation of a profile dos not mean that other profiles – if any – are affected.

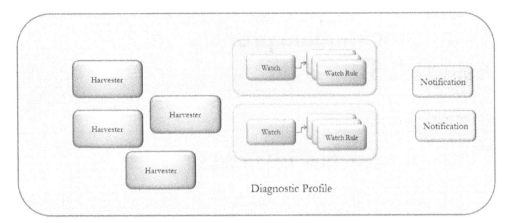

Figure 15.1: *Diagnostic Module Profile Example*

Profile Scopes

A previous chapter has already discussed different categories of profiles, named infrastructure profiles, service level profiles, application category profiles and application profiles.

All these categories can also be applied to diagnostic module profiles. Except for the application profiles these categories are normally rather unusual as they define only artifacts for a specific subject (like e.g. transactions).

Due to the fact that these profiles define a complete diagnostic module the most common usage will most likely be for application profiles. In this case this means that for each application an own profile can be defined. This can be defined either by the administration group or even by the developers as they now the application best.

Advantages and disadvantages

This granularity has a number of great advantages but also disadvantages which will be discussed in this section

Benefit of this approach:
- Independent profiles can be created without dependencies
- The administration group can maintain a list of application profiles
- The administration group does not need to have a deep knowledge of WLDF and WLST as the profiles can be developed by the application teams.

Disadvantages of this approach:
- Possible replication of component definitions in different profiles
- Course granularity
- Up to WLS 12.1.1 only one profile can be active and profile chaining is normally not supported for these profiles

Example Implementation

Due to the nature of WLST as a scripting environment it is – unfortunately – rather uncommon for administrators to pay a lot of attention to well written scripts with reuse and programming patterns in mind. It real life it is definitely more often the case that something is really needed immediately and afterwards saved for possible future reuse.

Implementing these diagnostic module profiles could therefore be done in two different flavors.

a) Res-use and extend the Jython classes defined in the previous chapter and extend those to complete diagnostic modules. This would require a lot of scripting knowledge and it is unlikely that e.g. project teams will be able to deliver ready-made profiles to the administrator group. The benefit though would be a nicely written collection of profiles with minimum replication, easily to use and easy to extend.

b) Implement a generic wrapper and profile manager script. Define a template which every profile must follow. The benefits would include that this easily be provided by project teams and will ease up the life of administrators, is easy to write and easy to understand. The disadvantage would be a high degree of replication and no reuse of module parts.

This chapter demonstrates an implementation of the second possibility. For that we will provide generic profile manager and a template for writing module profiles.

Template for module profiles

The following template is a very simple approach of providing a

```
"""
This defines a blueprint for all diagnostic profiles. The basic idea is to define a
 blueprint which can be used either by the administrators themselves or by project teams
 to create the required WLST functions to create a module.
"""

# get the desired module name
def getProfileName();
    return "xxx"

# define the installation mode
```

```
# possible values:
#    0 : leave all other modules unchanged
#    1 : untarget all other modules
#    2 : delete all other modules
def getProfileMode():
    return 0;
    # return 1;
    # return 2;

# return the targets of this module
# return as array of strings ['AdminServer','Cluster1']
def getTargets():
    return ['???']

# pre module setup activities , like SNMP / email / JMS configurations
def doPrerequisiteActivities():
    ...

# create module
# implement all parts of the module including module creation, module targeting, watches,
# notifications, events, ...
def createModule():
    ...

# implement activities which should be done after the nodule has been deleted,
# like SNMP / email / JMS cleanups
def doPostDeleteActivities():
    ...
```

Main execution scripts for administrators

In order to provide a better readability for the administrators the utility functions are outsourced into a library (see next section). The following script demonstrate a simple – (but fully functional !) – implementation of the main scripts an administrator will use to work with these profiles.

The first script iterates over all existing profiles and will print their names and their targets

```
import jarray

# include the library commands
execfile('./wldf_diagnosticmodules_lib.py')

#============================================================================
# Main
#============================================================================
if __name__ == "main":
    if len(sys.argv) < 4:
            print "Error: printAll_diagnosticProfiles.py 'user' 'password' 'connectURL' arguments
must be provided on command line"
            exit('1')

    # connect
    print 'Connect to '+ sys.argv[3]
    connect(sys.argv[1], sys.argv[2], sys.argv[3])

    print 'Found the following diagnostic modules configured:'
    printNamesAndTargetsOfAllDiagnosticModules()

    # disconnect
    disconnect()
    exit()
```

Example execution:

```
wlst.sh ./printAll_diagnosticProfiles.py weblogic xxxxxxxxx t3://localhost:7001

Initializing WebLogic Scripting Tool (WLST) ...

Connect to t3://localhost:7001
Connecting to t3://localhost:7001 with userid weblogic ...
Successfully connected to Admin Server "AdminServer" that belongs to domain "wl_server".

Found the following diagnostic modules configured:

Found diagnostic module MyTestModule_1
  Found targets :
            : AdminServer
            : TestCluster
Found diagnostic module DynamicClusterModule
  Found targets :
            : Cluster-0
Found diagnostic module AdminOnlyModule
  Found targets :
            : AdminServer
Disconnected from weblogic server: AdminServer
```

The second script shows how to delete all existing diagnostic profiles. In order to have a protocol what will be deleted, the script will print the current modules first.

```
import jarray

# include the library commands
execfile('./wldf_diagnosticmodules_lib.py')

#============================================================================
# Main
#============================================================================
if __name__ == "main":
    if len(sys.argv) < 4:
            print "Error: deleteAll_diagnosticProfiles.py 'user' 'password' 'connectURL'
arguments must be provided on command line"
            exit('1')

    # connect
    print 'Connect to '+ sys.argv[3]
    connect(sys.argv[1], sys.argv[2], sys.argv[3])

    print 'Found the following diagnostic modules configured:'
    printNamesAndTargetsOfAllDiagnosticModules()

    # delete all modules
    print 'All existing modules will be deleted'
    deleteAllDiagnosticModules()
    print 'All existing modules have been deleted'

    # disconnect
    disconnect()
    exit()
```

Example execution:

```
wlst.sh ./deleteAll_diagnosticProfiles.py weblogic xxxxxxxxx t3://localhost:7001

Initializing WebLogic Scripting Tool (WLST) ...

Connect to t3://localhost:7001
Connecting to t3://localhost:7001 with userid weblogic ...
Successfully connected to Admin Server "AdminServer" that belongs to domain "wl_server".

Found the following diagnostic modules configured:

Found diagnostic module MyTestModule_1
  Found targets :
            : AdminServer
            : TestCluster
```

```
Found diagnostic module DynamicClusterModule
  Found targets :
          : Cluster-0
Found diagnostic module AdminOnlyModule
  Found targets :
          : AdminServer
All existing modules will be deleted
Location changed to edit tree. This is a writable tree with
DomainMBean as the root. To make changes you will need to start
an edit session via startEdit().

For more help, use help('edit')
You already have an edit session in progress and hence WLST will
continue with your edit session.

Starting an edit session ...
Started edit session, please be sure to save and activate your
changes once you are done.
Deleting diagnostic module MyTestModule_1
Deleting diagnostic module DynamicClusterModule
Deleting diagnostic module AdminOnlyModule
Saving all your changes ...
Saved all your changes successfully.
Activating all your changes, this may take a while ...
The edit lock associated with this edit session is released
once the activation is completed.
Activation completed
All existing modules have been deleted
Disconnected from weblogic server: AdminServer
```

The last script shows the main tool, which installs a diagnostic profile as defined in a concrete definition.

```
# main script for dealing with diagnostic modules

import jarray


# include the library commands
execfile('./wldf_diagnosticmodules_lib.py')

#================================================================================
# Main
#================================================================================
if __name__ == "main":
    if len(sys.argv) < 5:
            print "Error: manage_diagnosticProfiles.py 'user' 'password' 'connectURL' 'module-
definition' arguments must be provided on command line"
            exit('1')

    # Try to load module defintion
    print 'Try to load module defintion'
    execfile(sys.argv[4])

    # connect
    print 'Connect to '+ sys.argv[3]
    connect(sys.argv[1], sys.argv[2], sys.argv[3])


    print 'Found the following diagnostic modules configured:'
    printNamesAndTargetsOfAllDiagnosticModules()

    # check if the module exists and if yes delete it
    if doesDiagnosticModuleExist(getProfileName()):
        print 'Profile: '+ getProfileName() + ' does exist and will be deleted.'
        deleteSpecifcDiagnosticModule(getProfileName())
        print 'Profile: '+ getProfileName() + ' has been deleted.'

    # check how to deal with other modules
    if getProfileMode() == 0:
        print 'All existing modules will be left unchanged'
    elif getProfileMode() == 1:
        print 'All existing modules will be untargeted'
        untargetAllDiagnosticModules()
        print 'All existing modules have been untargeted'
```

```
elif getProfileMode() == 2:
    print 'All existing modules will be deleted'
    deleteAllDiagnosticModules()
    print 'All existing modules have been deleted'

# create new module
print ''
print 'Diagnostic Module ' + getProfileName() + ' from the provided definition will be created'

# prerequisites
print '   1: Calling pre-requisite creation activities'
edit()
try:
    startEdit()
    doPrerequisiteActivities()
    activate()
except:
    dumpStack()
    cancelEdit('y')


# create the module
print ''
print '   2: Calling module creation activities'
edit()
try:
    startEdit()
    createModule()
    activate()
except:
    dumpStack()
    cancelEdit('y')

# do the targeting
print ''
print '   3: Target the module'
serverConfig()
myTargets = convertNamesToTargetMBeanList(getTargets())
edit()
try:
    startEdit()
    cd('/WLDFSystemResources/'+getProfileName())
    set('Targets', jarray.array(myTargets, ObjectName))
    activate()
except:
    dumpStack()
    cancelEdit('y')

# finish
print 'The diagnostic module has been created and targeted.'

# disconnect
disconnect()
exit()
```

This script will first of all load the concrete profile definition (which must be implemented with the API discussed in the template) using the "execfile(sys.argv[4])" call. It will then print all existing modules as a reference. Based on the mode defined in the profile definition this script might delete all existing profiles or un-target all of them or even do nothing.

If a module with the name equal to the name defined in the definition already exist then this script will delete this module first, otherwise the new one could not be created. Finally the new module will be created by executing the prerequisites first, then create the module and finally do the targeting.

Utility Library

As already show in the main script, a number of activities have been outsourced to own functions. These functions are called in this chapter the utility library. Please note that for the sake of the book these functions have been implemented in a simple and easy way with a focus on understanding. Jython offers much more advanced features like the library concept, object-oriented programming which is intentionally not used to keep the code small and simple. Also the exception handling is only minimal and can definitely be improved.

The first function checks if a given diagnostic module already exists:

```
# check if a specific module does exist
# return true or false
def doesDiagnosticModuleExist(name):
    domainConfig()
    cd ('/')
    # query module mbean
    moduleMBean = cmo.lookupWLDFSystemResource(name)

    if moduleMBean != None:
      return true
    else:
      return false
```

The next function has been introduced to print out a situation analysis, in case the administrator will later on restore this configuration. Here a lot of improvement could be done like a memory function which records the current state and allow for automatic re-creation and more.

```
# print names and targets of all modules
# can be used as debug output for verification or also for creating a protocol in
# case the old status nust be recreated at soma later time
def printNamesAndTargetsOfAllDiagnosticModules():
    domainConfig()
    cd ('/')
    listOfModules = cmo.WLDFSystemResources
    if listOfModules is not None:
        for moduleMbean in listOfModules:
            print 'Found diagnostic module ' + moduleMBean.getName()
            cd('/WLDFSystemResources/'+moduleMBean.getName())

        print '  Found targets : '
        modTargets = get('Targets')
        if modTargets is not None:
            for nextTarget in modTargets:
                # cd('/WLDFSystemResources/'+moduleMBean.getName()+'/Targets/')
                print '              : ' + nextTarget.getKeyProperty('Name')
```

A function to convert a name of a module into the according MBean reference.

```
# check if a specific module does exist
# return "None" or the MBean
def getDiagnosticModuleMBean(name):
    domainConfig()
    cd ('/')
    # query module mbean
    return cmo.lookupWLDFSystemResource(name)
```

The next function implements the destruction of a given module. This is used in the main code in order to delete a module – if one exists with the same name as the new module.

```
# delete only a specific module.  This is used if e.g. a module with the same name as the new
# module already exists in order to delete the old module. Otherwise the new one could not be created
def deleteSpecifcDiagnosticModule(name):
    try:
        edit()
        cd("/")
        if name is not None:
            startEdit()
            cmo.destroyWLDFSystemResource(cmo.lookupWLDFSystemResource(name))
            save()
            activate()
    except:
        cancelEdit('y')
```

The next function implements a complete cleanup by deleting all existing diagnostic modules.

```
# delete all modules in order to cleanup the server configuration before a new
# module is configured
def deleteAllDiagnosticModules():
    try:
        edit()
        cd('/')
        listOfModules = cmo.WLDFSystemResources
        if listOfModules is not None:
            startEdit()
            for moduleMbean in listOfModules:
                print 'Deleting diagnostic module ' + moduleMbean.getName()
                cmo.destroyWLDFSystemResource(moduleMbean)
            save()
            activate()
    except:
        dumpStack()
        cancelEdit('y')
```

The next function shows how to untarget (which is equal to disable) all existing modules.

```
# untarget all modules.  Note that since 12.1.2 disable is also possible, but then we would need to make a
# a distinction in the code if this script is running on WLS 12.1.2+ or below.
# for demonstration purpose this is enough
def untargetAllDiagnosticModules():
    try:
        edit()
        cd('/')
        listOfModules = cmo.WLDFSystemResources
        if listOfModules is not None:
            startEdit()
            for moduleMbean in listOfModules:
                print 'Untarget diagnostic module ' + moduleMbean.getName()
                cd('/WLDFSystemResources/'+moduleMbean.getName())
                # remove all targets
                set('Targets',jarray.array([], ObjectName))
            save()
            activate()
    except:
        dumpStack()
        cancelEdit('y')
```

The last function in his small library allows the admin to convert a list of Strings to a list of MBean references. This is used to create the list of target MBeans.

```
# Get a list of strings and return a list of MBeans (if Strings can be converted to MBeans
def convertNamesToTargetMBeanList(targetList):
    targetMBeans = array([],ObjectName)
    cd ('/')
    if targetList is not None:
      for targetName in targetList:
          print "Try to find MBean for the identifier: " + str(targetName)
          targetRef = cmo.lookupTarget(targetName)
          print "... found : " + str(targetRef)
          if targetRef != None:
              targetMBeans.append(targetRef.getObjectName())
              print "Append MBean " + targetRef.getName() + " instance to list of targets..."

    return targetMBeans
```

Example module profile

The following example is a very simple profile which is created out of a built-in profile of WebLogic (e.g. WLS 12.1.3).

The following profile definition is used.

```
# get the desired module name
def getProfileName():
    return 'MyTestModule_1'

# define the installation mode
def getProfileMode():
    return 1;   # means untarget all others


# return the targets of this module
def getTargets():
    return ['AdminServer','TestCluster']

# pre module setup activities , like SNMP / email / JMS configurations
def doPrerequisiteActivities():
    return

# create module
def createModule():
    cd('/')
    cmo.createWLDFSystemResourceFromBuiltin('MyTestModule_1', 'Medium')

    cd('/WLDFSystemResources/MyTestModule_1')
    cmo.setDescription('This is a test created by a template')


# implement activities which should be done after the nodule has been deleted,
# like SNMP / email / JMS cleanups
def doPostDeleteActivities():
    # nothing to do
    return
```

Please note that this code has demonstration quality only. By looking back at the previous book sections you all can imagine that the different function definitions might contain much more logic and code and, of course, might be much more complex.

In the example domain, the view of the diagnostic modules BEFORE executing the main script might look like:

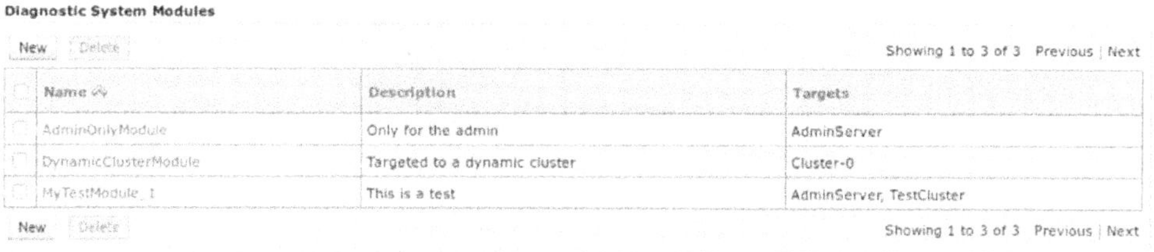

Diagnostic System Modules

Name	Description	Targets
AdminOnlyModule	Only for the admin	AdminServer
DynamicClusterModule	Targeted to a dynamic cluster	Cluster-0
MyTestModule_1	This is a test	AdminServer, TestCluster

New   Delete   Showing 1 to 3 of 3   Previous | Next

Figure 15.2: *View before script execution*

Now we will execute the script discussed above. In the following output you can see, that this script will load the definition, print all existing modules, untarget all existing modules. Then it detects that a module with the desired name already exists and will delete this module. Finally it will create and target this module:

```
wlst.sh ./manage_diagnosticProfiles.py weblogic xxx t3://localhost:7001  ./basicProfileExample.py

Initializing WebLogic Scripting Tool (WLST) ...

Try to load module defintion
Connect to t3://localhost:7001
Connecting to t3://localhost:7001 with userid weblogic ...
Successfully connected to Admin Server "AdminServer" that belongs to domain "wl_server".

Found the following diagnostic modules configured:

Found diagnostic module MyTestModule_1
  Found targets :
          : AdminServer
          : TestCluster
Found diagnostic module DynamicClusterModule
  Found targets :
          : Cluster-0
Found diagnostic module AdminOnlyModule
  Found targets :
          : AdminServer
Already in Domain Config Tree

Profile: MyTestModule_1 does exist and will be deleted.
Location changed to edit tree.

Starting an edit session ...
Saving all your changes ...
Saved all your changes successfully.
Activating all your changes, this may take a while ...
The edit lock associated with this edit session is released
once the activation is completed.
Activation completed

Profile: MyTestModule_1 has been deleted.
All existing modules will be untargeted
Already in Edit Tree

Starting an edit session ...
Started edit session, please be sure to save and activate your
changes once you are done.
Untarget diagnostic module DynamicClusterModule
Untarget diagnostic module AdminOnlyModule
Saving all your changes ...
Saved all your changes successfully.
Activating all your changes, this may take a while ...
```

```
Activation completed
All existing modules have been untargeted

Diagnostic Module MyTestModule_1 from the provided definition will be created
1: Calling pre-requisite creation activities
Already in Edit Tree

Starting an edit session ...
Started edit session, please be sure to save and activate your
changes once you are done.
Activating all your changes, this may take a while ...
The edit lock associated with this edit session is released
once the activation is completed.
Activation completed

2: Calling module creation activities
Already in Edit Tree

Starting an edit session ...
Started edit session, please be sure to save and activate your
changes once you are done.
Activating all your changes, this may take a while ...
The edit lock associated with this edit session is released
once the activation is completed.
Activation completed

3: Target the module

Try to find MBean for the identifier: AdminServer
... found : [MBeanServerInvocationHandler]com.bea:Name=AdminServer,Type=Server
Append MBean AdminServer instance to list of targets...
Try to find MBean for the identifier: TestCluster
... found : [MBeanServerInvocationHandler]com.bea:Name=TestCluster,Type=Cluster
Append MBean TestCluster instance to list of targets...

Starting an edit session ...
Started edit session, please be sure to save and activate your
changes once you are done.
Activating all your changes, this may take a while ...
The edit lock associated with this edit session is released
once the activation is completed.
Activation completed
The diagnostic module has been created and targeted.
Disconnected from weblogic server: AdminServer
```

Given this example, the view of the diagnostic modules AFTER executing the main script will look like:

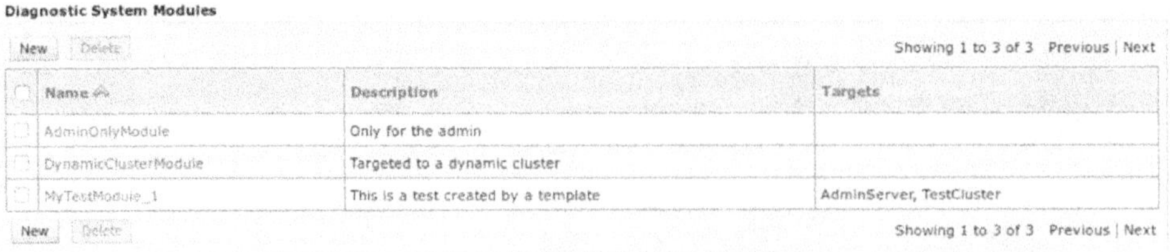

Diagnostic System Modules

	Name	Description	Targets
	AdminOnlyModule	Only for the admin	
	DynamicClusterModule	Targeted to a dynamic cluster	
	MyTestModule_1	This is a test created by a template	AdminServer, TestCluster

Showing 1 to 3 of 3   Previous | Next

Figure 15.3: *View after script has been executed*

Please note in the last screenshot, that all other modules has no targets any more. Furthermore the description of "MyTestModule_1" has changed and this is the only module with targets.

Comparison between profile types

The last chapter has discussed the more fine-grained component profiles. This chapter discussed the module profiles. Both have their advantages and disadvantages and there are different use cases for these two types of profiles. This section is a comparison based on the authors experience from real projects.

Component Profiles

Benefits

- Focus on specific subjects rather than on the complete module.

- Much better reuse. Can nicely be used for many different diagnostic modules if designed well.

Disadvantages

- These type of profiles will be used by WLS administrators only and will not be part of deployment handover from the project teams.

- Administrators need to have a great knowledge of WLST and WLDF to create and maintain these profiles well.

- If the same subject is required by different applications but with different content, then this might result in a number of similar profiles which might later be hard to distinguish

Should be used

- If admins are able to write and maintain WLST code (in particular WLDF related WLST).

- If most WLDF requirements are based on standard MBeans and attribute (good re-use).

Should not be used

- If projects often have special WLDF requirements as this leads to a lot of work for the administrators and to a uncontrolled growing component library.

- If administrators do not have the appropriate WLST and WLDF knowledge.

Diagnostic module Profiles

Benefits

- Describe a complete diagnostic profile.

- Depending on how they are implemented, they are easier to implement and maintain.

- Can be usually delivered from project teams to administrators.

- Can contain dye-injections as application specific elements. It is rather unusual to have component profile for dye injections.

Disadvantages

- If not constructed out of component profiles, will result in a lot of duplication

- It is an all or nothing approach (on module level). Older WebLogic versions only support one active diagnostic module.

Should be used

- By administrators who expect to get WLDF definitions as part of the application handover.

- Whenever it is required to produce complete scripts without dependencies which must be archived for audit and other reasons. Using component libraries cannot guarantee that the script will always execute the same functionality as underlying libraries might change.

Should not be used

- For generic tool implementations because this will result in duplications and many similar implementations.

- By experienced administrators with development experience who want to build an effective and reusable library.

Summary

This chapter completes the discussion about WLST profiles with the discussion of the most coarse grained profiles – the diagnostic module profiles. These profiles implement all aspects of a diagnostic profile, including targeting and if wanted even archive definitions. Basically we can distinguish about general purpose profiles which can be used by administrators to monitor general aspects of a domain like JVM, thread, networking, transaction or application specific profiles which can in addition also add injections and application specific monitoring.

Even though the complete discussion about profiling sounds very academic, it has been proven to be very useful in day to day administrative life if used in the right way. The biggest benefit for real projects and administrators is a framework which administrators get used to. Projects can be given guidelines to provide the profile implementations.

Also note that the approach discussed in the implementation has a very practical approach in mind.

This approach allows a group of administrators to concentrate on only a few main scripts, publish the template as required API and then let the projects themselves, without having any idea of existing libraries or script re-use option, create the module definitions and hand them over to the administrator group.

The administrators can use the provided templates with their own scripts without changing their scripts. Please note that the provided example is a much simplified implementation for the purpose of this book. Usually these scripts are much more complicated and might include getting credentials and URL from a database, using password stores or invoking the scripts for many different domains running on different machines.

Diagnostic profiles using JMX

Diagnostic profiles using JMX

All kinds of profiles were discussed in the last two chapters can these profiles also be implemented using JMX. In most cases, WLST will be used for WLDF configurations but in some use cases JMX is a very good alternative.

Introduction

This chapter discusses an implementation of the different profile types using JMX. Please consult the previous chapters for a detailed discussion about the idea and granularity of artifact profile, component profile and module profiles.

The implementation provided in this chapter will basically support all three types and each type can be constructed by reusing the finer grained profile types.

Use cases

Why use JMX and not WLST? WLST is easier to use, less code and available as readable script for administrators. In the world of automation and generation a lot of effort is done to provide more and more abstract views and generated processes. WLDF is still a pretty low level API. Many users wants to have nice UIs for providing drag and drop support for the generation of almost everything. Following this principal it might be easy to offer a tool which automatically discovers the applications running on the different WLS domains. Then this tool might offer – based e.g. on a knowledgebase of best practice possible harvesting, watches and notification suggestions. The user can combine these into potentially different profiles and then the tool will install these profiles into the different domains.

WLST is a very powerful scripting environment but it still has limitations - especially in the area of parallel processing. Therefore another use case for JMX might be automated tools collecting information from many different domains and doing WLDF setups and adjustments – maybe even depending on domain specific settings.

Architecture of the JMX Implementation

The basic idea of this implementation is that we will define the most fine grained artifact components first (own java package). This also includes all operations needed to test, create, update and delete these artifacts.

Then we will define component profiles (similar to those defined in the WLST component profile chapter) which make use of the artifact profiles and their operations. This also means that the implementation of a component profile is basically only a framework to combine existing artifacts into components and add usability functions where necessary.

Likewise the diagnostic module components use the component profiles and/or artifact components to define the most course grained module components. This implementation adds all functionality needed to test, create, update and delete diagnostic modules. In order to support a wide range of WLS versions this code supports the notion of enabling (WLS 12.1.2 and beyond) and also the notion of targeting/un-targeting of modules in order to activate/deactivate a module.

As JMX implementations usually have different use cases than WLST implementations the example implementation used in this chapter will be different to the WLST implementations discussed in the previous chapters. This example implementation will define all three granularity levels of profiles. For a maximum of code and configuration reuse components will be build out of artifacts and modules will be build out of components.

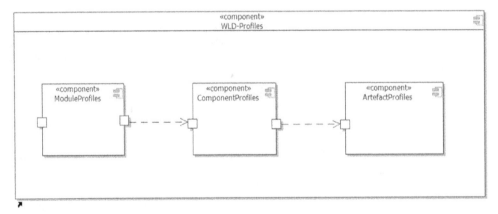

Figure 16.1: *Dependency diagram of dependencies*

The following diagram shows a class diagram of the profile implementation.

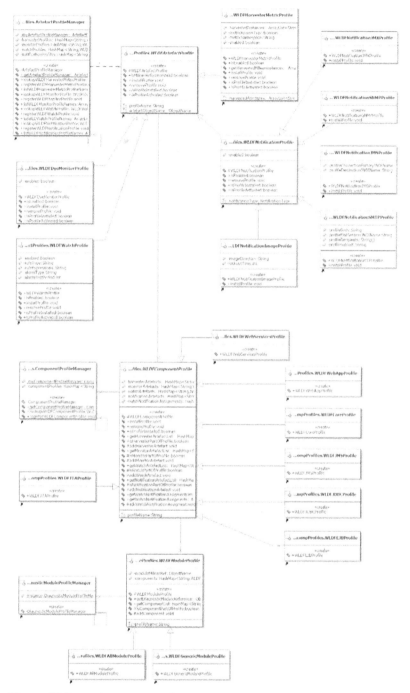

Figure 16.2: *Architecture and Class Diagram*

In addition to the three different level of profile implementation, the example also factors out all common activities into a number of utility class. The following utility classes are provided with the implementation.

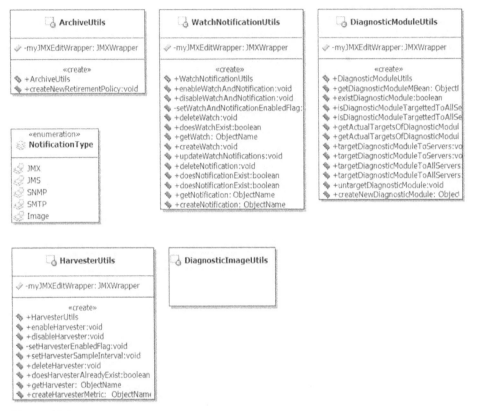

Figure 16.3: *Utility classes for the JMX profile implementations*

Artifact Profiles

This section describes the implementation of the artifact profiles – the most fine-grained profiles with the basic building blocks of WLDF.

Architecture and Overview

Every type is derived directly or indirectly (in case of the concrete notifications) from WLDFArtifactProfile. This allows for maximal generalization of code and to treat all instances of artifact profiles equally.

Figure 16.4: *Class diagram for artifact profiles*

Each subtype will only add type specific details which cannot be generalized.

Implementation

This section discusses the implementation details of the artifact profile solution. Due to size only fractions of the code are shown. Also code which was discussed in the previous WLDF building blocks chapters will not be shown again.

WLDFArtifactProfile

This class defines the base class for all artifact profiles.

```
public abstract class WLDFArtifactProfile
{
    // the name of this artifact profile
    private String profileName = "undefined";

    // the ObjectName (if known)
    private ObjectName artifactObjectName = null;

    protected WLDFArtifactProfile(String _name) {
        profileName = _name;
    }

    public String getProfileName() {
        return profileName;
    }

    public ObjectName getArtifactObjectName() {
        return artifactObjectName;
    }

    public void setArtifactObjectName(ObjectName _obName) {
        artifactObjectName = _obName;
    }

    public boolean isMBeanReferenceValid(JMXWrapper myJMXWrapper) {
        if (artifactObjectName != null)  {
            try {
                return myJMXWrapper.getConnection().isRegistered(artifactObjectName);
            }
            catch(Exception ex) {
                ex.printStackTrace();
                return false;     // just as a default
            }
        }
        else
            return false;
    }

    public abstract void installProfile(JMXWrapper _editwrapper, ObjectName myDiagnosticModule)
                    throws WLDFAutomationException;

    public abstract void removeProfile(JMXWrapper _editwrapper, ObjectName myDiagnosticModule)
                    throws WLDFAutomationException;

    public abstract boolean isProfileInstalled(JMXWrapper _editwrapper, ObjectName myDiagnosticMod)
                    throws WLDFAutomationException;

    public abstract boolean isProfileActivated(JMXWrapper _editwrapper, ObjectName myDiagnosticMod)
                    throws WLDFAutomationException;
}
```

As you can see, this class defines only some abstract base methods so that we can afterwards treat all artifact profiles equally. Beside the name and the MBean reference this class does not define any further data item.

All the different concrete types of artifact profiles are derived from the base class. Most of the functions are using very similar code than the one discussed earlier in the book, therefore only code examples will be printed here.

The harvester artifact profile

```
public class WLDFHarvesterMetricProfile  extends WLDFArtifactProfile
{
    private ArrayList<String> harvestedAttributes = new ArrayList<String>();

    private ArrayList<String> harvestedInstances = new ArrayList<String>();
```

```
    private boolean metricKnownType = true;

    private String metricNamespace = null;

    private boolean enabled = false;

    public WLDFHarvesterMetricProfile(String _name,
                                      boolean _enabled,
                                      ArrayList<String> _attribs,
                                      ArrayList<String> _instances, boolean isKnown)
    {
        super(_name);
        enabled = _enabled;
        arvestedAttributes.clear();
        metricKnownType = isKnown;

        if (_attribs != null)
            harvestedAttributes.addAll(_attribs);

        if (_instances != null)
            harvestedInstances = _instances;
    }

    public boolean isEnabled() {
            return enabled;
    }


    public ArrayList<String> getHarvestedAttributes() {
            return harvestedAttributes;
    }


    public ArrayList<String> getHarvestedMBeaninstances() {
            return harvestedInstances;
    }


    public void installProfile(JMXWrapper _editwrapper, ObjectName myDiagnosticModule)
            throws WLDFAutomationException {
        try {
          HarvesterUtils myHarvesterUtils = new HarvesterUtils(_editwrapper);

          if (! myHarvesterUtils.doesHarvesterAlreadyExist(myDiagnosticModule, getProfileName()))
              myHarvesterUtils.createHarvesterMetric(myDiagnosticModule, getProfileName(),
                              enabled, harvestedAttributes, harvestedInstances,
                              metricKnownType, metricNamespace);
        }
        catch(Exception ex) {
              ex.printStackTrace();
              throw new WLDFAutomationException(ex.getMessage());
        }
    }
    ...
}
```

The other artifact methods are implemented in a similar way. Please see the code depot for the complete implementation.

Notification profiles base class

Due to the fact that WLDF supports a number of notification types, it is better to add another level of inheritance in the class hierarchy. The notification base profile will implement the all the base methods except for "installProfile". The method "installProfile" is type specific. The following code shows the base class for all notification types.

```
public abstract class WLDFNotificationProfile  extends WLDFArtifactProfile
{
    private NotificationType notificationType = null;

    private boolean enabled = false;

    protected WLDFNotificationProfile(String _name, NotificationType _nType, boolean _enabled) {
            super(_name);
            notificationType = _nType;
            enabled = _enabled;
    }

    public boolean isEnabled() {
            return enabled;
    }

    public NotificationType getNotificationType() {
            return notificationType;
    }

    public void removeProfile(JMXWrapper _editwrapper, ObjectName myDiagnosticModule)
            throws WLDFAutomationException {
        try {
            WatchNotificationUtils myWatchNotificationUtils =
                            new WatchNotificationUtils(_editwrapper);

            if (myWatchNotificationUtils.doesNotificationExist(myDiagnosticModule, getProfileName()))
                    myWatchNotificationUtils.deleteNotification(myDiagnosticModule,
                                            notificationType, getProfileName());
        }
        catch(Exception ex) {
                ex.printStackTrace();
                throw new WLDFAutomationException(ex.getMessage());
        }
    }
    ...
}
```

The JMS notification profile

As a last example the following code explains how to implement a concrete
notification type. Note that only the install method needs to be implemented as all
others were already implemented in a generic way in the base class. Also note that this
class must inherit from WLDFNotificationProfile

```
public class WLDFNotificationJMSProfile extends WLDFNotificationProfile
{
    private String profileConnectionFactoryJNDIName = null;
    private String profileDestinationJNDIName = null;

    public WLDFNotificationJMSProfile(String name, boolean enabled, String cJName, String dJName) {
            super(name, NotificationType.JMS,enabled);
            profileConnectionFactoryJNDIName = cJName;
            profileDestinationJNDIName = dJName;
    }

    public void installProfile(JMXWrapper myJMXEditWrapper, ObjectName myDiagnosticModule)
            throws WLDFAutomationException {
        ObjectName notificationRef = null;
        try {
            WatchNotificationUtils myWatchNotificationUtils =
                            new WatchNotificationUtils(myJMXEditWrapper);

            if (myWatchNotificationUtils.doesNotificationExist(myDiagnosticModule,
                getProfileName()))
                    notificationRef = myWatchNotificationUtils.getNotification(
                                    myDiagnosticModule, getProfileName());
            else // create
                    notificationRef = myWatchNotificationUtils.createNotification(myDiagnosticModule,
                                    getNotificationType(), getProfileName());
```

```
            // enabled
            myJMXEditWrapper.setAttribute(notificationRef, new Attribute("Enabled",isEnabled()));

            // ConnectionFactoryJNDIName
            myJMXEditWrapper.setAttribute(notificationRef,
                    new Attribute("ConnectionFactoryJNDIName",profileConnectionFactoryJNDIName));

            // DestinationJNDIName
            myJMXEditWrapper.setAttribute(notificationRef,
                         new Attribute("DestinationJNDIName",profileDestinationJNDIName));
        }
        catch(Exception ex) {
            ex.printStackTrace();
            throw new WLDFAutomationException(ex.getMessage());
        }
    }
}
```

ArtifactProfileManager

The complete artifact profiles are maintained by a profile manager. This is a registry for profiles which can be used to store, retrieve and check for specific profiles.

```
public class ArtifactProfileManager
{
    // singleton
    private static ArtifactProfileManager myArtifactProfileManager = null;

    // harvester metric profiles
    private HashMap<String, WLDFHarvesterMetricProfile> harvesterProfiles =
                        new HashMap<String, WLDFHarvesterMetricProfile>();

    // monitor profiles
    private HashMap<String, WLDFDyeMonitorProfile> monitorProfiles =
                        new HashMap<String, WLDFDyeMonitorProfile>();

    // watch profiles
    private HashMap<String, WLDFWatchProfile> watchProfiles =
                        new HashMap<String, WLDFWatchProfile>();

    // notification profiles
    private HashMap<String, WLDFNotificationProfile> notificationProfiles =
                        new HashMap<String, WLDFNotificationProfile>();


    // singleton constructor
    private ArtifactProfileManager() {}

    public static ArtifactProfileManager getArtifactProfileManager()
    {
            if (myArtifactProfileManager == null)
            {
                    myArtifactProfileManager = new ArtifactProfileManager();
            }

            return myArtifactProfileManager;
    }


    public WLDFHarvesterMetricProfile lookupWLDFHarvesterMetricProfile(String name) {
            return harvesterProfiles.get(name);
    }

    public void registerWLDFHarvesterMetricProfile(WLDFHarvesterMetricProfile newProfile) {
            harvesterProfiles.put(newProfile.getProfileName(), newProfile);
    }

    public ArrayList<String> listWLDFHarvesterMetricProfileNames() {
            ArrayList<String> result = new ArrayList<String>();
            result.addAll(harvesterProfiles.keySet());
            return result;
    }
```

```
    ... lookupXXX, registerXXX and listXXX implementations for watches and more also available
}
```

There are a couple of important observations here. First of all this implementation uses different lists for different major types. The reason is that the profile names must only be unique within their own category.

Second, we note is that neither the implementation of the watches nor the implementation of the profile manager contains code which assign notification to watches. The reason is that all artifact profiles are independent from each other. This combination is done on the component profile level (see next session).

Initialization

The profile manager is only useful if it has profiles to manage. Therefore we need an implementation which also initializes the available profiles and add them to the profile manager.

This can be done in many different ways. I could be possible to generate these profiles on the fly from live domains, if could be possible that these profiles are defined in an external file – e.g. XML or these profiles could be stored in a central database. Where and how profiles are stored and maintained is really up to the user and the project needs.

The following example shows a static way where profiles are hardcoded into source code. This is the easiest way but by far not the most elegant or flexible way.

Example for initializing harvester artifacts

```
ArtifactProfileManager myArtifactProfileManager = ArtifactProfileManager.getArtifactProfileManager();

myArtifactProfileManager.registerWLDFHarvesterMetricProfile(new
WLDFHarvesterMetricProfile(ConstArtifactNames.workManagerType,          true, new
ArrayList<String>(Arrays.asList(new String[] {"StuckThreadCount" , "PendingRequests",
"CompletedRequests"})),null,false));

myArtifactProfileManager.registerWLDFHarvesterMetricProfile(new
WLDFHarvesterMetricProfile(ConstArtifactNames.srtType,          true, new
ArrayList<String>(Arrays.asList(new String[] {"OpenSocketsCurrentCount" ,
"SocketsOpenedTotalCount"})),null,false));

myArtifactProfileManager.registerWLDFHarvesterMetricProfile(new
WLDFHarvesterMetricProfile(ConstArtifactNames.clusterType,          true, new
ArrayList<String>(Arrays.asList(new String[] {"AliveServerCount"})),null,false));
```

Example for initializing watch artifacts

```
ArtifactProfileManager myArtifactProfileManager = ArtifactProfileManager.getArtifactProfileManager();

myArtifactProfileManager.registerWLDFWatchProfile(new
WLDFWatchProfile(ConstArtifactNames.stuckThreadWatch,          true, "${[" +
```

```
ConstArtifactNames.workManagerType + "]//StuckThreadCount} > 0", "Harvester",
"AutomaticReset",1000));

myArtifactProfileManager.registerWLDFWatchProfile(new
WLDFWatchProfile(ConstArtifactNames.serverHealthStateWatch ,true, "${[" + ConstArtifactNames.srtType
+"]//State} IN ('FAILED','FAILED_RESTARTING','FAILED_NOT_RESTARTABLE')", "Harvester",
"AutomaticReset",1000));

myArtifactProfileManager.registerWLDFWatchProfile(new
WLDFWatchProfile(ConstArtifactNames.clusterServerWatch,       true, "${[" +
ConstArtifactNames.clusterType +"]//AliveServerCount} = 0", "Harvester", "AutomaticReset",1000));
```

Example for initializing notification artifacts

```
ArtifactProfileManager myArtifactProfileManager =
ArtifactProfileManager.getArtifactProfileManager();

myArtifactProfileManager.registerWLDFNotificationProfile(new
WLDFNotificationJMXProfile(ConstArtifactNames.JMX_Core_Notification,true));

myArtifactProfileManager.registerWLDFNotificationProfile(new
WLDFNotificationImageProfile(ConstArtifactNames.Image_Core_Notification,
true, "/data/wldf_images/webapp", 100));

myArtifactProfileManager.registerWLDFNotificationProfile(new
WLDFNotificationJMXProfile(ConstArtifactNames.JMX_EJB_Notification,true));
```

Test

The following code shows a very simple test which will just query all registered
artifacts from the artifact manager and installs them into a given diagnostic module.

```
public static void main(String[] args) throws Exception {

    JMXWrapperRemote myJMXEditWrapper = new JMXWrapperRemote();

    myJMXEditWrapper.connectToAdminServer(true, true,  // edit tree of the domain
                    "weblogic", "test1234", "t3://localhost:11100");

    // init all profiles
    InitAllProfiles.initAllProfiles();

    // create a module
    DiagnosticModuleUtils myDiagnosticModuleUtils = new DiagnosticModuleUtils(myJMXEditWrapper);
    ObjectName modRef = myDiagnosticModuleUtils.createNewDiagnosticModule(
                    "DM_"+System.currentTimeMillis(),
                    "This is a test module to test the profile implementation");
    myDiagnosticModuleUtils.targetDiagnosticModuleToAllServers(modRef);

    // create all harvester
    ArtifactProfileManager myArtifactProfileManager =
                            ArtifactProfileManager.getArtifactProfileManager();

    ArrayList<String> harList = myArtifactProfileManager.listWLDFHarvesterMetricProfileNames();
    for (int i=0; i<harList.size(); i++)
        myArtifactProfileManager.lookupWLDFHarvesterMetricProfile(
                    harList.get(i)).installProfile(myJMXEditWrapper, modRef);

    // create all watches
    ArrayList<String> watchList = myArtifactProfileManager.listWLDFWatchProfileNames();
    for (int i=0; i<watchList.size(); i++)
        myArtifactProfileManager.lookupWLDFWatchProfile(
                    watchList.get(i)).installProfile(myJMXEditWrapper, modRef);
```

```
    // create all notifications
    ArrayList<String> notificationList = myArtifactProfileManager.listWLDFNotificationProfileNames();
        for (int i=0; i<notificationList.size(); i++)
            myArtifactProfileManager.lookupWLDFNotificationProfile(
                notificationList.get(i)).installProfile(myJMXEditWrapper, modRef);


    // do it
    myJMXEditWrapper.disconnectFromAdminServer(true);
}
```

After initializing all profiles the code connects to the admin server, creates a new diagnostic profile and installs all artifact profiles into this diagnostic module.

Component Profiles

The next level of granularity are component profiles. These have been discussed in chapter 14 with WLST and an interesting base library. Therefore this section will only discuss JMX specific implementations. Please see chapter 14 for more general information.

The implementation introduced here is in fact very similar to the WLST library. The following diagram shows the general class hierarchy. Most functionality is implemented in the base class and the profile manager.   Only specific value definitions are defined in derived classes.

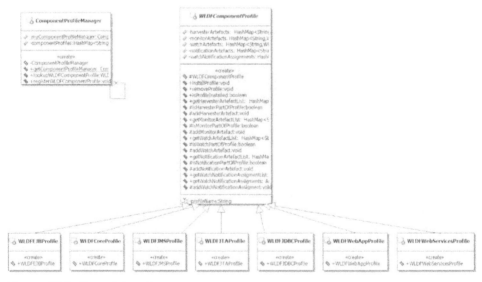

Figure 16.5: *General class diagram*

WLDFComponentProfile

This is the base class for all component profile types. It is an abstract definition which general functionality like installation of this profile, removal of this profile, or testing the profile.

The interesting aspect of this implementation is that all profile types are defined out of lower granularity profiles. As you can see in the implementation this base class maintains different lists of artifact profiles.

```
public abstract class WLDFComponentProfile
{
  private String profileName = "undefined";

  // Harvester
  private HashMap<String, WLDFHarvesterMetricProfile> harvesterArtifacts = new HashMap<String,
WLDFHarvesterMetricProfile>();

  // Monitors
  private HashMap<String, WLDFDyeMonitorProfile> monitorArtifacts = new HashMap<String,
WLDFDyeMonitorProfile>();

  // Watches
  private HashMap<String, WLDFWatchProfile> watchArtifacts = new HashMap<String, WLDFWatchProfile>();

  // Notifications
  private HashMap<String, WLDFNotificationProfile> notificationArtifacts = new HashMap<String,
WLDFNotificationProfile>();

  // Assign Watches to Notifications
  private HashMap<String, ArrayList<String>> watchNotificationAssignments = new HashMap<String,
ArrayList<String>>();

  protected WLDFComponentProfile(String _profileName)
  {
    profileName = _profileName;
  }

  public String getProfileName()
  {
    return profileName;
  }
...
```

One of its methods is a general implementation in order to install a component profile. Installation means installing all parts like watches, notifications or monitors.

```
  public void installProfile(JMXWrapper _editwrapper, ObjectName myDiagnosticModule) throws
WLDFAutomationException
  {
    try {
      // install first the harvesters
      Iterator<WLDFHarvesterMetricProfile> h_it = harvesterArtifacts.values().iterator();
      while (h_it.hasNext())
        h_it.next().installProfile(_editwrapper, myDiagnosticModule);

      // then install the monitors
      Iterator<WLDFDyeMonitorProfile> m_it = monitorArtifacts.values().iterator();
      while (m_it.hasNext())
        m_it.next().installProfile(_editwrapper, myDiagnosticModule);
```

```
    // then install the watches
    Iterator<WLDFWatchProfile> w_it = watchArtifacts.values().iterator();
    while (w_it.hasNext())
      w_it.next().installProfile(_editwrapper, myDiagnosticModule);

    // then the notifications
    Iterator<WLDFNotificationProfile> n_it = notificationArtifacts.values().iterator();
    while (n_it.hasNext())
      n_it.next().installProfile(_editwrapper, myDiagnosticModule);

    // then do the assignments
    WatchNotificationUtils myWatchNotificationUtils = new WatchNotificationUtils(_editwrapper);
    Iterator<String> a_it = watchNotificationAssignments.keySet().iterator();
    while (a_it.hasNext())
    {
      String nextWatch = a_it.next();
      ArrayList<String> assignedNotifications = watchNotificationAssignments.get(nextWatch);

      ObjectName[] notifications = new ObjectName[assignedNotifications.size()];

      for (int i=0;i<assignedNotifications.size();i++)
        notifications[i] = myWatchNotificationUtils.getNotification(
                      myDiagnosticModule, assignedNotifications.get(i));

      // update watch
      myWatchNotificationUtils.updateWatchNotifications(myDiagnosticModule, nextWatch,
                                            notifications);
    }
  }
  catch(Exception ex)
  {
    ex.printStackTrace();
  }
}
```

Another typical action is the removal of a profile. Note that even if multiple
component profiles are installed into the same diagnostic module it is possible to
remove only a specific profile as this class has the knowledge what belongs to this
profile.

```
public void removeProfile(JMXWrapper _editwrapper, ObjectName myDiagnosticModule)
          throws WLDFAutomationException
{
  try {
    // remove first the harvesters
    Iterator<WLDFHarvesterMetricProfile> h_it = harvesterArtifacts.values().iterator();
    while (h_it.hasNext())
      h_it.next().removeProfile(_editwrapper, myDiagnosticModule);

    // then remove the monitors
    Iterator<WLDFDyeMonitorProfile> m_it = monitorArtifacts.values().iterator();
    while (m_it.hasNext())
      m_it.next().removeProfile(_editwrapper, myDiagnosticModule);

    // then remove the watches
    Iterator<WLDFWatchProfile> w_it = watchArtifacts.values().iterator();
    while (w_it.hasNext())
      w_it.next().removeProfile(_editwrapper, myDiagnosticModule);

    // then remove the notifications
    Iterator<WLDFNotificationProfile> n_it = notificationArtifacts.values().iterator();
    while (n_it.hasNext())
      n_it.next().removeProfile(_editwrapper, myDiagnosticModule);
  }
  catch(Exception ex)
  {
    ex.printStackTrace();
  }
}
```

The next method does implement a simple check if the profile is installed. As this implementation is a stacked implementation and component profiles are defined out of artifact profiles, this method simply asks every artifact profile to check if it is installed. Only if all are of the components are installed, this method returns "true".

```java
public boolean isProfileInstalled(JMXWrapper _editwrapper, ObjectName myDiagnosticModule)
             throws WLDFAutomationException
{
  try {
    boolean result = true;     // well we hope so ;-)

    // install first the harvesters
    Iterator<WLDFHarvesterMetricProfile> h_it = harvesterArtifacts.values().iterator();
    while (h_it.hasNext())
      if (! h_it.next().isProfileInstalled(_editwrapper, myDiagnosticModule))
        result = false;  // something is already missing

    // then install the monitors
    Iterator<WLDFDyeMonitorProfile> m_it = monitorArtifacts.values().iterator();
    while (m_it.hasNext())
      if (! m_it.next().isProfileInstalled(_editwrapper, myDiagnosticModule))
        result = false;  // something is already missing

    // then install the watches
    Iterator<WLDFWatchProfile> w_it = watchArtifacts.values().iterator();
    while (w_it.hasNext())
      if (! w_it.next().isProfileInstalled(_editwrapper, myDiagnosticModule))
        result = false;  // something is already missing

    // then the notifications
    Iterator<WLDFNotificationProfile> n_it = notificationArtifacts.values().iterator();
    while (n_it.hasNext())
      if (! n_it.next().isProfileInstalled(_editwrapper, myDiagnosticModule))
        result = false;  // something is already missing

    return result;
  }
  catch(Exception ex)
  {
    ex.printStackTrace();
    throw new WLDFAutomationException(ex.getMessage());
  }
}
```

Beside these methods the base class has a number of other methods for adding, removing and testing different types of artifacts. These are omitted here due to size limitations.

WLDFCoreProfile

The following code shows as an example the core profile. It has similar functionality to the core profiles defined in WLST. The difference is that this profile is constructed out of artifact profiles.

```java
public class WLDFCoreProfile extends WLDFComponentProfile
{
  /**
   * Constructor: This constructor will define all the attributes and the watch definitions.
   * The value containers are defined in the base class
   */
  public WLDFCoreProfile(String profileName)  {
    super(profileName);
    try {
      ArtifactProfileManager apm = ArtifactProfileManager.getArtifactProfileManager();
```

```
    // add harvester artifacts

addHarvesterArtifact(apm.lookupWLDFHarvesterMetricProfile(ConstArtifactNames.workManagerType));

addHarvesterArtifact(apm.lookupWLDFHarvesterMetricProfile(ConstArtifactNames.srtType));
addHarvesterArtifact(apm.lookupWLDFHarvesterMetricProfile(ConstArtifactNames.clusterType));
addHarvesterArtifact(apm.lookupWLDFHarvesterMetricProfile(ConstArtifactNames.threadPoolType));
addHarvesterArtifact(apm.lookupWLDFHarvesterMetricProfile(ConstArtifactNames.jvmType));
addHarvesterArtifact(apm.lookupWLDFHarvesterMetricProfile(ConstArtifactNames.jrockitType));

    // add watches artifacts
addWatchArtifact(apm.lookupWLDFWatchProfile(ConstArtifactNames.stuckThreadWatch));
addWatchArtifact(apm.lookupWLDFWatchProfile(ConstArtifactNames.serverHealthStateWatch));
addWatchArtifact(apm.lookupWLDFWatchProfile(ConstArtifactNames.clusterServerWatch));
addWatchArtifact(apm.lookupWLDFWatchProfile(ConstArtifactNames.heapWatch));
addWatchArtifact(apm.lookupWLDFWatchProfile(ConstArtifactNames.jRockitHeapWatch));
addWatchArtifact(apm.lookupWLDFWatchProfile(ConstArtifactNames.jRockitCPUWatch));
addWatchArtifact(apm.lookupWLDFWatchProfile(ConstArtifactNames.serverLogWatch));
addWatchArtifact(apm.lookupWLDFWatchProfile(ConstArtifactNames.serverLifeCycleWatch));
addWatchArtifact(apm.lookupWLDFWatchProfile(ConstArtifactNames.clusterHealthWatch));

    // add notification artifacts
addNotificationArtifact(apm.lookupWLDFNotificationProfile(
        ConstArtifactNames.JMX_Core_Notification));
addNotificationArtifact(apm.lookupWLDFNotificationProfile(
        ConstArtifactNames.Image_Core_Notification));

    // assign notifications to watches
addWatchNotificationAssigment(ConstArtifactNames.stuckThreadWatch,
    new ArrayList<String>(Arrays.asList(new String[]
    {ConstArtifactNames.JMX_Core_Notification,
    ConstArtifactNames.Image_Core_Notification})) );
addWatchNotificationAssigment(ConstArtifactNames.serverHealthStateWatch,
    new ArrayList<String>(Arrays.asList(new String[]
    {ConstArtifactNames.JMX_Core_Notification})) );
addWatchNotificationAssigment(ConstArtifactNames.clusterServerWatch,
    new ArrayList<String>(Arrays.asList(new String[]
    {ConstArtifactNames.JMX_Core_Notification})) );
addWatchNotificationAssigment(ConstArtifactNames.heapWatch,
    new ArrayList<String>(Arrays.asList(new String[]
    {ConstArtifactNames.JMX_Core_Notification})) );
addWatchNotificationAssigment(ConstArtifactNames.jRockitHeapWatch,
    new ArrayList<String>(Arrays.asList(new String[]
    {ConstArtifactNames.JMX_Core_Notification})) );
addWatchNotificationAssigment(ConstArtifactNames.jRockitCPUWatch,
    new ArrayList<String>(Arrays.asList(new String[]
    {ConstArtifactNames.JMX_Core_Notification})) );
addWatchNotificationAssigment(ConstArtifactNames.serverLogWatch,
    new ArrayList<String>(Arrays.asList(new String[]
    {ConstArtifactNames.JMX_Core_Notification})) );
addWatchNotificationAssigment(ConstArtifactNames.serverLifeCycleWatch,
    new ArrayList<String>(Arrays.asList(new String[]
    {ConstArtifactNames.JMX_Core_Notification})) );
addWatchNotificationAssigment(ConstArtifactNames.clusterHealthWatch,
    new ArrayList<String>(Arrays.asList(new String[]
    {ConstArtifactNames.JMX_Core_Notification})) );
    }
    catch(Exception ex) {
        ex.printStackTrace();
    }
  }
 }
}
```

All other profiles like JTA, JDBC, and JMS are constructed in exactly the same way. Only the combination of artifact profiles is different. Therefore the others are omitted from the chapter. Please consult the code base for more details.

Profile Manager

The profile manager is a useful class which simplifies the handling of component profiles. It is a single point of contact to register and lookup component profiles.

```
public class ComponentProfileManager
{
    // singleton
    private static ComponentProfileManager myComponentProfileManager = null;

    // all component profiles
    private HashMap<String, WLDFComponentProfile> componentProfiles =
            new HashMap<String, WLDFComponentProfile>();


    // singleton constructor
    private ComponentProfileManager() {}

    // get the singelton implementation
    public static ComponentProfileManager getComponentProfileManager()
    {
            if (myComponentProfileManager == null)
            {
                    myComponentProfileManager = new ComponentProfileManager();
            }

            return myComponentProfileManager;
    }

    // search for a specific profile
    public WLDFComponentProfile lookupWLDFComponentProfile(String name)
    {
            return componentProfiles.get(name);
    }

    // register a new profile
    public void registerWLDFComponentProfile(WLDFComponentProfile newProfile)
    {
            componentProfiles.put(newProfile.getProfileName(), newProfile);
    }

    // list all available profiles
    public ArrayList<String> listComponentProfileNames()
    {
            ArrayList<String> result = new ArrayList<String>();
            result.addAll(componentProfiles.keySet());
            return result;
    }
}
```

Examples

This library is designed for ease of use and ease of extension as the main design factors. The following three examples provide an impression how to use this library.

Init profiles

The first example shows how to initialize the component profile library. After creating an instance of the profile manager, it is required to instantiate and add all concrete profiles. As already discussed every profile will create all required artifact instances.

```
// init the default profiles
```

```
ComponentProfileManager myMgr = ComponentProfileManager.getComponentProfileManager();

// add the profiles
myMgr.registerWLDFComponentProfile(new WLDFCoreProfile(ConstComponentNames.CoreComponentProfile));
myMgr.registerWLDFComponentProfile(new WLDFEJBProfile(ConstComponentNames.EJBComponentProfile));
myMgr.registerWLDFComponentProfile(new WLDFJDBCProfile(ConstComponentNames.JDBCComponentProfile));
myMgr.registerWLDFComponentProfile(new WLDFJMSProfile(ConstComponentNames.JMSComponentProfile));
myMgr.registerWLDFComponentProfile(new WLDFJTAProfile(ConstComponentNames.JTAComponentProfile));
myMgr.registerWLDFComponentProfile(new WLDFWebAppProfile(ConstComponentNames.WebAppCompProfile));
```

Create a module with only one profile

Assuming that all initializations have been done, the following example will create a diagnostic module. After that this code will install only the core profile into the module.

```
// create a module
DiagnosticModuleUtils myDiagnosticModuleUtils = new DiagnosticModuleUtils(myJMXEditWrapper);

ObjectName modRef = myDiagnosticModuleUtils.createNewDiagnosticModule("TestModule",
            "This is a test module to test the profile implementation");
myDiagnosticModuleUtils.targetDiagnosticModuleToAllServers(modRef);

ComponentProfileManager myMgr = ComponentProfileManager.getComponentProfileManager();

// create only core
myMgr.lookupWLDFComponentProfile(ConstComponentNames.CoreComponentProfileName).
            installProfile(myJMXEditWrapper, modRef);
```

Create a module with only all profiles

Assuming that all initializations have been done, the following example will create a diagnostic module. After that this code will install all available profiles into this module.

```
// create a module
DiagnosticModuleUtils myDiagnosticModuleUtils = new DiagnosticModuleUtils(myJMXEditWrapper);

ObjectName modRef = myDiagnosticModuleUtils.createNewDiagnosticModule("TestModule",
            "This is a test module to test the profile implementation");
myDiagnosticModuleUtils.targetDiagnosticModuleToAllServers(modRef);

ComponentProfileManager myMgr = ComponentProfileManager.getComponentProfileManager();

// create all profiles
ArrayList<String> compNames = myMgr.listComponentProfileNames();
for (int i=0; i<compNames.size(); i++)
    myMgr.lookupWLDFComponentProfile(compNames.get(i)).installProfile(myJMXEditWrapper, modRef);
```

Diagnostic module Profiles

The last level of granularity are diagnostic profiles. These have been discussed in chapter 15 with WLST.

The implementation introduced here is different from the WLST discussion. In the WLST chapter we discussed black-box profiles which means that all was just defined in these profiles. The implementation discussed in this section is different as it reuses the code and functionality discussed above. Diagnostic profiles discussed in this section are constructed out of component profiles which themselves are constructed out of artifact profiles. This allows for the best possible reuse and avoids duplication of definitions.

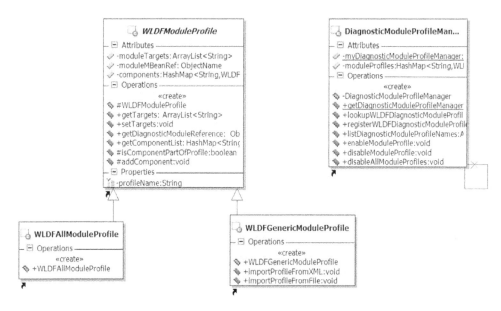

Figure 16.6: *Class diagram of diagnostic profiles*

This class diagram is rather small as it is expected that additional classes are added for new applications or usage scenarios.

WLDFModuleProfile base class

Likewise the other profile types all profiles will be derived from a base class which contains all common functionality. The following code snippet of this class shows that this profile type essentially consists of a number of component profiles. One specialty though is that this base class also contains some more information like targets. This is needed as a profile of this type describes a complete diagnostic module.

```
public abstract class WLDFModuleProfile
{
    private String profileName = "undefined";

    private ArrayList<String> moduleTargets = new ArrayList<String>();

    private ObjectName  moduleMBeanRef = null;

    // components
    private HashMap<String, WLDFComponentProfile> components =
```

```
                new HashMap<String, WLDFComponentProfile>();

    protected WLDFModuleProfile(String _profileName)
    {
            profileName = _profileName;
    }

    public String getProfileName()
    {
            return profileName;
    }

    public ArrayList<String> getTargets()
    {
            return moduleTargets;
    }
...
```

DiagnosticProfileManager

The profile manager implements a simple collection of profiles for easier maintenance of larger number of profiles. It also offers method to enable or disable a module.

Examples and Extensions

As this profile type represents a complete diagnostic module there are many different examples possible. Like generic modules for e.g. monitoring a WebLogic subsystem like JDBC or application specific modules which together with injection can also monitor application specific details.

An interesting implementation would also be a generic type which reads its details out of a configuration file.

Using Profiles in Real Life

After talking so much about the different profile types and technologies a valid question arises: How can this be useful in real production systems?

Real administrator life is almost always a constant reacting to issues which no time to do proper development of solutions. Nevertheless if WLDF is used intensively for many different problems and situations a carefully designed profile library will allow administrators to react much faster to real life issues. Over time the library will grow with more and more solutions. As administrators usually prefer scripting WLST is definitely the technology of choice for administrators.

In complex enterprise systems there exists many different software solutions, including monitoring, troubleshooting and management solutions. These solutions must think about generic implementation in order to be able to cope with as many different situations as possible. For these software solutions JMX/Java as discussed in this chapter is the better alternative as it allows a much more structured way and allows the developers to stay with Java.

Summary

This chapter has discussed the handling of WLDF using the Java JMX API. There are a number of occasions where JMX is a better alternative than WLST. In almost all cases this has to do with some kind of embedded code into other applications.

As the reader has seen, all WLDF functionality and also all the different notions of profiles which we have seen in WLST can also be used with Java JMX.

It is the decision of the individual user which language (WLST or JMS) he prefers to deal with WLDF. Project experience has shown that for all use cases which do not have to embed WLDF code in other application WLST is the better choice but for embedded code JMX is the clear winner.

Part V

Using and Visualizing WLDF Data

The fifth part of the book discusses possible ways to access, use, and visualize data collected by WLDF.

Getting access to diagnostic data

Data Accessor

So far all previous chapters have discussed different ways to capture data or getting notified when specific conditions have occurred. After such a condition or error situation has occurred it is now essential to get access to the recorded data in order to do the analysis for the issue. WLDF defines the "data accessor" API for exactly this purpose. Let's take a closer look.

Introduction

Data recorded by other WLDF components (especially the different harvester components) will be kept in the data archives. Depending on the WebLogic version, the WLDF configuration and other factors different archives are available which contain different categories of information like harvester data and log data.

The API defined in WLDF allows the user to access the data from the different data stores. If the server is running, then access is possible by using the Administration Console, JMX, or WLST.

In order to better understand the data accessor component it is important to understand how WLDF keeps the diagnostic data. WLDF by itself is not using network communication, therefore all the data recorded in a WebLogic server (admin or managed-server) is kept on this server in the data archives. The data Accessor therefore has to work on the basis of individual servers and has to provide access capabilities on a per server basis. Each server may maintain several data stores.

Which data stores are available?

Data recorded by WLDF is stored in different logical data stores. The distribution is based on the type of the data. Examples for the different types include harvested data, server logs, http access logs and others.

The content of these stores is similar to tabular data. Similar to a table each row corresponds to one entry in the store and the headlines of each column describe the content.

The following list includes the different types of data stores which can be maintained on a WebLogic server:

- HTTP_LOG
- HARVESTED_DATA_ARCHIVE
- EVENTS_DATA_ARCHIVE
- SERVER_LOG
- DOMAIN_LOG
- HTTP_ACCESS_LOG
- WEBAPP_LOG
- CONNECTOR_LOG
- JMS_MESSAGE_LOG
- CUSTOM_LOG

Because not every WebLogic instance will always provide all kinds of stores, every automation should check if the desired data store is available on any particular WebLogic server.

WebLogic offers a special MBean for this purpose which is called WLDFAccessRuntimeMBean. This MBean can be used to get a list of available data stores, find out about the data and of course retrieve data from these data stores. This can be done using WLST and JMX.

```
com.bea:Name=Accessor,ServerRuntime=AdminServer,Type=WLDFAccessRuntime,WLDFRuntime=WLDFRuntime
        Attribute: AvailableDiagnosticDataAccessorNames   of Type : [Ljava.lang.String;
        Attribute: DataAccessRuntimes   of Type : [Ljavax.management.ObjectName;
        Attribute: Name   of Type : java.lang.String
        Attribute: Parent   of Type : javax.management.ObjectName
        Attribute: Type   of Type : java.lang.String
        Attribute: WLDFDataAccessRuntimes   of Type : [Ljavax.management.ObjectName;
        Operation: java.lang.Void  preDeregister()
        Operation: javax.management.ObjectName  lookupWLDFDataAccessRuntime(.String: String  )
        Operation: javax.management.ObjectName  lookupDataAccessRuntime(String: String  )
```

This MBean offers one interesting attribute called "WLDFDataAccessRuntimes" which returns the logical names of all available data stores and a lookup method called "lookupWLDFDataAccessRuntime" to get the store specific MBean instance based on a given data store name.

The following example shows how to discover the available data stores using WLST:

```
connect('weblogic','<pw>','t3://<host>:<port>')
serverRuntime()
cd ('/WLDFRuntime/WLDFRuntime/WLDFAccessRuntime/Accessor')
```

```
availNames = cmo.getAvailableDiagnosticDataAccessorNames()

print 'Availables Names\n----------------------------'
for name in availNames:
    print '   ' + name
```

The same functionality is also available in JMX. The next example shows how to use this API in JMX:

```
public void getAllAccessorNames(JMXWrapperRemote myJMXRuntimeWrapper) throws Exception
{
    // get WLDF Runtime from the server runtime
    ObjectName myWLDFRuntime = (ObjectName)myJMXRuntimeWrapper.getAttribute(
            myJMXRuntimeWrapper.getMyOwnServerRuntime(), "WLDFRuntime");

    // now from the WLDF runtime we need to get the accessor runtime
    ObjectName myWLDFAccessRuntime = (ObjectName)
            myJMXRuntimeWrapper.getAttribute(myWLDFRuntime, "WLDFAccessRuntime");

    // finally from the accessor runtime we can query all available accessor names
    String[] myAccessorNames = (String[]) myJMXRuntimeWrapper.
            getAttribute(myWLDFAccessRuntime, "AvailableDiagnosticDataAccessorNames");

    // and print them
    System.out.println("Available data Accessors :\n=========================");

    for (int i=0;i<myAccessorNames.length;i++)
        System.out.println("   "+ myAccessorNames[i]);
}
```

The above script (as same as the Java program) will produce an output similar to the following:

```
Available data Accessors :
=================================================
    HarvestedDataArchive
    HTTPAccessLog
    DataSourceLog
    DomainLog
    ServerLog
    EventsDataArchive
```

Get Information about data store content

For each data store WebLogic offers another MBean called WLDFDataAccessRuntimeMBean, which can be used to get information about the concrete data store.

```
com.bea:Name=HarvestedDataArchive,ServerRuntime=AdminServer,Type=WLDFDataAccessRuntime,WLDFAccessRunt
ime=Accessor,WLDFRuntime=WLDFRuntime
        Attribute: ColumnIndexMap   of Type : java.util.Map
        Attribute: ColumnInfoMap    of Type : java.util.Map
        Attribute: ColumnTypeMap    of Type : java.util.Map
        Attribute: Columns   of Type : [Lweblogic.diagnostics.accessor.ColumnInfo;
        Attribute: DataArchiveParameters   of Type : java.util.Map
        Attribute: EarliestAvailableTimestamp   of Type : java.lang.Long
        Attribute: LatestAvailableTimestamp   of Type : java.lang.Long
        Attribute: LatestRecordId   of Type : java.lang.Long
        Attribute: Name   of Type : java.lang.String
        Attribute: Parent   of Type : javax.management.ObjectName
        Attribute: TimestampAvailable   of Type : java.lang.Boolean
        Attribute: Type   of Type : java.lang.String
        Operation: java.util.Iterator   retrieveDataRecords(...)
        Operation: java.lang.String   openCursor(...)
        Operation: java.util.Iterator   retrieveDataRecords(...)
```

```
Operation: [Ljava.lang.Object;  fetch(...)
Operation: java.lang.Void  preDeregister()
Operation: java.lang.String  openCursor(...)
Operation: java.lang.Integer  getDataRecordCount(...)
Operation: [Ljava.lang.Object;  fetch(...)
Operation: java.lang.String  openCursor(...)
Operation: java.util.Iterator  retrieveDataRecords(...)
Operation: java.lang.Void  closeArchive()
Operation: java.lang.Integer  getDataRecordCount(...)
Operation: java.lang.Integer  deleteDataRecords(...)
Operation: java.lang.Void  closeCursor(...)
Operation: java.lang.Boolean  hasMoreData(...)
Operation: java.lang.Integer  getDataRecordCount(...)
Operation: java.util.Iterator  retrieveDataRecords(...)
```

As an example, it is possible to print out the layout of the data stores. This includes the different columns with their column types. It is also possible get information about available data and the time period covered in this data store.

Unfortunately WebLogic uses two WebLogic specific data structures. The first class with the name "ColumnInfo" provides information about the different columns. Information include name and data type:

```
class weblogic.diagnostics.accessor.ColumnInfo

    // get the name of the column
    public String getColumnName()
    // get the type as type code (type codes are defined in this class
    public int getColumnType()
    // get type as string
    public String getColumnTypeName()

    // type codes defined in this class
    COLTYPE_INT = 1;
    COLTYPE_LONG = 2;
    COLTYPE_FLOAT = 3;
    COLTYPE_DOUBLE = 4;
    COLTYPE_STRING = 5;
    COLTYPE_OBJECT = 6;
```

The second structure defined by WebLogic is a data structure which will be used to transport all data of one data record (or table row) from the server back to the client. All data is transported as java.lang.Object:

```
class weblogic.diagnostics.accessor.DataRecord

    // get all values as array
    public Object[] getValues();
    // get a specific element
    public Object get(int index);
    // set data
    public void setValues(Object[] data);
```

The following WLST script can be used to get data store information.

```
connect('weblogic',<pw>,'t3://<host>:<port>')
serverRuntime()
cd
('/WLDFRuntime/WLDFRuntime/WLDFAccessRuntime/Accessor/WLDFDataAccessRuntimes/HarvestedDataArchive')
ls()
```

Note that this script does not use nice printing, it will just issue an "ls()" to list the MBean content. This script is also a very basic test, as it only looks at one specific data store. More sophisticated scripts will loop over all available types and print all data stores.

The result from a script run will display the MBean information like this:

```
Your environment has been set.

Initializing WebLogic Scripting Tool (WLST) ...

Welcome to WebLogic Server Administration Scripting Shell


-r--   ColumnIndexMap                          {NAME=5, RECORDID=0, ATTRNAME=6, ATTRVALUE=8,
TIMESTAMP=1, DOMAIN=2, ATTRTYPE=7, SERVER=3, TYPE=4, WLDFMODULE=9}
-r--   ColumnInfoMap                           {NAME=ColumnInfo{NAME,5},
RECORDID=ColumnInfo{RECORDID,2}, ATTRNAME=ColumnInfo{ATTRNAME,5}, ATTRVALUE=ColumnInfo{ATTRVALUE,6},
TIMESTAMP=ColumnInfo{TIMESTAMP,2}, DOMAIN=ColumnInfo{DOMAIN,5}, ATTRTYPE=ColumnInfo{ATTRTYPE,1},
SERVER=ColumnInfo{SERVER,5}, TYPE=ColumnInfo{TYPE,5}, WLDFMODULE=ColumnInfo{WLDFMODULE,5}}
-r--   ColumnTypeMap                           {NAME=java.lang.String, RECORDID=java.lang.Long,
ATTRNAME=java.lang.String, ATTRVALUE=java.lang.Object, TIMESTAMP=java.lang.Long,
DOMAIN=java.lang.String, ATTRTYPE=java.lang.Integer, SERVER=java.lang.String, TYPE=java.lang.String,
WLDFMODULE=java.lang.String}
-r--   Columns
weblogic.diagnostics.accessor.ColumnInfo[ColumnInfo{RECORDID,2}, ColumnInfo{TIMESTAMP,2},
ColumnInfo{DOMAIN,5}, ColumnInfo{SERVER,5}, ColumnInfo{TYPE,5}, ColumnInfo{NAME,5},
ColumnInfo{ATTRTYPE,1}, ColumnInfo{ATTRVALUE,6}, ColumnInfo{WLDFMODULE,5}]
-rw-   DataArchiveParameters
{storeDir=/domains/martinTest/domains/martinTest_1/servers/AdminServer/data/store/diagnostics}
-r--   EarliestAvailableTimestamp                1405697595346
-r--   LatestAvailableTimestamp                  1407422211880
-r--   LatestRecordId                            3276756
-r--   Name                                      HarvestedDataArchive
-r--   TimestampAvailable                        true
-r--   Type                                      WLDFDataAccessRuntime
```

The same functionality is also available from Java using the JMX API. Using JMX to print the layout of the store:

```java
public void getAccessorDetails(JMXWrapperRemote myWrapper) throws Exception
{
    // get WLDF Runtime from the server runtime
    ObjectName myWLDFRuntime = (ObjectName)myWrapper.getAttribute(
            myWrapper.getMyOwnServerRuntime(), "WLDFRuntime");

    // now from the WLDF runtime we need to get the accessor runtime
    ObjectName myWLDFAccessRuntime = (ObjectName)
            myWrapper.getAttribute(myWLDFRuntime, "WLDFAccessRuntime");

    // finally from the accessor runtime we can query all available accessor names
    ObjectName[] myAccessors = (ObjectName[])
            myWrapper.getAttribute(myWLDFAccessRuntime, "WLDFDataAccessRuntimes");

    // and print them
    for (int i=0;i<myAccessors.length;i++)  {
        System.out.println("\n=============================================");

        System.out.println("    Name: "+ myWrapper.getAttribute(myAccessors[i], "Name"));
        System.out.println("    Type: "+ myWrapper.getAttribute(myAccessors[i], "Type"));
        System.out.println("    TimestampAvailable: "+
                myWrapper.getAttribute(myAccessors[i], "TimestampAvailable"));
        System.out.println("    EarliestAvailableTimestamp: "+
                myWrapper.getAttribute(myAccessors[i], "EarliestAvailableTimestamp"));
        System.out.println("    LatestAvailableTimestamp: "+
                myWrapper.getAttribute(myAccessors[i], "LatestAvailableTimestamp"));
        System.out.println("    LatestRecordId: "+
                myWrapper.getAttribute(myAccessors[i], "LatestRecordId"));
        System.out.println("\n");
```

```
    printMap("ColumnIndexMap",(Map) myWrapper.getAttribute(myAccessors[i], "ColumnIndexMap"));
    printMap("ColumnInfoMap",(Map) myWrapper.getAttribute(myAccessors[i], "ColumnInfoMap"));
    printMap("ColumnTypeMap",(Map) myWrapper.getAttribute(myAccessors[i], "ColumnTypeMap"));
    printMap("ArchiveParam",(Map) myWrapper.getAttribute(myAccessors[i], "DataArchiveParameters"));
  }
}
```

This program does a little bit more than the very basic WLST script. It iterates over all types and print information about all data stores.

The output will look similar to:

```
Name: HarvestedDataArchive
Type: WLDFDataAccessRuntime
TimestampAvailable: true
EarliestAvailableTimestamp: 1405697595346
LatestAvailableTimestamp: 1407406671880
LatestRecordId: 3271576


ColumnIndexMap:
    Key: NAME  => Value: 5
    Key: RECORDID  => Value: 0
    Key: ATTRNAME  => Value: 6
    Key: ATTRVALUE  => Value: 8
    Key: TIMESTAMP  => Value: 1
    Key: DOMAIN  => Value: 2
    Key: ATTRTYPE  => Value: 7
    Key: SERVER  => Value: 3
    Key: TYPE  => Value: 4
    Key: WLDFMODULE  => Value: 9
ColumnInfoMap:
    Key: NAME  => Value: ColumnInfo{NAME,5}
    Key: RECORDID  => Value: ColumnInfo{RECORDID,2}
    Key: ATTRNAME  => Value: ColumnInfo{ATTRNAME,5}
    Key: ATTRVALUE  => Value: ColumnInfo{ATTRVALUE,6}
    Key: TIMESTAMP  => Value: ColumnInfo{TIMESTAMP,2}
    Key: DOMAIN  => Value: ColumnInfo{DOMAIN,5}
    Key: ATTRTYPE  => Value: ColumnInfo{ATTRTYPE,1}
    Key: SERVER  => Value: ColumnInfo{SERVER,5}
    Key: TYPE  => Value: ColumnInfo{TYPE,5}
    Key: WLDFMODULE  => Value: ColumnInfo{WLDFMODULE,5}
ColumnTypeMap:
    Key: NAME  => Value: java.lang.String
    Key: RECORDID  => Value: java.lang.Long
    Key: ATTRNAME  => Value: java.lang.String
    Key: ATTRVALUE  => Value: java.lang.Object
    Key: TIMESTAMP  => Value: java.lang.Long
    Key: DOMAIN  => Value: java.lang.String
    Key: ATTRTYPE  => Value: java.lang.Integer
    Key: SERVER  => Value: java.lang.String
    Key: TYPE  => Value: java.lang.String
    Key: WLDFMODULE  => Value: java.lang.String
DataArchiveParameters:
    Key: storeDir => Value:
/domains/martinTest/domains/martinTest_1/servers/AdminServer/data/store/diagnostics
```

Access Diagnostic data using the accessor API

Each store specific WLDFDataAccessRuntimeMBean instance offers different methods to query data from the store. This MBean offers methods to get all selected rows as a bulk. These methods are called retrievedataRecords and the MBean offers a few methods with this name but different signature.

Especially for large queries and result sets this MBean also offers a kind of paging mechanism called "Cursor". Then the client can decide how many data rows are returned with every call (argument of the "fetch" method).

```
com.bea:Name=HarvestedDataArchive,ServerRuntime=AdminServer,Type=WLDFDataAccessRuntime,WLDFAccessRunt
ime=Accessor,WLDFRuntime=WLDFRuntime

Operation: java.util.Iterator  retrieveDataRecords(...)

Operation: [Ljava.lang.Object; fetch(...)
Operation: java.lang.String  openCursor(...)
Operation: java.lang.Integer  getDataRecordCount(...)
Operation: [Ljava.lang.Object; fetch(...)
Operation: java.lang.String  openCursor(...)
Operation: java.lang.Void  closeArchive()
Operation: java.lang.Integer  getDataRecordCount(...)
Operation: java.lang.Void  closeCursor(...)
Operation: java.lang.Boolean  hasMoreData(...)
```

 Important note: WLDF defines a query language which can be used to provide queries in order to specify the data which should be retrieved. A query string can be provided based on this query language. Note that "**NULL**" can be provided in order to get all data.

In addition to a query string the desired time period must be provided. The API requires this as value in milliseconds base on the standard JDK time notation.

The following example implements an example in JMX which will retrieve data from a data store.

```
public void getDataRecords(String storeName, JMXWrapperRemote myWrapper,
                    Long startTime, Long endTime, String query)
{
    // get WLDF Runtime from the server runtime
    ObjectName myWLDFRuntime = (ObjectName)myWrapper.getAttribute(
            myJMXRuntimeWrapper.getMyOwnServerRuntime(), "WLDFRuntime");

    // now from the WLDF runtime we need to get the accessor runtime
    ObjectName myWLDFAccessRuntime = (ObjectName)
            myWrapper.getAttribute(myWLDFRuntime, "WLDFAccessRuntime");

    // finally from the accessor runtime we can query all available accessor names
    ObjectName myAccessor = (ObjectName) myWrapper.invoke(myWLDFAccessRuntime,
        "lookupWLDFDataAccessRuntime",
        new Object[]{new String(storeName)}, new String[]{String.class.getName()});

    // now get the data from this
    ColumnInfo[] dataStoreInfo = (ColumnInfo[])myWrapper.getAttribute(myAccessor, "Columns");

    int entryCounter = 0;

    Iterator<DataRecord> myIterator = (Iterator<DataRecord>) myWrapper.invoke(myAccessor,
            "retrieveDataRecords", new Object[]{startTime, endTime, query},
            new String[]{Long.class.getName(),Long.class.getName(),String.class.getName()});

    while (myIterator.hasNext())  {
        DataRecord nextRecord = myIterator.next();
        System.out.println("\nDataStore-Entry (" + entryCounter + "): ");
        Object[] values = nextRecord.getValues();
```

```
    for (int colno=0; colno < values.length; colno++) {
        System.out.println("[" + colno + "] " + dataStoreInfo[colno].getColumnName() +
        " (" + dataStoreInfo[colno].getColumnTypeName() + "): " +
        ( ("TIMESTAMP".equalsIgnoreCase(dataStoreInfo[colno].getColumnName())) ?
        DateUtils.getLocaleTimeRepresentation((Long)values[colno])  : values[colno]));
    }
    entryCounter++;
  }
}
```

This method will get the store which is defines in the argument "storeName". Then the will look up the data content definition which is provided as array of ColumnInfo and finally retrieve that data from the saver as one bulk using the retrieveDataRecord operation. The data will then be printed enriched with information from the table metadata (ColumnInfo).

Here is an example: Call the above method using the arguments "Long(0), Long.MAX_VALUE, null" for data selection. The output looks like:

```
DataStore-Entry (0):
[0] RECORDID (java.lang.Long): 3019960
[1] TIMESTAMP (java.lang.Long): 21.07.2014 20:12:15:346
[2] DOMAIN (java.lang.String): martinTest_1
[3] SERVER (java.lang.String): AdminServer
[4] TYPE (java.lang.String): weblogic.management.runtime.WebAppComponentRuntimeMBean
[5] NAME (java.lang.String):
com.bea:ApplicationRuntime=bea_wls_deployment_internal,Name=AdminServer_/bea_wls_deployment_internal,
ServerRuntime=AdminServer,Type=WebAppComponentRuntime
[6] ATTRNAME (java.lang.String): OpenSessionsCurrentCount
[7] ATTRTYPE (java.lang.Integer): 4
[8] ATTRVALUE (java.lang.Object): 0
[9] WLDFMODULE (java.lang.String): wldf-server-low

DataStore-Entry (1):
[0] RECORDID (java.lang.Long): 3019967
[1] TIMESTAMP (java.lang.Long): 21.07.2014 20:12:15:346
[2] DOMAIN (java.lang.String): martinTest_1
[3] SERVER (java.lang.String): AdminServer
[4] TYPE (java.lang.String): weblogic.management.runtime.JVMRuntimeMBean
[5] NAME (java.lang.String): com.bea:Name=AdminServer,ServerRuntime=AdminServer,Type=JVMRuntime
[6] ATTRNAME (java.lang.String): HeapFreePercent
[7] ATTRTYPE (java.lang.Integer): 4
[8] ATTRVALUE (java.lang.Object): 36
[9] WLDFMODULE (java.lang.String): wldf-server-low

DataStore-Entry (2):
[0] RECORDID (java.lang.Long): 3019968
[1] TIMESTAMP (java.lang.Long): 21.07.2014 20:12:15:346
[2] DOMAIN (java.lang.String): martinTest_1
[3] SERVER (java.lang.String): AdminServer
[4] TYPE (java.lang.String): weblogic.management.runtime.ThreadPoolRuntimeMBean
[5] NAME (java.lang.String):
com.bea:Name=ThreadPoolRuntime,ServerRuntime=AdminServer,Type=ThreadPoolRuntime
[6] ATTRNAME (java.lang.String): HoggingThreadCount
[7] ATTRTYPE (java.lang.Integer): 4
[8] ATTRVALUE (java.lang.Object): 0
```

Note that in the example code above the timestamp was converted to a readable format, there the output shows human readable times.

Selection query can be rather complex (see Oracle documentation for complete syntax) and can be based on all fields of the recorded data.

In the following example we select only for the attribute HeapFreePercent. Therefore the method will be called with the parameters: "Long(0), Long.MAX_VALUE, **_"ATTRNAME = 'HeapFreePercent'"_**" for data selection. As you can see we are selecting the records based on the field name ATTRNAME whereas this field must be equal to 'HeapFreepercent'. Please note that with these argument we do not restrict the time period.

Then – as expected – the output will only contain records based on this field.

```
DataStore-Entry (0):
[0] RECORDID (java.lang.Long): 3019967
[1] TIMESTAMP (java.lang.Long): 21.07.2014 20:12:15:346
[2] DOMAIN (java.lang.String): martinTest_1
[3] SERVER (java.lang.String): AdminServer
[4] TYPE (java.lang.String): weblogic.management.runtime.JVMRuntimeMBean
[5] NAME (java.lang.String): com.bea:Name=AdminServer,ServerRuntime=AdminServer,Type=JVMRuntime
[6] ATTRNAME (java.lang.String): HeapFreePercent
[7] ATTRTYPE (java.lang.Integer): 4
[8] ATTRVALUE (java.lang.Object): 36
[9] WLDFMODULE (java.lang.String): wldf-server-low

DataStore-Entry (1):
[0] RECORDID (java.lang.Long): 3019987
[1] TIMESTAMP (java.lang.Long): 21.07.2014 20:13:15:346
[2] DOMAIN (java.lang.String): martinTest_1
[3] SERVER (java.lang.String): AdminServer
[4] TYPE (java.lang.String): weblogic.management.runtime.JVMRuntimeMBean
[5] NAME (java.lang.String): com.bea:Name=AdminServer,ServerRuntime=AdminServer,Type=JVMRuntime
[6] ATTRNAME (java.lang.String): HeapFreePercent
[7] ATTRTYPE (java.lang.Integer): 4
[8] ATTRVALUE (java.lang.Object): 36
[9] WLDFMODULE (java.lang.String): wldf-server-low

DataStore-Entry (2):
[0] RECORDID (java.lang.Long): 3020007
[1] TIMESTAMP (java.lang.Long): 21.07.2014 20:14:15:346
[2] DOMAIN (java.lang.String): martinTest_1
[3] SERVER (java.lang.String): AdminServer
[4] TYPE (java.lang.String): weblogic.management.runtime.JVMRuntimeMBean
[5] NAME (java.lang.String): com.bea:Name=AdminServer,ServerRuntime=AdminServer,Type=JVMRuntime
[6] ATTRNAME (java.lang.String): HeapFreePercent
[7] ATTRTYPE (java.lang.Integer): 4
[8] ATTRVALUE (java.lang.Object): 36
[9] WLDFMODULE (java.lang.String): wldf-server-low
```

As already mentioned earlier, each data store has a different set of fields, therefore also the valid query syntax varies between stores.

Of course, these data queries can also be done using WLST. The following example shows the equivalent functionality using a WLST script.

```
# connect to server
connect('<user>','<password>','t3://<host>:<port>')

# switch to the server runtime
# (if connected to the admin you need to use domainRuntime and switch to the desired server runtime)
serverRuntime()

# change to the accessor runtime
cd ('WLDFRuntime/WLDFRuntime/WLDFAccessRuntime/Accessor/WLDFDataAccessRuntimes')

# change to the desired runtime (archive specific)  - in this case the harvester data
cd ('HarvestedDataArchive')

# as an example , request all data -None means no selection
```

```
# the result is an java iterator
it = cmo.retrieveDataRecords(Long(0), Long.MAX_VALUE, None)

# use the java iterator methods to iterate over the data
while it.hasNext():
  # get the next data record
  nextRecord = it.next()
  # get the values from the data record
  values = nextRecord.getValues()
  # just print the complete data array as an example
  print values
```

The output of this script will look like the following example. Due to the simplicity of the script the output is no formatted or classified like the output from the JMX program.

```
array(java.lang.Object,[76263L, 1408740738371L, 'base_domain', 'AdminServer',
'weblogic.management.runtime.JMSDestinationRuntimeMBean',
'com.bea:JMSServerRuntime=WLDFJMSServer,Name=WLDFJMSSystemResource!WLDFMonitoringQueue,ServerRuntime=
AdminServer,Type=JMSDestinationRuntime', 'MessagesCurrentCount', 4, 0L, 'wldf-server-low'])
array(java.lang.Object,[76264L, 1408740738371L, 'base_domain', 'AdminServer',
'weblogic.management.runtime.ServerRuntimeMBean', 'com.bea:Name=AdminServer,Type=ServerRuntime',
'State', 5, 'RUNNING', 'wldf-server-low'])
array(java.lang.Object,[76265L, 1408740738371L, 'base_domain', 'AdminServer',
'weblogic.management.runtime.ServerRuntimeMBean', 'com.bea:Name=AdminServer,Type=ServerRuntime',
'OpenSocketsCurrentCount', 4, 1, 'wldf-server-low'])
array(java.lang.Object,[76266L, 1408740738371L, 'base_domain', 'AdminServer',
'weblogic.management.runtime.JTARuntimeMBean',
'com.bea:Name=JTARuntime,ServerRuntime=AdminServer,Type=JTARuntime', 'ActiveTransactionsTotalCount',
4, 0, 'wldf-server-low'])
array(java.lang.Object,[76267L, 1408740738371L, 'base_domain', 'AdminServer',
'weblogic.management.runtime.JTARuntimeMBean',
'com.bea:Name=JTARuntime,ServerRuntime=AdminServer,Type=JTARuntime', 'SecondsActiveTotalCount', 4,
0L, 'wldf-server-low'])
```

If the result set is getting too big then you need to use the other set of query methods provided by the WLDF MBeans – paging using the Cursor. In order to cursors, the MBeans define a number of methods.

Methods related to cursors:

```
closeCursor            Void : String(java.lang.String)
deleteDataRecords      Integer : Long(long),Long(long),String(java.lang.String)
fetch                  Object[] : String(java.lang.String)
fetch                  Object[] : String(java.lang.String),Integer(int)
getDataRecordCount     Integer : Long(long),Long(long),Long(long),String(java.lang.String)
getDataRecordCount     Integer : Long(long),Long(long),String(java.lang.String)
getDataRecordCount     Integer : String(java.lang.String)
hasMoreData            Boolean : String(java.lang.String)
openCursor             String : Long(long),Long(long),Long(long),String(java.lang.String)
openCursor             String : Long(long),Long(long),Long(long),String(String),Long(long)
openCursor             String : Long(long),Long(long),String(java.lang.String)
openCursor             String : Long(long),Long(long),String(java.lang.String),Long(long)
openCursor             String : String(java.lang.String)
openCursor             String : String(java.lang.String),Long(long)
```

Cursors implement a kind of paging mechanism. First of all it is necessary to open a cursor for a given query ("openCursor") and then you can retrieve data ("fetch") if more data is available ("hasMoreData").

Example to get the first 10 data rows:

```
# connect to server
```

```
connect('<user>','<password>','t3://<host>:<port>')

# switch to the server runtime
# (if connected to the admin you need to use domainRuntime and switch to the desired server runtime)
serverRuntime()

# change to the accessor runtime
cd ('WLDFRuntime/WLDFRuntime/WLDFAccessRuntime/Accessor/WLDFDataAccessRuntimes')

# change to the desired runtime (archive specific)  - in this case the harvester data
cd ('HarvestedDataArchive')

# open the cursor and save it into "myCursor"
myCursor = cmo.openCursor(Long(0), Long.MAX_VALUE, None)
print str(cmo.hasMoreData(myCursor))

# print the first 10 data rows
print cmo.fetch(myCursor,10)
```

The result from this script will look like this:

```
1
array(java.lang.Object,[array(java.lang.Object,[1L, 1403259636077L, 'base_domain', 'AdminServer',
'weblogic.management.runtime.WebAppComponentRuntimeMBean',
'com.bea:ApplicationRuntime=bea_wls_diagnostics,Name=AdminServer_/bea_wls_diagnostics,ServerRuntime=A
dminServer,Type=WebAppComponentRuntime', 'OpenSessionsCurrentCount', 4, 0, 'wldf-server-low']) ,
array(java.lang.Object,[2L, 1403259636077L, 'base_domain', 'AdminServer',
'weblogic.management.runtime.WebAppComponentRuntimeMBean',
'com.bea:ApplicationRuntime=bea_wls_management_internal2,Name=AdminServer_/bea_wls_management_interna
l2,ServerRuntime=AdminServer,Type=WebAppComponentRuntime', 'OpenSessionsCurrentCount', 4, 0, 'wldf-
server-low']) , array(java.lang.Object,[3L, 1403259636077L, 'base_domain', 'AdminServer',
'weblogic.management.runtime.WebAppComponentRuntimeMBean', 'com.bea:ApplicationRuntime=wls-
wsat,Name=AdminServer_/wls-wsat,ServerRuntime=AdminServer,Type=WebAppComponentRuntime',
'OpenSessionsCurrentCount', 4, 0, 'wldf-server-low']) , array(java.lang.Object,[4L, 1403259636077L,
'base_domain', 'AdminServer', 'weblogic.management.runtime.WebAppComponentRuntimeMBean',
'com.bea:ApplicationRuntime=bea_wls_deployment_internal,Name=AdminServer_/bea_wls_deployment_internal
,ServerRuntime=AdminServer,Type=WebAppComponentRuntime', 'OpenSessionsCurrentCount', 4, 0, 'wldf-
server-low']) , array(java.lang.Object,[5L, 1403259636077L, 'base_domain', 'AdminServer',
'weblogic.management.runtime.WebAppComponentRuntimeMBean',
'com.bea:ApplicationRuntime=consoleapp,Name=AdminServer_/consolehelp,ServerRuntime=AdminServer,Type=W
ebAppComponentRuntime', 'OpenSessionsCurrentCount', 4, 0, 'wldf-server-low']) ,
array(java.lang.Object,[6L, 1403259636077L, 'base_domain', 'AdminServer',
'weblogic.management.runtime.WebAppComponentRuntimeMBean',
'com.bea:ApplicationRuntime=bea_wls_internal,Name=AdminServer_/bea_wls_internal,ServerRuntime=AdminSe
rver,Type=WebAppComponentRuntime', 'OpenSessionsCurrentCount', 4, 0, 'wldf-server-low']) ,
array(java.lang.Object,[7L, 1403259636077L, 'base_domain', 'AdminServer',
'weblogic.management.runtime.WebAppComponentRuntimeMBean',
'com.bea:ApplicationRuntime=consoleapp,Name=AdminServer_/console,ServerRuntime=AdminServer,Type=WebAp
pComponentRuntime', 'OpenSessionsCurrentCount', 4, 1, 'wldf-server-low']) ,
array(java.lang.Object,[8L, 1403259636077L, 'base_domain', 'AdminServer',
'weblogic.management.runtime.WebAppComponentRuntimeMBean',
'com.bea:ApplicationRuntime=bea_wls9_async_response,Name=AdminServer_/_async,ServerRuntime=AdminServe
r,Type=WebAppComponentRuntime', 'OpenSessionsCurrentCount', 4, 0, 'wldf-server-low']) ,
array(java.lang.Object,[9L, 1403259636077L, 'base_domain', 'AdminServer',
'weblogic.management.runtime.LogBroadcasterRuntimeMBean',
'com.bea:Name=TheLogBroadcaster,ServerRuntime=AdminServer,Type=LogBroadcasterRuntime',
'MessagesLogged', 4, 0L, 'wldf-server-low']) , array(java.lang.Object,[10L, 1403259636077L,
'base_domain', 'AdminServer', 'weblogic.management.runtime.JVMRuntimeMBean',
'com.bea:Name=AdminServer,ServerRuntime=AdminServer,Type=JVMRuntime', 'HeapFreePercent', 4, 55,
'wldf-server-low']) ])
```

The real power of the cursors become visible as soon as you want to load a large result set in small pieces. The following WLST script will load the complete result set in chunks of 10 datarows each.

```
# connect to server
connect('<user>','<password>','t3://<host>:<port>')

# switch to the server runtime
# (if connected to the admin you need to use domainRuntime and switch to the desired server runtime)
serverRuntime()
```

```
# change to the accessor runtime
cd ('WLDFRuntime/WLDFRuntime/WLDFAccessRuntime/Accessor/WLDFDataAccessRuntimes')

# change to the desired runtime (archive specific)  - in this case the harvester data
cd ('HarvestedDataArchive')

# open the cursor
myCursor = cmo.openCursor(Long(0), Long.MAX_VALUE, None)

# while more data is available, read the next 10 rows and print them
while cmo.hasMoreData(myCursor):
    print cmo.fetch(myCursor,10)
    print ""
    print ""
```

Offline Access using WLST

WLST provides a special operation called "exportDiagnosticData". This operation allows the user to extract diagnostic data in offline mode. Node that this method can only be used if the server is not running. If the server is running the archive is locked and calling this method will result in a WLST error.

Another important aspect is that you do not have access to the MBeans of WebLogic, therefore you cannot query configuration or runtime information like for example the available data store instances.

This function takes a number of input arguments like filename, store directory, begin and end-time and of course a selection query. Use "help('exportDiagnosticData')" in the WLST interactive mode to get more information. The default harvester data archive name is WLS_DIAGNOSTICS000000.DAT.

Example for querying all data from a server log file (note that this must run on the machine where the server is usually running and when calling this operation the server must be down):

```
exportDiagnosticData(logicalName='HarvestedDataArchive',
logName='/opt/tests/domains/martinTest_1/servers/AdminServer/data/store/diag
nostics/WLS_DIAGNOSTICS000000.DAT', logRotationDir='.',
storeDir='/opt/tests/domains/martinTest_1/servers/AdminServer/data/store/dia
gnostics', query='', exportFileName='myExport.xml', elfFields='',
beginTimestamp=0L, endTimestamp=9223372036854775807L)
```

Note that this is running in offline mode, therefore no "connect" to the server is required. This call needs concrete file and directory names as this call directly operates on the local file system.

So why exporting data from the local file-system to another file on the local file-system? Well the difference is that the original files are either in binary format just contain all details even if you are only interested in a fraction of this data. This function not only converts data, it filters the data and converts it into an Oracle defined XML format. This allows other tools like XLST based tools to work with exactly the data you are interested in.

Here is an example: The exportDiagnosticData function operated on the harvester data will result into the following XML file:

```
<?xml version='1.0' encoding='utf-8'?>
<DiagnosticData xmlns:xsi="http://www.w3.org/2001/XMLSchema-instance"
xsi:schemaLocation="http://www.bea.com/ns/weblogic/90/diagnostics/accessor/export.xsd export.xsd"
xmlns="http://www.bea.com/ns/weblogic/90/diagnostics/accessor/Export">
  <DataInfo>
    <ColumnInfo><Name>RECORDID</Name><Type>java.lang.Long</Type></ColumnInfo>
    <ColumnInfo><Name>TIMESTAMP</Name><Type>java.lang.Long</Type></ColumnInfo>
    <ColumnInfo><Name>DOMAIN</Name><Type>java.lang.String</Type></ColumnInfo>
    <ColumnInfo><Name>SERVER</Name><Type>java.lang.String</Type></ColumnInfo>
    <ColumnInfo><Name>TYPE</Name><Type>java.lang.String</Type></ColumnInfo>
    <ColumnInfo><Name>NAME</Name><Type>java.lang.String</Type></ColumnInfo>
    <ColumnInfo><Name>ATTRNAME</Name><Type>java.lang.String</Type></ColumnInfo>
    <ColumnInfo><Name>ATTRTYPE</Name><Type>java.lang.Integer</Type></ColumnInfo>
    <ColumnInfo><Name>ATTRVALUE</Name><Type>java.lang.Object</Type></ColumnInfo>
    <ColumnInfo><Name>WLDFMODULE</Name><Type>java.lang.String</Type></ColumnInfo>
  </DataInfo>

<DataRecord><ColumnData>3507160</ColumnData><ColumnData>1408113471880</ColumnData><ColumnData>martinT
est_1</ColumnData><ColumnData>AdminServer</ColumnData><ColumnData>weblogic.management.runtime.WebAppC
omponentRuntimeMBean</ColumnData><ColumnData>com.bea:ApplicationRuntime=bea_wls_deployment_internal,N
ame=AdminServer_/bea_wls_deployment_internal,ServerRuntime=AdminServer,Type=WebAppComponentRuntime</C
olumnData><ColumnData>OpenSessionsCurrentCount</ColumnData><ColumnData>4</ColumnData><ColumnData>0</C
olumnData><ColumnData>wldf-server-low</ColumnData></DataRecord>

<DataRecord><ColumnData>3507161</ColumnData><ColumnData>1408113471880</ColumnData><ColumnData>martinT
est_1</ColumnData><ColumnData>AdminServer</ColumnData><ColumnData>weblogic.management.runtime.WebAppC
omponentRuntimeMBean</ColumnData><ColumnData>com.bea:ApplicationRuntime=consoleapp,Name=AdminServer_/
consolehelp,ServerRuntime=AdminServer,Type=WebAppComponentRuntime</ColumnData><ColumnData>OpenSession
sCurrentCount</ColumnData><ColumnData>4</ColumnData><ColumnData>0</ColumnData><ColumnData>wldf-
server-low</ColumnData></DataRecord>
...
```

Online Access using WLST

WLST also provides a special operation in order to query diagnostic data online (local or remote) from running WebLogic servers. This operation is called "exportDiagnosticDataFromServer". This operation allows the user to extract diagnostic data in online mode. Note that this method can only be used if the server is running. Another important aspect is that in online mode you also have access to the MBeans of WebLogic, therefore you can query configuration or runtime information like the available data store instances.

This operation is using one of the internal WebLogic applications which is deployed by default. Its name is "bea_wls_diagnostics". If the domain is running in "production" mode, WebLogic - due to security restrictions - only allows downloading diagnostic data over a secure connection. This means that the "connect" method must use a secure connection like t3s to connect to the server.

If an insecure connection is used, this operation results in an error. See the following WLST example:

```
connect('<user>','password','t3://localhost:port')
exportDiagnosticDataFromServer(logicalName="HarvestedDataArchive", exportFileName="myExport.xml")
```

This results in the following WLST error:

```
Connecting to http://localhost:port with userid weblogic ...
Traceback (innermost last):
  File "<console>", line 1, in ?
  File "<iostream>", line 1847, in exportDiagnosticDataFromServer
        at
weblogic.diagnostics.accessor.AccessorScriptHandler.exportDiagnosticDataFromServer(AccessorScriptHand
ler.java:34)
        at
weblogic.management.scripting.WLScriptContext.exportDiagnosticDataFromServer(WLScriptContext.java:433
)
        at sun.reflect.NativeMethodAccessorImpl.invoke0(Native Method)
        at sun.reflect.NativeMethodAccessorImpl.invoke(NativeMethodAccessorImpl.java:57)
        at sun.reflect.DelegatingMethodAccessorImpl.invoke(DelegatingMethodAccessorImpl.java:43)
        at java.lang.reflect.Method.invoke(Method.java:601)

weblogic.management.scripting.ScriptException: weblogic.management.scripting.ScriptException:
Response: '401: Unauthorized' for url:
'http://localhost:<port>/bea_wls_diagnostics/accessor?logicalName=HarvestedDataArchive&query=&beginTi
mestamp=0&endTimestamp=9223372036854775807'
```

It is therefore required to use secure connections in WLST. Therefore the WLST interpreter must be started with a few additional arguments. Here it is important to know which certificate is used by the WebLogic server. There are two different possibilities: Either the default "Demo" certificate or a custom certificate.

If the default "Demo" certificate is used by the server then the following arguments must be added to the WLST startup command:

```
-Dweblogic.security.SSL.ignoreHostnameVerification=true -Dweblogic.security.TrustKeyStore=DemoTrust
```

If a custom certificate is being used then these parameter must be added:

```
-Dweblogic.security.SSL.ignoreHostnameVerification=true -
Dweblogic.security.CustomTrustKeyStoreType="JKS" -Dweblogic.security.TrustKeyStore=CustomTrust -
Dweblogic.security.CustomTrustKeyStoreFileName="/somewhere/my_truststore.jks"
```

Note that it is necessary to trust the server. It is not necessary to provide a private certificate for authentication. The authentication will be done using user/password as usual.

e.g. for a server with the demo certificate start WLST:

```
java -cp $CLASSPATH -Dweblogic.security.SSL.ignoreHostnameVerification=true -
Dweblogic.security.TrustKeyStore=DemoTrust weblogic.WLST exportData.py
```

Whereas the exportData.py contains:

```
# note:  you MUST use t3s  and the ssl port of your server
connect('weblogic','test1234','t3s://<host>:<ssl-port>')

# get the data
```

```
exportDiagnosticDataFromServer(logicalName="HarvestedDataArchive",
exportFileName="myExport_online.xml")
```

Output:

```
Connecting to t3s://<host>:<ssl-port> with userid weblogic ...

<Aug 25, 2014 8:09:22 AM UTC> <Info> <Security> <BEA-090905> <Disabling the CryptoJ JCE Provider
self-integrity check for better startup performance. To enable this check, specify -
Dweblogic.security.allowCryptoJDefaultJCEVerification=true.>

<Aug 25, 2014 8:09:22 AM UTC> <Info> <Security> <BEA-090906> <Changing the default Random Number
Generator in RSA CryptoJ from ECDRBG to FIPS186PRNG. To disable this change, specify -
Dweblogic.security.allowCryptoJDefaultPRNG=true.>

Successfully connected to Admin Server "AdminServer" that belongs to domain "martinTest_1".

Exported diagnostic data to myExport_online.xml
```

The data saved in the XML file has the same format as already discussed in the offline section above.

Using the exported data

Unfortunately Oracle does not offer any tool to work with the exported data. It is up to the user to create these tools.
e.g. http://www.oracle.com/technetwork/articles/entarch/mining-wldf-xslt2-092743.html shows a way to use XLST.

Summary

This chapter has discussed the API included in WLDF in order to access the data collected. Different diagnostic data types like harvester data, log files and others are supported.

The API can be used with Java by using standard JMX calls as well as with the WLST scripting environment.

In addition WLDF extends WLST with two operations to extract data and transforms it to XML which allows other tools like XLST to consume and work with the diagnostic data. Both online and offline mode is supported.

Visualizing and Analyzing data with Mission Control

WLDF and Flight Recorder information

Inherited from JRockit, JDK versions starting with JDK 1.7.0_40 include an important tool named "Mission Control". One part of Mission Control is a recording feature called flight recorder. WLDF provides an integration and can create diagnostic data and events which can be analyzed using Flight Recorder.

Introduction

First, note that Mission Control is not part of WLDF. Instead, Mission Control is an external tool which is part of the JDK and may need to be licensed separately. WLDF can generate the data which can then be analyzed using Flight Recorder, which is part of Mission Control.

The Flight Recorder is a java profiler and monitoring framework which can collect continuous performance and diagnostic data. This data is recorded in a so-called JFR file. The Oracle documentation compares this to an aircraft black-box because the collected data can be used to reconstruct what happened in the time period monitored.

The interesting aspect is that flight recorder includes APIs which allows it to also monitor events from other systems or components. And exactly this feature is used to integrate it with WLDF so that WLDF events can be analyzed using flight recorder.

Activating flight recorder features in a JVM. Note that the order of arguments here is important !

```
-XX:+UnlockCommercialFeatures -XX:+FlightRecorder
```

WLDF and Flight Recorder

The WLDF implementation provides a number of features. Diagnostic images in WLDF automatically includes a data archive which implements the syntax used by flight recorder – a JRF file. The integration also adds improvements to WLST since WebLogic has added WLST commands for downloading the flight recorder information from a diagnostic archive (see chapter about archives).

Amount of WLDF Data recorded by Flight Recorder

WebLogic offers a setting for each WebLogic server instance in order to define the amount of data which should be recorded. This can be found on each server on th "General" configuration tab.

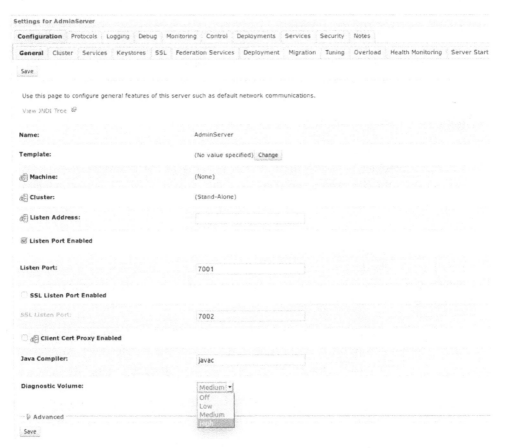

Figure 18.1: *Define the level of data recording*

Please consult the Oracle documentation for a detailed list which events are captured for which level.

Of course this can also be set using WLST. The following WLST script can be used:

```
connect (…)
startEdit ()

cd('/Servers/AdminServer/ServerDiagnosticConfig/AdminServer')
cmo.setWLDFDiagnosticVolume('High')

activate ()
```

Example Data

The following information is created based on the file FlightRecoder.jfr from a diagnostic image. Please see the diagnostic image chapter for more information of how to lookup diagnostic images and how to download images or even parts (e.g. FlightRecorder.jfr) from an image.

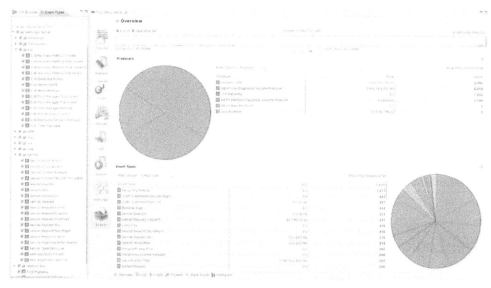

Figure 18.2: *View after opening the FlightRecorder.jfr file*

The screenshot above shows the de default view of the "Event" section in flight recorder. Note especially on the left side that it is possible to select which types of events should be considered in the right hand analysis. Many different event types are supported.

Code section

Flight recorder does not only offer events captured but also much more like code coverage:

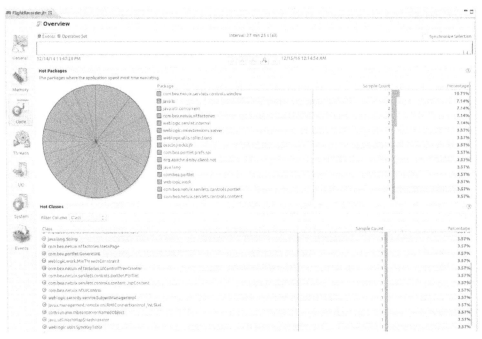

Figure 18.3: *Code coverage view*

WebLogic plugin

Oracle offers also a WebLogic plugin for mission control, which extends the features of Mission Control with WebLogic specific views.

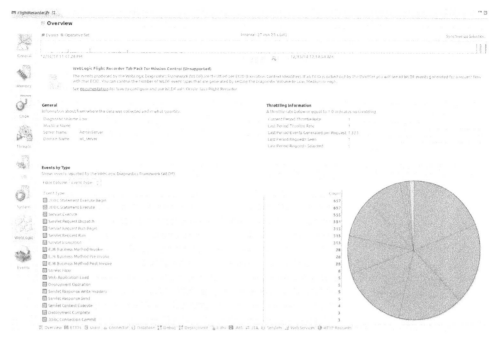

Figure 18.4: *WebLogic extension*

Note the amount of sub-sections implemented by tabs on the bottom. These are all WebLogic specific views.

The next picture will demonstrate the servlet view of the WebLogic plugin, which provides a number of information for the different servlet invocations.

Figure 18.5: *Servlet view of the WebLogic extension*

Summary

WebLogic offers an integration of WLDF with the Flight Recorder of Mission Control. This integration allows flight recorder to analyze events and more created by WLDF and stored in the FlightRecorder.jfr file which is part of a diagnostic image. This offers a number of powerful analysis and monitoring possibilities.

Visualizing data with the WLDF Dashboard

Visualizing data with the Dashboard

The WebLogic diagnostic framework comes along with a Dashboard which is built into the standard WebLogic console. This feature offers a nice way to display WLDF data and also offers a number of extension options for visualizing data.

Introduction

WebLogic has integrated this dashboard into the WebLogic console. This means that this dashboard can be invoked from the main WLS console (see next screenshot) and will open in a new tab. If this is not wanted, then you can also run the dashboard in its own browser.

From the main WebLogic console portal (by clicking on the "Home" button on the top left corner) you can navigate to the WLDF dashboard by selecting "Monitoring dashboard" on this page.

Figure 19.1: *Select Monitoring Dashboard to get to the WLDF dashboard*

The WLDF dashboard has a limited number of sources from which it can obtain its values. On one hand this could be data provided by run-time MBeans from the running WebLogic server domain, or on the other hand this can be archived values which had formerly been collected by one of the harvester defined in one of the WLDF modules of this domain.

The Oracle documentation calls the first type "polled metrics" and the archived data type "collected metrics".

The WLDF dashboard distinguishes between two types of views – built-in views which are provided by WebLogic and Custom views which can be defined by administrators as extensions to the dashboard.

After opening the dashboard the user will see on the left hand side the list of available views.

WebLogic Diagnostic Framework

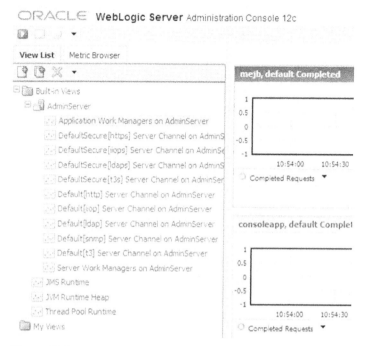

Figure 19.2: *WLDF view browser in the dashboard*

Built-In Views

For each server (including the admin server), WebLogic offers a number of pre-defined views. You can select them from the list and then click the green little button on the top in order start them. Note that by default all views are deactivated in order to save CPU and memory resources.

After the view has been started, the icon in the tree list will be changed to bold so that you can see which views are currently active.

As an example, if you activate the application view, you will see a default dashboard like this:

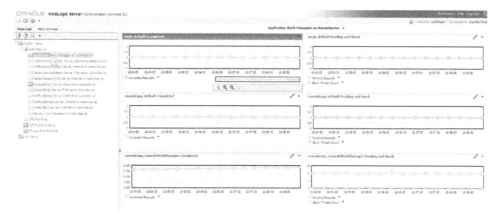

Figure 19.3: *Default dashboard of the application view*

Another example is the http connector view which offers a few standard values for http connections.

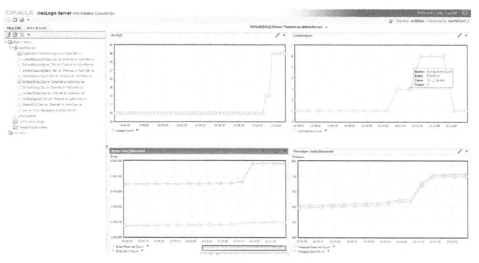

Figure 19.4: *Default dashboard of the http view*

Built-in views can also contain data from more than one server of this domain. An example is the provided view of the JVM heap which shows the heap of all running server of the current domain

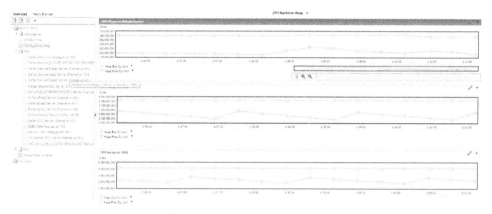

Figure 19.5: *JVM view of the current domain*

The standard views cannot be changed or extended with more metrics. In order to get more complex and most likely more meaningful views, it is possible to create custom views.

Custom Views

The dashboard allows users to define custom views with the metrics customers need to see. The view layout will be saved in the configuration file under the adminserver configuration tree in the file system.

The first step needed is to create a new custom view. This can be done by selecting the appropriate menu option.

Figure 19.6: *Select "New View" to create a custom view*

Then charts can be added to the new view.

Figure 19.7: *Add a new chart to a view*

Charts are empty by default, therefore it is required to select the metrics you want to see from the metrics browser. After selecting "Server", "Type", "Instance" and "Metric" you can drag and drop this metric to the chart to which you want to add the metric.

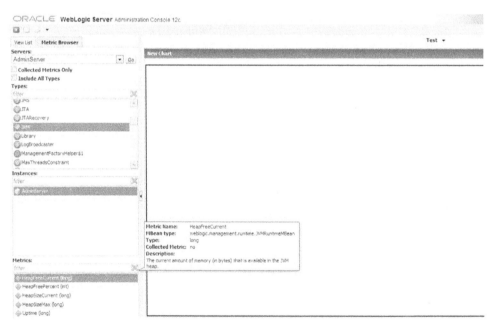

Figure 19.8: *Select the require metric which should be added to the view*

This view is called the "Metric Browser". It is a view with filter capabilities on the repository of available metrics.

This browser requests the user to select one of the server of the domain. Note that only RUNNING servers can be selected.

Then this view allows you to filter for thy type you are interested in and based on the type the following filter will narrow the selection down to a specific instance of the selected type. Finally in the last section you will then be able to select a metric from this specific instance. This metric can then be moved (drag and drop) to the view.

Figure 19.9: *The metrics browser*

This browser is the GUI view and access to the repository of all available metrics.

Custom View Example

The custom views are stored in a file called ConsolePreferences. This file is located at:

```
<domain>/servers/AdminServer/data/console/ConsolePreferences.xml
```

The following example view has 4 different metrics (even different types) and each metric has values from different servers – either from MS1 and MS2 or even from all servers including the adminserver. The configuration file looks like:

```
<?xml version='1.0' encoding='US-ASCII'?>
<?xml version='1.0' encoding='utf-8'?>
<portlet-preferences>
  <portlet-preference definitionLabel="dashboard" user="weblogic">
    <preference name="view_7437925023-1416318135765" description=
                "Test view for demo purpose" isModifiable="true" isMultivalued="false"
value="{&quot;name&quot;:&quot;TestMonitor&quot;,&quot;id&quot;:&quot;7437925023-
1416318135765&quot;,&quot;panels&quot;:[[{&quot;type&quot;:&quot;chart&quot;,&quot;state&quot;:{&quot
;name&quot;:&quot;Test-
JVM&quot;,&quot;type&quot;:&quot;linePlot&quot;,&quot;background&quot;:&quot;#FFFFFF&quot;,&quot;colo
r&quot;:&quot;#000000&quot;,&quot;highlight&quot;:&quot;#FBC8CA&quot;,&quot;units&quot;:&quot;&quot;,
&quot;timeRange&quot;:&quot;current&quot;,&quot;metrics&quot;:[{&quot;name&quot;:&quot;HeapSizeCurren
t@MS1&quot;,&quot;metric&quot;:{&quot;on&quot;:&quot;com.bea:Name=MS1,ServerRuntime=MS1,Type=JVMRunti
me&quot;,&quot;a&quot;:&quot;HeapSizeCurrent&quot;,&quot;type&quot;:&quot;weblogic.management.runtime
.JVMRuntimeMBean&quot;,&quot;server&quot;:&quot;MS1&quot;},&quot;color&quot;:&quot;#33CCFF&quot;,&quo
t;markerShape&quot;:&quot;diamond&quot;,&quot;markerFill&quot;:true},{&quot;name&quot;:&quot;HeapFree
Current@MS1&quot;,&quot;metric&quot;:{&quot;on&quot;:&quot;com.bea:Name=MS1,ServerRuntime=MS1,Type=JV
MRuntime&quot;,&quot;a&quot;:&quot;HeapFreeCurrent&quot;,&quot;type&quot;:&quot;weblogic.management.r
untime.JVMRuntimeMBean&quot;,&quot;server&quot;:&quot;MS1&quot;},&quot;color&quot;:&quot;#CC3333&quot
;,&quot;markerShape&quot;:&quot;triangleUp&quot;,&quot;markerFill&quot;:true},{&quot;name&quot;:&quot
;HeapSizeMax@MS1&quot;,&quot;metric&quot;:{&quot;on&quot;:&quot;com.bea:Name=MS1,ServerRuntime=MS1,Ty
pe=JVMRuntime&quot;,&quot;a&quot;:&quot;HeapSizeMax&quot;,&quot;type&quot;:&quot;weblogic.management.
runtime.JVMRuntimeMBean&quot;,&quot;server&quot;:&quot;MS1&quot;},&quot;color&quot;:&quot;#669966&quo
t;,&quot;markerShape&quot;:&quot;triangleDown&quot;,&quot;markerFill&quot;:true},{&quot;name&quot;:&q
uot;HeapSizeCurrent@MS2&quot;,&quot;metric&quot;:{&quot;on&quot;:&quot;com.bea:Name=MS2,ServerRuntime
=MS2,Type=JVMRuntime&quot;,&quot;a&quot;:&quot;HeapSizeCurrent&quot;,&quot;type&quot;:&quot;weblogic.
management.runtime.JVMRuntimeMBean&quot;,&quot;server&quot;:&quot;MS2&quot;},&quot;color&quot;:&quot;
#009999&quot;,&quot;markerShape&quot;:&quot;diamond&quot;,&quot;markerFill&quot;:false},{&quot;name&q
uot;:&quot;HeapSizeMax@MS2&quot;,&quot;metric&quot;:{&quot;on&quot;:&quot;com.bea:Name=MS2,ServerRunt
ime=MS2,Type=JVMRuntime&quot;,&quot;a&quot;:&quot;HeapSizeMax&quot;,&quot;type&quot;:&quot;weblogic.m
anagement.runtime.JVMRuntimeMBean&quot;,&quot;server&quot;:&quot;MS2&quot;},&quot;color&quot;:&quot;#
990099&quot;,&quot;markerShape&quot;:&quot;triangleUp&quot;,&quot;markerFill&quot;:false},{&quot;name
&quot;:&quot;HeapFreeCurrent@MS2&quot;,&quot;metric&quot;:{&quot;on&quot;:&quot;com.bea:Name=MS2,Serv
erRuntime=MS2,Type=JVMRuntime&quot;,&quot;a&quot;:&quot;HeapFreeCurrent&quot;,&quot;type&quot;:&quot;
weblogic.management.runtime.JVMRuntimeMBean&quot;,&quot;server&quot;:&quot;MS2&quot;},&quot;color&quo
t;:&quot;#666699&quot;,&quot;markerShape&quot;:&quot;square&quot;,&quot;markerFill&quot;:true}],&quot
;autoRange&quot;:true,&quot;rangeMin&quot;:0,&quot;rangeMax&quot;:100,&quot;thresholdMin&quot;:null,&
quot;thresholdMax&quot;:null,&quot;markerIndex&quot;:5,&quot;timeStart&quot;:{&quot;name&quot;,&quot;timeD
uration&quot;:&quot;&quot;}},{&quot;type&quot;:&quot;chart&quot;,&quot;state&quot;:{&quot;name&quot;:
&quot;Heap-Free (%) of all
servers&quot;,&quot;type&quot;:&quot;radialGauge&quot;,&quot;background&quot;:&quot;#FFFFFF&quot;,&qu
ot;color&quot;:&quot;#000000&quot;,&quot;highlight&quot;:&quot;#FBC8CA&quot;,&quot;units&quot;:&quot;
&quot;,&quot;timeRange&quot;:&quot;current&quot;,&quot;metrics&quot;:[{&quot;name&quot;:&quot;HeapFre
ePercent@MS1&quot;,&quot;metric&quot;:{&quot;on&quot;:&quot;com.bea:Name=MS1,ServerRuntime=MS1,Type=J
VMRuntime&quot;,&quot;a&quot;:&quot;HeapFreePercent&quot;,&quot;type&quot;:&quot;weblogic.management.
runtime.JVMRuntimeMBean&quot;,&quot;server&quot;:&quot;MS1&quot;},&quot;color&quot;:&quot;#FFCC33&quo
t;,&quot;markerShape&quot;:&quot;circle&quot;,&quot;markerFill&quot;:true},{&quot;name&quot;:&quot;He
apFreePercent@MS2&quot;,&quot;metric&quot;:{&quot;on&quot;:&quot;com.bea:Name=MS2,ServerRuntime=MS2,T
ype=JVMRuntime&quot;,&quot;a&quot;:&quot;HeapFreePercent&quot;,&quot;type&quot;:&quot;weblogic.manage
ment.runtime.JVMRuntimeMBean&quot;,&quot;server&quot;:&quot;MS2&quot;},&quot;color&quot;:&quot;#33CCF
F&quot;,&quot;markerShape&quot;:&quot;diamond&quot;,&quot;markerFill&quot;:true},{&quot;name&quot;:&q
uot;HeapFreePercent@AdminServer&quot;,&quot;metric&quot;:{&quot;on&quot;:&quot;com.bea:Name=AdminServ
er,ServerRuntime=AdminServer,Type=JVMRuntime&quot;,&quot;a&quot;:&quot;HeapFreePercent&quot;,&quot;ty
pe&quot;:&quot;weblogic.management.runtime.JVMRuntimeMBean&quot;,&quot;server&quot;:&quot;AdminServer
&quot;},&quot;color&quot;:&quot;#CC3333&quot;,&quot;markerShape&quot;:&quot;triangleUp&quot;,&quot;ma
rkerFill&quot;:true}],&quot;autoRange&quot;:true,&quot;rangeMin&quot;:0,&quot;rangeMax&quot;:100,&quo
```

t;thresholdMin":null,"thresholdMax":null,"markerIndex":3,"timeStart&quo
t;:"","timeDuration":""}}],[{"type":"chart","s
tate":{"name":"Test-
Threadpool","type":"linePlot","background":"#FFFFFF",&qu
ot;color":"#000000","highlight":"#FBC8CA","units":"
","timeRange":"current","metrics":[{"name":"Execute
ThreadIdleCount@ThreadPoolRuntime","metric":{"on":"com.bea:Name=ThreadP
oolRuntime,ServerRuntime=MS1,Type=ThreadPoolRuntime","a":"ExecuteThreadIdleCount&
quot;,"type":"weblogic.management.runtime.ThreadPoolRuntimeMBean","server&qu
ot;:"MS1"},"color":"#33CCFF","markerShape":"diamond&quot
;,"markerFill":true},{"name":"ExecuteThreadTotalCount@ThreadPoolRuntime&quot
;,"metric":{"on":"com.bea:Name=ThreadPoolRuntime,ServerRuntime=MS1,Type=Thre
adPoolRuntime","a":"ExecuteThreadTotalCount","type":"weblogic
.management.runtime.ThreadPoolRuntimeMBean","server":"MS1"},"color&quot
;:"#CC3333","markerShape":"triangleUp","markerFill":true},{&q
uot;name":"HoggingThreadCount@ThreadPoolRuntime","metric":{"on":&q
uot;com.bea:Name=ThreadPoolRuntime,ServerRuntime=MS1,Type=ThreadPoolRuntime","a":&quot
;HoggingThreadCount","type":"weblogic.management.runtime.ThreadPoolRuntimeMBean&q
uot;,"server":"MS1"},"color":"#669966","markerShape&quot
;:"triangleDown","markerFill":true},{"name":"PendingUserRequestCou
nt@ThreadPoolRuntime","metric":{"on":"com.bea:Name=ThreadPoolRuntime,Se
rverRuntime=MS1,Type=ThreadPoolRuntime","a":"PendingUserRequestCount","
type":"weblogic.management.runtime.ThreadPoolRuntimeMBean","server":"MS
1"},"color":"#666699","markerShape":"square","marke
rFill":true},{"name":"StandbyThreadCount@ThreadPoolRuntime","metric&quo
t;:{"on":"com.bea:Name=ThreadPoolRuntime,ServerRuntime=MS1,Type=ThreadPoolRuntime&quot
;,"a":"StandbyThreadCount","type":"weblogic.management.runtime.Thr
eadPoolRuntimeMBean","server":"MS1"},"color":"#009900",&
quot;markerShape":"bar","markerFill":true}],"autoRange":true,&quot
;rangeMin":0,"rangeMax":100,"thresholdMin":null,"thresholdMax":nul
l,"markerIndex":12,"timeStart":"","timeDuration":""
}},{"type":"chart","state":{"name":"Test-.https
Channel","type":"linePlot","background":"#FFFFFF","
color":"#000000","highlight":"#FBC8CA","units":"&qu
ot;,"timeRange":"current","metrics":[{"name":"AcceptCoun
t@DefaultSecure[https]","metric":{"on":"com.bea:Name=DefaultSecure[http
s],ServerRuntime=MS2,Type=ServerChannelRuntime","a":"AcceptCount","type
":"weblogic.management.runtime.ServerChannelRuntimeMBean","server":"MS2
"},"color":"#FFCC33","markerShape":"circle","marker
Fill":true},{"name":"BytesReceivedCount@DefaultSecure[https]","metric&q
uot;:{"on":"com.bea:Name=DefaultSecure[https],ServerRuntime=MS2,Type=ServerChannelRunt
ime","a":"BytesReceivedCount","type":"weblogic.management.run
time.ServerChannelRuntimeMBean","server":"MS2"},"color":"#33C
CFF","markerShape":"diamond","markerFill":true},{"name":
"BytesSentCount@DefaultSecure[https]","metric":{"on":"com.bea:Name
=DefaultSecure[https],ServerRuntime=MS2,Type=ServerChannelRuntime","a":"BytesSent
Count","type":"weblogic.management.runtime.ServerChannelRuntimeMBean","
server":"MS2"},"color":"#CC3333","markerShape":"tri
angleUp","markerFill":true},{"name":"MessagesReceivedCount@DefaultSecur
e[https]","metric":{"on":"com.bea:Name=DefaultSecure[https],ServerRunti
me=MS2,Type=ServerChannelRuntime","a":"MessagesReceivedCount","type&quo
t;:"weblogic.management.runtime.ServerChannelRuntimeMBean","server":"MS2&quo
t;},"color":"#669966","markerShape":"triangleDown","mark
erFill":true},{"name":"AcceptCount@DefaultSecure[https]","metric":
{"on":"com.bea:Name=DefaultSecure[https],ServerRuntime=MS1,Type=ServerChannelRuntime&q
uot;,"a":"AcceptCount","type":"weblogic.management.runtime.ServerC
hannelRuntimeMBean","server":"MS1"},"color":"#666699",&q
uot;markerShape":"square","markerFill":true},{"name":"BytesRe
ceivedCount@DefaultSecure[https]","metric":{"on":"com.bea:Name=DefaultS
ecure[https],ServerRuntime=MS1,Type=ServerChannelRuntime","a":"BytesReceivedCount
","type":"weblogic.management.runtime.ServerChannelRuntimeMBean","serve
r":"MS1"},"color":"#009900","markerShape":"bar&quot
;,"markerFill":true},{"name":"BytesSentCount@DefaultSecure[https]",&quo
t;metric":{"on":"com.bea:Name=DefaultSecure[https],ServerRuntime=MS1,Type=ServerC
hannelRuntime","a":"BytesSentCount","type":"weblogic.manageme
nt.runtime.ServerChannelRuntimeMBean","server":"MS1"},"color":&quo
t;#990000","markerShape":"halfCircleLeft","markerFill":true},{&quo
t;name":"ConnectionsCount@DefaultSecure[https]","metric":{"on":&qu
ot;com.bea:Name=DefaultSecure[https],ServerRuntime=MS1,Type=ServerChannelRuntime","a":
"ConnectionsCount","type":"weblogic.management.runtime.ServerChannelRuntimeM
Bean","server":"MS1"},"color":"#000099","markerShap
e":"halfCircleRight","markerFill":true},{"name":"MessagesRece
ivedCount@DefaultSecure[https]","metric":{"on":"com.bea:Name=DefaultSec
ure[https],ServerRuntime=MS1,Type=ServerChannelRuntime","a":"MessagesReceivedCoun
t","type":"weblogic.management.runtime.ServerChannelRuntimeMBean","serv
er":"MS1"},"color":"#999900","markerShape":"circle&
quot;,"markerFill":false},{"name":"MessagesSentCount@DefaultSecure[https]&qu
ot;,"metric":{"on":"com.bea:Name=DefaultSecure[https],ServerRuntime=MS1,Type

```
=ServerChannelRuntime&quot;,&quot;a&quot;:&quot;MessagesSentCount&quot;,&quot;type&quot;:&quot;weblog
ic.management.runtime.ServerChannelRuntimeMBean&quot;,&quot;server&quot;:&quot;MS1&quot;},&quot;color
&quot;:&quot;#009999&quot;,&quot;markerShape&quot;:&quot;diamond&quot;,&quot;markerFill&quot;:false}]
,&quot;autoRange&quot;:true,&quot;rangeMin&quot;:0,&quot;rangeMax&quot;:100,&quot;thresholdMin&quot;:
null,&quot;thresholdMax&quot;:null,&quot;markerIndex&quot;:4,&quot;timeStart&quot;:&quot;&quot;,&quot
;timeDuration&quot;:&quot;&quot;}}]],&quot;activeState&quot;:true}"/>
    <preference name="lastViewId" description="The description" isModifiable="true"
isMultivalued="false" value="7437925023-1416318135765"/>
    <preference name="splitterClosed" description="The description" isModifiable="true"
isMultivalued="false" value="false"/>
    <preference name="splitterWidth" description="The description" isModifiable="true"
isMultivalued="false" value="300"/>
  </portlet-preference>
</portlet-preferences>
```

Unfortunately Oracle has not documented this syntax so that there is no possibility to generate the custom views from this code. I am also not aware of any tools – open source or commercial – which are making use of this syntax and which are generating custom views.

In the WLS console this custom view will look like:

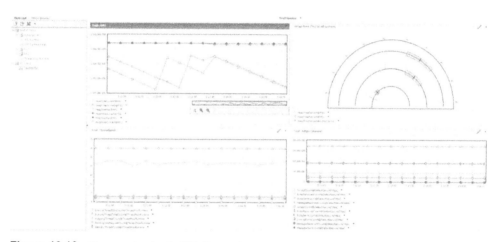

Figure 19.10: *Custom view in the WLS console*

All charts in the different views have zoom-in and zoom-out capabilities available. You can select in the small rectangle underneath the chart which time frame you want to see. See the selection made inside the circle in the next picture. The selected timeframe is marked with a darker grey rectangle (sometimes difficult to see).

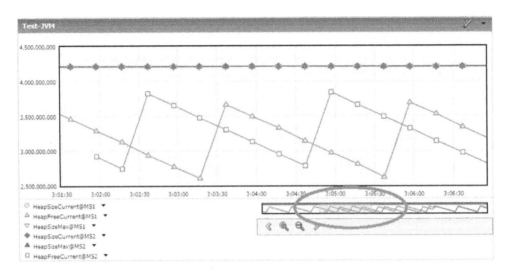

Figure 19.11: *Zoom into a time frame*

Outlook

The dashboard is the WLDF standard offering in order to visualize collected data. As Oracle is moving all future development in the direction of the Fusion Middleware Console, Oracle will not invest more into this dashboard. So it is not expected to see new features in this dashboard. Nevertheless it is also in its current shape a useful tool which can be used with the standard WebLogic console. This makes it easy for everybody with the appropriate rights to use it and get some visualization of their data.

Summary

This chapter introduces another way of using the collected data. Beside the API discussed in the previous chapter, WebLogic offers a built-in dashboard which offers virtualization. The charming detail of this dashboard is that it is built into the WLS console and therefore can be used without any additional tool. Albeit Oracle is not going to extend this dashboard it is a valuable tool for all administrators. Please see the Oracle documentation for details on all aspects of the charts and chart types.

Part VI

Advanced Concepts

The next section of the book depicts the powerful advanced concepts that enable WLDF to be used for application-specific monitoring, which is not possible using standard JMX and MBeans.

Extending WLDF with its own Monitoring Access Points

Using WLDF Instrumentation

With code level instrumentation that is based upon "aspect oriented" programming concepts, WLDF offers a powerful set of features for many advanced monitoring and alerting possibilities. This chapter provides an overview with basic examples.

Introduction to WLDF Instrumentation

WLDF is not restricted to the data provided by MBeans. MBeans are a convenient way to get data using a standardized API (JMX). But the obvious limitation is that only data provided by those MBeans can be used for the monitoring. Up to this point the book has discussed WLDF features based on MBean access. But WLDF offers monitoring capabilities beyond JMX which are based on aspect oriented (AOP) technologies and allow the user to inject monitoring code into WebLogic and also into application code. This feature is called WLDF instrumentation.

WLDF instrumentation is a very comprehensive topic and a full discussion is beyond the scope of this book. This chapter provides an overview and some basic examples in order to demonstrate the abilities of WLDF instrumentation. For details about the following topics and especially details about the configuration items and possibilities please consult the Oracle documentation.

What is AOP?

Before moving to the WLDF implementation it is important to understand the rationality and concepts behind AOP.

Consider the following example:

A complex application has been built over a number of years and is now in production or a standard application from a software vendor has been bought, customized and is now running in production. Now, due to management decisions, (or audit requirements) additional application logs or workflow information must be captured. Also assume that there is no way to change this system due to costs, timeline or because of the external software vendor. Therefore an extension is needed which can get the necessary logs in certain conditions or in certain software modules. The existing code must be extended without the ability to change and recompile the original source code.

Second example:

During the architecture phase the architects decided that they do not want to have standard tasks which are not part of the business logic in the business code in order to keep this code easier to maintain and easier to understand. It is common knowledge that the non-business tasks like logging or security can sometimes consume 50-80% of the overall source code. So they developed the software and only consider the business requirements (also called functional requirements) and they expected that a code extension will implement the non-functional requirements as a so called "cross cutting" extension. Cross cutting here means concerns which are required in many different software modules but should be developed only once and used everywhere in the system.

Both examples describe a need for software which can be written independently from the original software and can be "injected" at well-defined points in order to extend the original code. This is the idea of AOP. AOP is all about developing aspects which can then be injected into existing systems in order to extend them with additional functionality.

Terminology

Standard terminology used in Aspect-oriented programming may include:

- **Cross-cutting concerns:** Even though most classes in an OO model will perform a single, specific function, they often share common, secondary requirements with other classes. For example, we may want to add logging to classes within the data-access layer and also to classes in the UI layer whenever a thread enters or exits a method. Even though each class has a very different primary functionality, the code needed to perform the secondary functionality is often identical.

- **Advice:** This is the additional code that you want to apply to your existing model. In our example, this is the logging code that we want to apply whenever the thread enters or exits a method.

- **Pointcut:** This is the term given to the point of execution in the application at which cross-cutting concern needs to be applied. In our example, a pointcut is reached when the thread enters a method, and another pointcut is reached when the thread exits the method.

- **Aspect:** The combination of the pointcut and the advice is termed an aspect. In the example above, we add a logging aspect to our application by defining a pointcut and giving the correct advice.

(© http://en.wikipedia.org/wiki/Aspect-oriented_programming with permission)

WLDF instrumentation

WebLogic offers standard MBeans for almost everything, therefore instrumentation on the core WebLogic classes is not needed very often. The really exciting aspect of this instrumentation is that it is possible to inject monitoring code into application code which was never be designed to provide monitoring information.

WLDF provides essentially three key capabilities:

Diagnostic monitors.

- A diagnostic monitor is a dynamically manageable unit of diagnostic code that is inserted into server or application code at specific locations.

- You define monitors by scope (system or application) and type (standard, delegating, or custom).

Diagnostic actions.

A diagnostic action is the action a monitor takes when it is triggered during program execution.

Diagnostic context

A diagnostic context is contextual information, such as unique request identifier and flags that indicate the presence of certain request properties such as originating IP address or user identity. The diagnostic context provides a means for tracking program execution and for controlling when monitors trigger their diagnostic actions.

(© Oracle documentation , WebLogic 12.1.3, WLDF)

The WLDF offering contains a number of predefined diagnostic monitors and actions but it is also possible to create monitors for your own applications. These two different capabilities of WLDF have to be configured in different locations. Instrumentations for the WebLogic core like server, resources or cluster have to be configured into the WebLogic configuration. As discussed in the first part of the book this will be stored in a XML file located in <domain>/config/diagnostics subfolder.

New for this book are the instrumentation techniques for the application level. These will NOT be part of the WebLogic configuration but part of the application deployment. A new file – called weblogic-diagnostics.xml – must be added to the application under the META-INF folder which contains all the application level configurations.

Based on the AOP terminology, WLDF defines three main concepts which result in configuration items in the XML configuration files which defines the concrete injection points. WLDF defines a **joinpoint** as the concrete injection point within a java class. A **pointcut** in WLDF is a well-defined rule which defines a number of joinpoints. And finally a diagnostic **location** describes how the monitoring injection should be performed. The code can either be performed before the injection point, after the injection point or even around the injection point.

WLDF also distinguishes three types of diagnostic monitors, which are called "standard monitor", "delegating monitor" and "custom monitor". The types differ due to locations and actions.

WLDF specifies a number of possible actions for the delegation or custom monitor configuration. It is really important to specify the action in the appropriate XML configuration file so that the implementation knows what this monitor configuration should perform. According to the Oracle documentation the following types of actions are available in WLDF: DisplayArgumentsAction, MethodInvocationStatisticsAction, MethodMemoryAllocationStatisticsAction, StackDumpAction, ThreadDumpAction, TraceAction, TraceElapsedTimeAction and TraceMemoryAllocationAction.

Defining Watches on Instrumentation Events

Of course, it is possible to create watches and notifications which react to instrumentation events.

The following XML snippet from a configuration shows a watch which will be triggered is a specific standard monitor for a given server and given domain has been called.

```
<watch>
    <name>my_WLDF_test_Watch</name>
    <enabled>true</enabled>
    <rule-type>EventData</rule-type>
    <rule-expression>
            (MONITOR LIKE 'EJB_Around_SessionEjbBusinessMethods') AND
            (DOMAIN = 'MartinTestDomain') AND
            (SERVER = 'MS1') AND
            ((TYPE = 'ThreadDumpAction') OR (TYPE = 'TraceElapsedTimeAction'))
    </rule-expression>
    <notification>MyJMXNotification</notification>
</watch>
```

DyeInjection Monitor

WLDF also provides a powerful tracing and filtering capability out of the box. WLDF offers a possibility to uniquely mark requests and create a trace of these requests while these requests are processed in the system. WLDF even provides a filtering capability such that the administrator can specify that only certain requests like requests from specific users or from specific source IP addresses will be considered. For this component WLDF uses two parts - a unique ID and fields for request characteristics which is also called dye vector.

How to use the DyeInjection ?

First of all you need to the DyeInjection module. All incoming requests will be checked against the dye values and for every match the appropriate flag (bit) will be set in the context. During the request begin processed by the system, whenever a diagnostic monitor (system or application scope level) meets the dye mask and the configured conditions the configured actions are performed.

The ID created and used by DYE injection is a unique ID which is passed around. It could be quite handy to also re-use this ID for own purposes, like enriching your own logs with this ID. WebLogic offers an API which allows you to get access to this ID – but of course only if DYE injection is activated and used.

Example code to get the DYE ID:

```
import weblogic.diagnostics.context.DiagnosticContextHelper;
DiagnosticContextHelper.getContextId()
```

Example 1: Using a standard monitor to observe HTTP sessions

It is a very common problem that administrators and other stakeholders would like to know how often data is placed and accessed from a HTTP session. This does not only provide information to calculate the required resources like memory but also provides data to make further application decision like e.g. the need for session replication and the costs associated with this.

Oracle provides a build-in standard monitor to collect this data.

A standard monitor performs specific, predefined diagnostic actions at specific, predefined pointcuts and locations. These actions, pointcuts, and locations are hard-coded in the monitor. You can enable or disable the monitor, but you cannot modify its behavior. The only standard server-scoped monitor is the DyeInjection monitor, which you can use to create diagnostic context and to configure dye injection at the server level. The only standard application-scoped monitor is *HttpSessionDebug*, which you can use to inspect an HTTP Session object.
(© Oracle Documentation)

This example will utilize this HTTPSessionDebug standard monitor for data gathering.

Creating the diagnostic module

First of all we need to create a diagnostic module and enable instrumentation. As discussed in the first part of the book this can be done using the WebConsole, WLST or JMX.

Figure 20.1: *Creation of a diagnostic module using the WebConsole*

As a second step it is required to enable instrumentation for this diagnostic module and target it to the desired servers and/or clusters.

Figure 20.2: *Enable Instrumentation*

The XML definition of the diagnostic module can be found at <domain>/config/diagnostics/<name>.xml. As this module only contains the activation of the instrumentation layer, the definition does is very simple.

```
<?xml version='1.0' encoding='UTF-8'?>
<wldf-resource xmlns="http://xmlns.oracle.com/weblogic/weblogic-diagnostics"
xmlns:sec="http://xmlns.oracle.com/weblogic/security"
xmlns:wls="http://xmlns.oracle.com/weblogic/security/wls"
xmlns:xsi="http://www.w3.org/2001/XMLSchema-instance"
xsi:schemaLocation="http://xmlns.oracle.com/weblogic/weblogic-diagnostics
http://xmlns.oracle.com/weblogic/weblogic-diagnostics/1.0/weblogic-
diagnostics.xsd">
  <name>SessionInstrumentationModule</name>
  <instrumentation>
    <enabled>true</enabled>
  </instrumentation>
</wldf-resource>
```

Instrument the application

Create a web application which uses session data in order to monitor session usage or instrument and existing application by adding the following weblogic-diagnostics.xml file to the application deployment.

```
<?xml version="1.0" encoding="UTF-8"?>
<wldf-resource … >
    <name>Martin-WebApp-Monitor</name>
    <instrumentation>
          <enabled>true</enabled>
          <wldf-instrumentation-monitor>
                <name>HttpSessionDebug</name>
                <enabled>true</enabled>
          </wldf-instrumentation-monitor>
    </instrumentation>
</wldf-resource>
```

It is important that this file will be added to the META-INF directory and that the application will then be redeployed (if already deployed).

Please note that the above XML code is NOT part of the config.xml or the diagnostic module definition (see above). This XML is part of the application deployment! Please note that the above XML is incomplete. The "…" in "<wldf-resource …>" require some more details but these depend on the WLS version. Please consult the WLS documentation for details.

Example 2: Using custom monitors to monitor special EJB methods

The second example uses an EJB application and instruments the EJB calls with WLDF monitors.

In this example we will be actually looking at two different scenarios. WLDF out of the box offers a number of standard monitors which also offer EJB method instrumentation. These instrumentations will be applied to all calls of the standard EJB implementation.

Very often EJBs are just wrapper which allow architects to use the container resources like transactions and security but the methods themselves are not doing anything but calling delegate implementations which are implemented as POJOs. If you want to do tracing or even time measurement of these calls, then you need custom monitors.

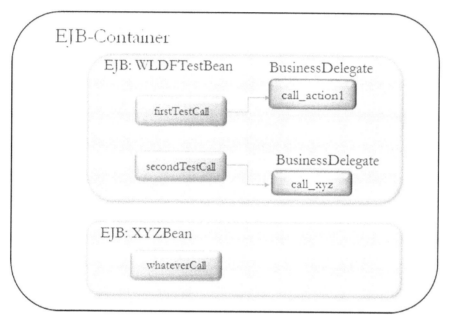

Figure 20.3: *Example setup*

In this example we will look at the instrumentation of the EJB calls like "firstTestCall" or "whateverCall". We will also look at the instrumentation of customer code in the delete POJO objects like the "call_action1".

Example setup

This very simple example is using the following implementation. The WLDF TestBean is a very simple stateless session bean with two main business calls. These business calls will forward incoming calls to the BusinessDelegate implementation.

Code of the WLDFTestBean:

```
package com.martin.wldf.ejb.test;

import javax.ejb.Stateless;

@Stateless
public class WLDFTestBean {

    public void firstTestCall(int action, int simulateTime)
    {
      BusinessDelegate myBusinessDelegate = new BusinessDelegate();

      // call business
      myBusinessDelegate.call_action1();
    }

    public int secondTestCall(int action, int simulateTime)
    {
      BusinessDelegate myBusinessDelegate = new BusinessDelegate();

      // call business
      return myBusinessDelegate.call_xyz();
    }
}
```

Code of the BusinessDelegate:

```
package com.martin.wldf.ejb.test;

/**
 * @author Martin Heinzl
 *
 */
public class BusinessDelegate
{
    public void call_action1() {
        try {
            // ... do something
        }
        catch (Exception e) {
            e.printStackTrace();
        }
    }

    public int call_xyz() {
        try {
            // ... do something
            return /* something */ createRandomValue();
        }
        catch (Exception e) {
            e.printStackTrace();
        }
    }
}
```

Note that the implementation details of the methods are not shown here. It could basically be any business logic.

Configuration of the WLDF Instrumentation

First of all it is required to create a diagnostic module with instrumentation enabled. Please see the first example because the steps required here are identical.

Now we need to create the weblogic-diagnostics.xml which will be deployed with the application.

First option:
Only instrument the standard EJB calls using the WLDF standard monitors

Example weblogic-diagnostics.xml:

```xml
<?xml version='1.0' encoding='UTF-8'?>
<wldf-resource>
    <name>Test EJB standard instrumentation</name>
    <instrumentation>
        <enabled>true</enabled>

        <wldf-instrumentation-monitor>
            <name>EJB_Around_SessionEjbBusinessMethods</name>
            <enabled>true</enabled>
            <action>TraceElapsedTimeAction</action>
        </wldf-instrumentation-monitor>


        <wldf-instrumentation-monitor>
            <name>EJB_After_SessionEjbMethods</name>
            <enabled>true</enabled>
            <action>TraceAction</action>
        </wldf-instrumentation-monitor>

    </instrumentation>
</wldf-resource>
```

WLDF defines a number of standard monitors like: EJB_Around_SessionEjbMethods EJB_Around_SessionEjbBusinessMethods, EJB_After_SessionEjbMethods, EJB_After_SessionEjbBusinessMethods, EJB_After_SessionEjbSemanticMethods, EJB_Before_SessionEjbBusinessMethods, EJB_Before_SessionEjbBusinessMethods EJB_Before_SessionEjbSemanticMethods and many other.

This example uses two of them. The "Around" flavor in order to measure the business calls of all EJBs and the "After" flavor in order to measure the lifecycle methods like ejbCreate. Please consult the Oracle documentation for all possible combinations of flavors, method types and actions.

Also for business methods we would like to measure the time spend in these methods (=>TraceElapsedTimeAction action) and for lifecycle methods we just want to trace them being called (=>TraceAction)

Back to our example, this WLDF configuration would do a time tracing for all EJB business calls. In our example these are WLDFTestBean:firstTestCall, WLDFTestBean:secondTestCall and also XZYBean:whateverCall.

Second option:

Only instrument the business delegate implementation calls using WLDF custom monitors. Note in this case we cannot use the predefined monitors but we have to define our own pointcuts.

Example weblogic-diagnostics.xml:

```
<wldf-resource>
    <name>Test EJB custom instrumentation</name>
    <instrumentation>
        <enabled>true</enabled>
        <wldf-instrumentation-monitor>
            <name>BusinessDelegate Data</name>
            <enabled>true</enabled>
            <action>TraceElapsedTimeAction</action>
            <location-type>around</location-type>
            <pointcut>
                    execution( * com.martin.wldf.ejb.test.BusinessDelegate call*(...));
            </pointcut>
        </wldf-instrumentation-monitor>
    </instrumentation>
</wldf-resource>
```

Note that with this configuration all methods from the BusinessDelegate starting with "call" will be instrumented. Also note that none of the EJB lifecycle calls and nothing from XYZBean will instrumented.

Third option:
Of course both configurations can be combined in case you want to have both configurations.

Example weblogic-diagnostics.xml:

```
<?xml version='1.0' encoding='UTF-8'?>
<wldf-resource>
    <name>Test EJB standard AND custom instrumentation</name>
    <instrumentation>
        <enabled>true</enabled>

        <wldf-instrumentation-monitor>
            <name>EJB_Around_SessionEjbBusinessMethods</name>
            <enabled>true</enabled>
            <action>TraceElapsedTimeAction</action>
        </wldf-instrumentation-monitor>


        <wldf-instrumentation-monitor>
            <name>EJB_After_SessionEjbMethods</name>
            <enabled>true</enabled>
            <action>TraceAction</action>
        </wldf-instrumentation-monitor>


        <wldf-instrumentation-monitor>
            <name>BusinessDelegate Data</name>
            <enabled>true</enabled>
            <action>TraceElapsedTimeAction</action>
            <location-type>around</location-type>
            <pointcut>
                    execution( * com.martin.wldf.ejb.test.* call*(...));
            </pointcut>
        </wldf-instrumentation-monitor>

    </instrumentation>
</wldf-resource>
```

Example 3: Using DyeInjection and DYE Monitors

The third example shows how to use DYE injection and DYE filters. DyeInjection is the only standard server filter, which can be enabled without adding a weblogic-diagnostic.xml file to your application.

The following example will use a web application which calls an EJB which itself will call POJO objects. In all system component we use the over discussed WebLogic API in order to print the context information. For demonstration purpose this application will use 3 different call paths which are shown in the following diagram.

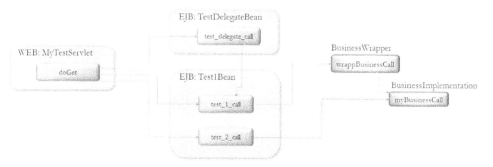

Figure 20.4: *Call paths through the application*

Implementation of the Example

For a better understanding, this section will list the important code parts. Please note that for better readability this code does not make use of proper exception handling or other essential J2EE patterns.

The first listing shows the demo implementation of the business implementation. In a real implementation all the real business functionality will be placed here.

```
package de.martin.test_dye.pojo;

import java.util.Random;

import weblogic.diagnostics.context.DiagnosticContextHelper;

public class BusinessImplementation {

    public BusinessImplementation() {}

    public void myBusinessCall()
    {
        String myDYEMessageID_in_Business = DiagnosticContextHelper.getContextId();

        System.out.println("[INFO] Enter BusinessImplementation:myBusinessCall_call with "+
                    "DYE ID="+myDYEMessageID_in_Business);
```

```
            // do your business here
    }
}
```

The second listing shows the demo implementation of the business wrapper. A
wrapper may be implemented to provide an additional level of API in front of the
business code which can be beneficial for many different reasons.

```
package de.martin.test_dye.pojo;

import weblogic.diagnostics.context.DiagnosticContextHelper;

public class BusinessWrapper {

    public BusinessWrapper() {}

    public void wrappBusinessCall()
    {
            String myDYEMessageID_in_Wrapper = DiagnosticContextHelper.getContextId();

            System.out.println("INFO] Enter BusinessWrapper:wrappBusinessCall_call with "+
                            "DYE ID="+myDYEMessageID_in_Wrapper);

            // call business function
            (new BusinessImplementation()).myBusinessCall();
    }
}
```

The third listing shows the implementation of the Test1Bean which is a stateless
session and offers access to the business functionality.

```
package de.martin.test_dye.ejb;

import javax.ejb.Stateless;

import weblogic.diagnostics.context.DiagnosticContextHelper;
import de.martin.test_dye.pojo.*;

@Stateless(mappedName = "Test1")
public class Test1Bean implements Test1BeanLocal, Test1BeanRemote{

    public Test1Bean() {}

    public void test_1_call()
    {
      try {
         String myDYEMessageID_in_EJB = DiagnosticContextHelper.getContextId();

         System.out.println("INFO] Enter Test1Bean:test_1_call with DYE ID="+myDYEMessageID_in_EJB);

         // call business using the business wrapper
         (new BusinessWrapper()).wrappBusinessCall();
      }
      catch(Exception ex) {
         ex.printStackTrace();
      }
    }

    public void test_2_call()
    {
      try {
         String myDYEMessageID_in_EJB = DiagnosticContextHelper.getContextId();

         System.out.println("INFO] Enter Test1Bean:test_2_call with DYE ID="+myDYEMessageID_in_EJB);

         // call business directly
         (new BusinessImplementation()).myBusinessCall();
      }
      catch(Exception ex) {
```

```
            ex.printStackTrace();
        }
    }
}
```

The second EJB is an EJB which might implement some additional features and makes use of the other EJB to call the real business.

```
package de.martin.test_dye.ejb;

import javax.ejb.Stateless;
import javax.naming.InitialContext;

import weblogic.diagnostics.context.DiagnosticContextHelper;

@Stateless(mappedName = "TestDelegateBean")
public class TestDelegateBean  implements TestDelegateBeanLocal,TestDelegateBeanRemote {

    public TestDelegateBean() {}

    public void test_delegate_call()
    {
      try {
          String myDYEMessageID_in_EJB = DiagnosticContextHelper.getContextId();

          System.out.println("INFO] Enter TestDelegateBean:test_delegate_call with "+
                             "DYE ID="+myDYEMessageID_in_EJB);

          // call delegate bean
          Test1BeanRemote myTest1BeanRemote =
                      (Test1BeanRemote)(new InitialContext()).lookup("Test1 ");
          myTest1BeanRemote.test_1_call();
      }
      catch(Exception ex) {
              ex.printStackTrace();
      }
    }
}
```

And finally the servlet does nothing else but calls one of the possible call paths.

```
package de.martin.test_dye.servlet;

import java.io.IOException;

import javax.naming.InitialContext;
import javax.servlet.ServletException;
import javax.servlet.http.*;
import weblogic.diagnostics.context.DiagnosticContextHelper;
import de.martin.test_dye.ejb.*;

public class MyTestServlet extends HttpServlet {
    private InitialContext ctx;
    private Test1BeanRemote myTest1Bean;
    private TestDelegateBeanRemote myTestDelegateBean;

    public MyTestServlet() {
        super();
        try {
            ctx = new InitialContext();
            myTest1Bean = (Test1BeanRemote)ctx.lookup("Test1 ");
            myTestDelegateBean = (TestDelegateBeanRemote)ctx.lookup("TestDelegateBean ");
        }
        catch(Exception ex) {
            ex.printStackTrace();
        }
    }

    protected void doGet(HttpServletRequest request, HttpServletResponse response)
                throws ServletException, IOException
    {
        try {
```

```
        String myDYEMessageID_in_Web = DiagnosticContextHelper.getContextId();
        String taskID = request.getParameter("id");

        System.out.println("INFO] Enter MyTestServlet:doGet_call "+
                    "(called with taskID="+taskID+") with DYE ID="+myDYEMessageID_in_Web);

          if (taskID==null || "1".equalsIgnoreCase(taskID))
              myTest1Bean.test_1_call();
          else if ("2".equalsIgnoreCase(taskID))
              myTest1Bean.test_2_call();
          else if ("3".equalsIgnoreCase(taskID))
              myTestDelegateBean.test_delegate_call();
          else
              System.out.println("INFO] NO :-( valid task id found with DYE "+
                            "ID="+myDYEMessageID_in_Web);
        }
      catch(Exception ex) {
        ex.printStackTrace();
      }
    }
  }
}
```

Running the example

The first step is to compile the example, build the EAR application and deploy it. After the application got deployed, it is possible to hit the servlet with taskID 1, 2 or 3.

The following will be the output:

```
INFO] Enter MyTestServlet:doGet_call (called with taskID=3) with DYE ID=null
INFO] Enter TestDelegateBean:test_delegate_call with DYE ID=null
INFO] Enter Test1Bean:test_1_call with DYE ID=null
INFO] Enter BusinessWrapper:wrappBusinessCall_call with DYE ID=null
INFO] Enter BusinessImplementation:myBusinessCall_call with DYE ID=null

INFO] Enter MyTestServlet:doGet_call (called with taskID=1) with DYE ID=null
INFO] Enter Test1Bean:test_1_call with DYE ID=null
INFO] Enter BusinessWrapper:wrappBusinessCall_call with DYE ID=null
INFO] Enter BusinessImplementation:myBusinessCall_call with DYE ID=null
```

As you can see, the example works but the "DYE ID" is always null.

Creating the diagnostic module

In order to make use of the DYE-ID it is only necessary to create a diagnostic module and activate the standard system monitor called "DYE injection".

The first step is to create a new diagnostic module.

Figure 20.5: *New diagnostic module*

After the module was created, it is necessary to enable the instrumentation for this module (similar to the enabling of previous examples). On the instrumentation section of the diagnostic module the "enabled" flag has to be set. On the same section it is possible to add diagnostic monitors.

Figure 20.6: *Instrumentation section of the diagnostic module*

As a next step it is now necessary to add the "DYE Injection" monitor.

Add/Remove Monitors From Library

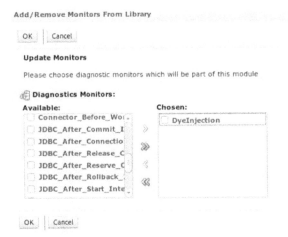

Figure 20.7: *Selection and addition the DyeInjection monitor*

As a last step it is possible (but not necessary) to add a diagnostic filter. This will limit the amount of events being generated.

Figure 20.8: *Optionally defining a DYE filter*

The complete module configuration will finally look like:

```
<?xml version='1.0' encoding='UTF-8'?>
```

```
<wldf-resource xmlns="http://xmlns.oracle.com/weblogic/weblogic-diagnostics"
xmlns:sec="http://xmlns.oracle.com/weblogic/security"
xmlns:wls="http://xmlns.oracle.com/weblogic/security/wls"
xmlns:xsi="http://www.w3.org/2001/XMLSchema-instance"
xsi:schemaLocation="http://xmlns.oracle.com/weblogic/weblogic-diagnostics
http://xmlns.oracle.com/weblogic/weblogic-diagnostics/1.0/weblogic-diagnostics.xsd">
  <name>TestDYEInjection</name>
  <instrumentation>
    <enabled>true</enabled>
    <wldf-instrumentation-monitor>
      <name>DyeInjection</name>
      <description>Set ADDR1 to localhost</description>
      <dye-mask xsi:nil="true"></dye-mask>
      <properties>ADDR1=localhost</properties>
    </wldf-instrumentation-monitor>
  </instrumentation>
</wldf-resource>
```

Running the example again

After the module is created we will run the same example (without any change or redeployment) again.

```
INFO] Enter MyTestServlet:doGet_call (called with taskID=1) with DYE ID=9e687275-9bde-4237-a40a-
018a4feae65b-000000e5
INFO] Enter Test1Bean:test_1_call with DYE ID=9e687275-9bde-4237-a40a-018a4feae65b-000000e5
INFO] Enter BusinessWrapper:wrappBusinessCall_call with DYE ID=9e687275-9bde-4237-a40a-018a4feae65b-
000000e5
INFO] Enter BusinessImplementation:myBusinessCall_call with DYE ID=9e687275-9bde-4237-a40a-
018a4feae65b-000000e5
INFO] Enter MyTestServlet:doGet_call (called with taskID=2) with DYE ID=9e687275-9bde-4237-a40a-
018a4feae65b-000000e7
INFO] Enter Test1Bean:test_2_call with DYE ID=9e687275-9bde-4237-a40a-018a4feae65b-000000e7
INFO] Enter BusinessImplementation:myBusinessCall_call with DYE ID=9e687275-9bde-4237-a40a-
018a4feae65b-000000e7
INFO] Enter MyTestServlet:doGet_call (called with taskID=3) with DYE ID=9e687275-9bde-4237-a40a-
018a4feae65b-000000e9
INFO] Enter TestDelegateBean:test_delegate_call with DYE ID=9e687275-9bde-4237-a40a-018a4feae65b-
000000e9
INFO] Enter Test1Bean:test_1_call with DYE ID=9e687275-9bde-4237-a40a-018a4feae65b-000000e9
INFO] Enter BusinessWrapper:wrappBusinessCall_call with DYE ID=9e687275-9bde-4237-a40a-018a4feae65b-
000000e9
INFO] Enter BusinessImplementation:myBusinessCall_call with DYE ID=9e687275-9bde-4237-a40a-
018a4feae65b-000000e9
INFO] Enter MyTestServlet:doGet_call (called with taskID=4) with DYE ID=9e687275-9bde-4237-a40a-
018a4feae65b-000000ea
INFO] NO :-( valid task id found with DYE ID=9e687275-9bde-4237-a40a-018a4feae65b-000000ea
```

As you can see, now we get a unique DYE-ID for each request like DYE ID=9e687275-9bde-4237-a40a-018a4feae65b-000000e5. You can also see in the output above that printing the ID in each step in the call path will always result in the same ID for the actual call.

This really is a powerful but unfortunately very little known feature of WebLogic to enable call path tracking in WebLogic.

Combination with Instrumentation

As a next step we will define instrumentation monitors. Let us define standard monitors for Servlet and EJBs and custom monitors for the POJO objects.

```xml
<?xml version="1.0" encoding="UTF-8"?>
<wldf-resource>
    <name>DYE INjection Test</name>
    <instrumentation>

        <enabled>true</enabled>

        <wldf-instrumentation-monitor>
            <name>Servlet_Before_Service</name>
            <enabled>true</enabled>
            <action>TraceAction</action>
        </wldf-instrumentation-monitor>

        <wldf-instrumentation-monitor>
            <name>EJB_Around_SessionEjbBusinessMethods</name>
            <enabled>true</enabled>
            <action>TraceAction</action>
        </wldf-instrumentation-monitor>

        <wldf-instrumentation-monitor>
            <name>POJO-Business</name>
            <enabled>true</enabled>
            <action>TraceElapsedTimeAction</action>
            <location-type>around</location-type>
            <pointcut>execution( * de.martin.test_dye.pojo.BusinessImplementation
myBusinessCall*(...));</pointcut>
        </wldf-instrumentation-monitor>

        <wldf-instrumentation-monitor>
            <name>POJO-Wrapper</name>
            <enabled>true</enabled>
            <action>TraceElapsedTimeAction</action>
            <location-type>around</location-type>
            <pointcut>execution( * de.martin.test_dye.pojo.BusinessWrapper
wrappBusinessCall*(...));</pointcut>
        </wldf-instrumentation-monitor>
    </instrumentation>
</wldf-resource>
```

If we now ran the example again, we will not only see the System out messages in the standout log file as shown above but we will also see entries in the Event log file. S yu can see in the next screenshot, the second column contains the DYE-ID

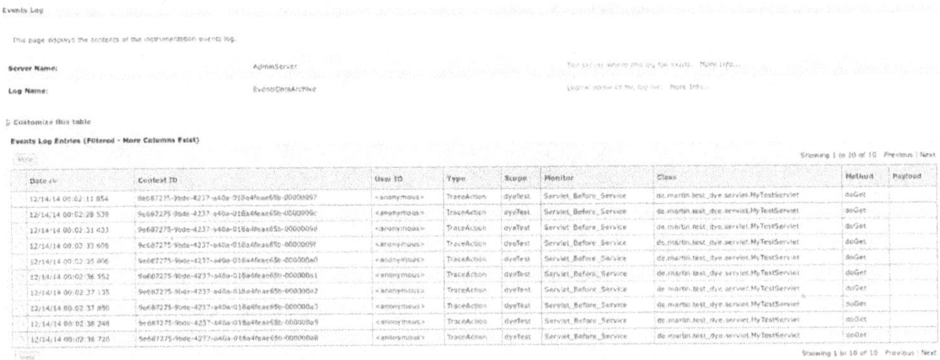

Figure 20.9: *Event log file entries*

Example 4: Mining WebLogic Diagnostic Data with XSLT

The following example is based on a blog written by Philip Aston (thanks for the permission)

Using WLDF, you can monitor and record pretty much anything you want to about the behavior of a running WebLogic Server domain. The standard tools can be used to extract harvested data and events from the diagnostic archive but provide little to allow you to build a composite picture from the harvested data. This example uses advanced WebLogic and WLDF techniques to show how to use XSLT to reformat diagnostic data and generate hierarchical HTML reports from the WLDF diagnostic data.

This example shows how to perform a number of useful transformations to the collected data, like reformat diagnostic data as a comma-separated value file so it can be easily imported into spreadsheet tools and recombine raw event data into a hierarchical structure and present that data as an HTML report. In conjunction with the WLDF diagnostic context, this can be used to show the flow of events across multiple WebLogic Server instances.

Process Overview

The example uses a number of stylesheets to process the diagnostic data. The following depicts the overall process for a better understanding.

WebLogic Server stores collected metrics and event data in its diagnostic archive. WLST can then be used to export the data into XML files (events.xml and harvest.xsl). Stylesheets are used afterwards to convert this exported data to comma-separated value (CSV) format to merge two exported data files into one, to build up an XML file that is structured according to the event tree (eventsToTree.xsl). Finally an HTL report will be generated.

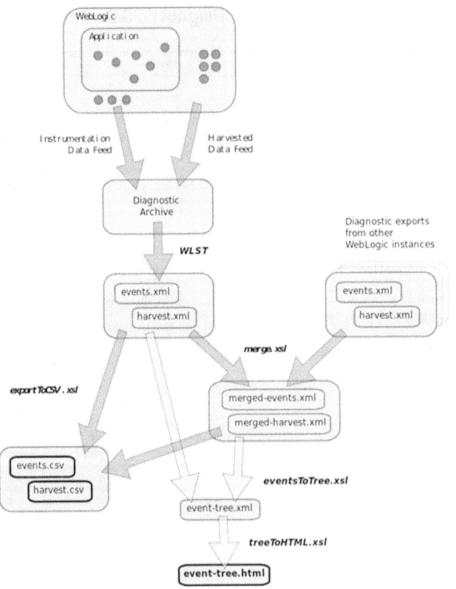

Figure 20.10: *The process overview*

First Step: Instrument Your System

First, configure WLDF to instrument your application code to produce event data and to regularly harvest metric data from interesting MBeans. WebLogic Server will store this information in its diagnostic archive.

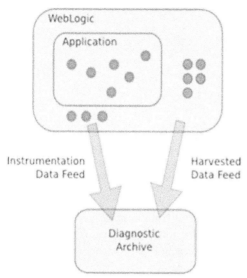

Figure 20.11: *WebLogic Server stores WLDF data in its diagnostic archive.*

It is necessary to add instrumentation instructions to your application deployment. To specify the instrumentation, add a **weblogic-diagnostics.xml** file to the META-INF directory of your application. Make sure you include plenty of delegating monitors or custom monitors with a diagnostic location type of around and a TraceElapsedTimeAction action. These record the time taken by a particular operation when it completes. You'll be needing this data later to build event trees.

This example captures a variety of servlet and EJB operations:

```xml
<?xml version="1.0" encoding="UTF-8"?>

<wldf-resource xmlns="http://www.bea.com/ns/weblogic/90/diagnostics">
  <instrumentation>
    <enabled>true</enabled>

    <wldf-instrumentation-monitor>
      <name>Trace_Servlet_Around_Service</name>
      <action>TraceElapsedTimeAction</action>
      <location-type>around</location-type>
      <pointcut>execution(* +javax.servlet.Servlet service(+javax.servlet.ServletRequest,
+javax.servlet.ServletResponse))</pointcut>
    </wldf-instrumentation-monitor>

    <wldf-instrumentation-monitor>
```

```
    <name>Trace_EJB_Session_Business_Methods</name>
    <action>TraceElapsedTimeAction</action>
    <location-type>around</location-type>
    <pointcut>execution(* +javax.ejb.SessionBean * (...))
      AND NOT execution(* * __WL* (...))
      AND NOT execution(* * ejbCreate (...))
      AND NOT execution(* * ejbRemove ())
      AND NOT execution(* * ejbActivate ())
      AND NOT execution(* * ejbPassivate ())
      AND NOT execution(* * setSessionContext (...))
    </pointcut>
</wldf-instrumentation-monitor>

<wldf-instrumentation-monitor>
    <name>Trace_EJB_Session_Home_Methods</name>
    <action>TraceElapsedTimeAction</action>
    <location-type>around</location-type>
    <pointcut>execution(* +javax.ejb.EJBHome * (...))
          AND execution(* *Impl * (...))
    </pointcut>
</wldf-instrumentation-monitor>

<wldf-instrumentation-monitor>
    <name>Trace_EJB_Stub_Calls</name>
    <action>TraceElapsedTimeAction</action>
    <location-type>around</location-type>
    <pointcut>call(* +wldfexample.SessionEJBRemote * (...))
      AND NOT call(* *_EOImpl* * (...))
    </pointcut>
</wldf-instrumentation-monitor>

  </instrumentation>
</wldf-resource>
```

This example specifies monitors with own custom pointcuts, rather than rely on the standard delegating monitors. This provides more control over precisely which events are captured. For example, the last monitor traces only EJB stubs for the test EJB I have been deployed (wldfexample.SessionEJBRemote).

Add a system diagnostic module to your domains

The instrumentation specified in an application's weblogic-diagnostics.xml file will not be applied unless there is a system diagnostic module with instrumentation enabled, and the system diagnostic module is targeted to the WebLogic Server instance.

If you change the targeting of the system diagnostic module, or change whether instrumentation is enabled, you must fully redeploy your application for the change to take effect. Only a full redeployment will perform the AOP weaving process and change the instrumentation. Stopping and starting the application through the WebLogic console is not sufficient. It is required to either use the WLST redeploy() command or to fully redeploy (untarget, change and retarget) the application. Afterwards restart your servers.

Whenever you change weblogic-diagnostics.xml, you must also do a full redeployment. You can create a system diagnostic module using the WebLogic console. This results in a file in the config/diagnostics directory of your domain.

The following listing shows an example for such a diagnostic module:

```
<?xml version='1.0' encoding='UTF-8'?>
<wldf-resource xmlns="http://www.bea.com/ns/weblogic/90/diagnostics"
 xmlns:sec="http://www.bea.com/ns/weblogic/90/security"
 xmlns:xsi="http://www.w3.org/2001/XMLSchema-instance"
 xmlns:wls="http://www.bea.com/ns/weblogic/90/security/wls"
 xsi:schemaLocation="http://www.bea.com/ns/weblogic/90/diagnostics
http://www.bea.com/ns/weblogic/920/diagnostics.xsd">
  <name>MySystemDiagnosticModule</name>
  <instrumentation>
    <enabled>true</enabled>
  </instrumentation>
  <harvester>
    <enabled>true</enabled>
    <sample-period>10000</sample-period>
    <harvested-type>
      <name>weblogic.management.runtime.WorkManagerRuntimeMBean</name>
      <harvested-attribute>CompletedRequests</harvested-attribute>
      <harvested-attribute>PendingRequests</harvested-attribute>
      <harvested-attribute>StuckThreadCount</harvested-attribute>
      <harvested-
instance>com.bea:ApplicationRuntime=WLDF,Name=default,ServerRuntime=AdminServer,Type=WorkManagerRunti
me</harvested-instance>
    </harvested-type>
    <harvested-type>
      <name>weblogic.management.runtime.JTAStatisticsRuntimeMBean</name>
      <harvested-attribute>TransactionCommittedTotalCount</harvested-attribute>
      <harvested-attribute>TransactionRolledBackTotalCount</harvested-attribute>
      <harvested-
instance>com.bea:Name=JTARuntime,ServerRuntime=AdminServer,Type=JTARuntime</harvested-instance>
    </harvested-type>
  </harvester>
  <watch-notification></watch-notification>
</wldf-resource>
```

In addition to the instrumentation the diagnostic module which is defined in the above configuration also configured a number of MBean harvesters.

The Diagnostic Context

An interesting feature of WLDF not commonly found in other tools is its ability to create and propagate a diagnostic "context". This diagnostic context uniquely identifies a particular request, and flows across synchronous calls to other WebLogic Server instances. The diagnostic context includes a unique ID (for example, 583c10bfdbd326ba:-43487c71:112bda0af31:-7ff4-00000000000001b7). You can use this ID to trace event flows across servers.

Related to the diagnostic context is the notion of requesting **dyeing**. A **DyeInjectionMonitor** can be used to filter the events that are recorded based on various request characteristics (user identity, protocol type, IP address, and so on). This is a powerful way of focusing what you record and could be a very beneficial extension to this example (not used here to reduce the complexity).

The diagnostic context adds a very small processing overhead: essentially, it's the cost of generating the unique ID, and passing it around with every request. This overhead is negligible. This diagnostic context is generated only if a DyeInjectionMonitor is enabled or if instrumentation is enabled.

WebLogic stores diagnostics in a diagnostic archive local to each server. WLST can be used to extract data from the diagnostic archive

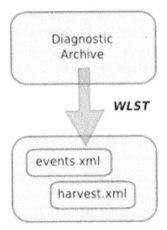

Figure 20.12: *WLST is used to export data from the diagnostic archive*

The diagnostic archive contains event and harvested metric data in a binary format. This data can be exported to an XML format using the WebLogic Scripting Tool (WLST), using either the exportDiagnosticData or exportDiagnosticDataFromServer commands.

For example:

```
exportDiagnosticData(storeDir="/work/domain/servers/server1/data/store/diagnostics",
  logicalName="EventsDataArchive", exportFileName="server1-events.xml")
```

This example uses two types of data, event data (logicalName="EventsDataArchive") and harvested metric data (logicalName="HarvestedDataArchive"). Both exportDiagnosticData and exportDiagnosticDataFromServer have options that allow you to filter data, by time or through a full WLDF query. You should use these filter options to limit the size of the exported XML files.

Here's an example of filtering by a particular diagnostic context ID:

```
exportDiagnosticData(storeDir="/work/domain/servers/server1/data/store/diagnostics",
  logicalName="EventsDataArchive", exportFileName="events.xml",
  query="CONTEXTID='583c10bfdbd326ba:58f87d21:1126b53f6ec:-7ff3-0000000000000c2a'")
```

If you look at the exported XML data, you'll see the XML conforms to an abstract schema that models a set of DataRecords consisting of ColumnData values for various columns. The XML file starts with a DataInfo element that contains the names of the columns and their Java types. These columns are slightly different for the event and harvested data files in which we are interested.

How to Run an XSLT Stylesheet

So now we have some XML. Before we get to our first XSLT stylesheet, here's a useful Jython script you can use to process an XML document with a stylesheet:

```python
import sys

from java.io import FileReader, PrintWriter
from java.lang import System
from javax.xml.transform import TransformerFactory, Transformer
from javax.xml.transform.stream import StreamSource, StreamResult

def transform(source, stylesheet, result, parameters):
    transformer = TransformerFactory.newInstance().newTransformer(stylesheet)

    for (p, v) in parameters: transformer.setParameter(p, v)

    transformer.transform(source, result)

if __name__ == '__main__':
    args = sys.argv[1:]
    parameters = []

    while args and args[0].startswith('-'):
        try:
            i = args[0].index('=')
        except ValueError:
            parameters.append((args[0], ""))
        else:
            parameters.append((args[0][1:i], args[0][i+1:]))

        args = args[1:]

    if len(args) == 1:   source = StreamSource(System.in)
    elif len(args) == 2: source = StreamSource(FileReader(args[1]))
    else: raise "Usage: <jython|wlst> process.py -<parameter>=<value> <stylesheetfile> [inputfile]"

    stylesheet = StreamSource(FileReader(args[0]))
    result = StreamResult(PrintWriter(System.out))

    transform(source, stylesheet, result, parameters)

    stylesheet.reader.close()
    source.reader and source.reader.close()
    result.writer.close()
```

The above WLST script can be called using the following command:

```
java weblogic.WLST process.py stylesheet.xsl input.xml > output.xml
```

The output will go to stdout, so we use shell redirection to send it to output.xml. Alternatively, you might use the shell pipe operator to chain multiple process.py processes together.

Some of our stylesheets take parameters that control their behavior. process.py lets you specify stylesheet parameters as follows:

```
java weblogic.WLST process.py -myparameter=value stylesheet.xsl input.xml >
output.xml
```

Merging Data

The first stylesheet simply merges the exported data from two diagnostic archives. This is a useful way to combine data from multiple WebLogic Server instances. First, extract the data from each server, filtering as appropriate using WLST; then create a combined file for further processing using this stylesheet.

```xml
<?xml version="1.0" encoding="utf-8"?>

<xsl:stylesheet xmlns:xsl="http://www.w3.org/1999/XSL/Transform" version="1.0"
xmlns:e="http://www.bea.com/ns/weblogic/90/diagnostics/accessor/Export">

  <xsl:output method="xml"/>

  <xsl:variable name="TIMESTAMP" select="count(//e:ColumnInfo[e:Name='TIMESTAMP']/preceding-
sibling::*) + 1"/>

  <xsl:param name="document2"/>
  <xsl:param name="offset" select="0"/>

  <xsl:template match="e:DiagnosticData">
    <xsl:copy>
      <xsl:apply-templates select="@*"/>
      <xsl:apply-templates/>

      <xsl:variable name="d2" select="document($document2)" />

      <xsl:for-each select="$d2/e:DiagnosticData/e:DataRecord">
        <xsl:copy>
          <xsl:apply-templates select="@*" mode="d2"/>
          <xsl:apply-templates mode="d2"/>
        </xsl:copy>

        <xsl:text>
</xsl:text>
      </xsl:for-each>

    </xsl:copy>
  </xsl:template>

  <xsl:template match="e:ColumnData[$TIMESTAMP]" mode="d2">
    <xsl:copy>
      <xsl:value-of select=". + $offset"/>
    </xsl:copy>
  </xsl:template>

  <xsl:template match="node()|@*">
    <xsl:copy>
      <xsl:apply-templates select="@*"/>
      <xsl:apply-templates/>
    </xsl:copy>
  </xsl:template>

  <xsl:template match="node()|@*" mode="d2">
    <xsl:copy>
      <xsl:apply-templates select="@*"/>
      <xsl:apply-templates/>
    </xsl:copy>
  </xsl:template>
</xsl:stylesheet>
```

This stylesheet takes two parameters: document2 is the name of a document to merge with its main input document; and offset is an optional time offset in milliseconds. If offset is specified, its value is added to all the timestamps in document2. This is useful where the times of the systems that host the WebLogic Server instances are not fully synchronized.

Here is an example of using the stylesheet to merge two event data export files:

```
java weblogic.WLST process.py -document2=server2-events.xml merge.xsl
server1-events.xml > events.xml
```

It makes sense to merge two event data files or two harvested metric files. It does not make sense to merge an event data file with a harvested metric file, since these file types have different column sets.

Producing a Comma-separated Value (csv) spreadsheet File

The next stylesheet does something more useful. It converts an export file into a comma-separated value file that can be imported into Microsoft Excel and other spreadsheet tools.

The stylesheet takes no parameters.

```xml
<?xml version="1.0" encoding="utf-8"?>

<xsl:stylesheet xmlns:xsl="http://www.w3.org/1999/XSL/Transform" version="1.0"
xmlns:e="http://www.bea.com/ns/weblogic/90/diagnostics/accessor/Export">

  <xsl:output method="text"/>

  <xsl:template match="e:DiagnosticData">
    <xsl:apply-templates/>
  </xsl:template>

  <xsl:template match="e:DataInfo"/>

  <xsl:template match="e:DataRecord">
    <xsl:variable name="record" select="."/>

    <xsl:for-each select="/e:DiagnosticData/e:DataInfo[1]/e:ColumnInfo">
      <xsl:variable name="p" select="position()"/>
      <xsl:value-of select="$record/e:ColumnData[$p]"/>
      <xsl:if test="$p != last()">
        <xsl:text>, </xsl:text>
      </xsl:if>
    </xsl:for-each>

    <xsl:text>
</xsl:text>
  </xsl:template>

  <!-- Work around known issue in Java 5 (Sun bug 6413803 inherited
  from XALAN-2230) which means that the xsl:stripspace directive
  doesn't work with XML name spaces. We explicitly trim text nodes.
  -->
  <xsl:template match="text()">
    <xsl:value-of select="normalize-space(.)"/>
  </xsl:template>

</xsl:stylesheet>
```

Producing an Event Tree File

The exported data files have information about the individual events but don't record the relationships between the events. By using the timing information, we can reconstruct the event tree, which gives us an idea of which parts of the code were called by other parts. To build the event tree, we'll use the difference in times between before and after events recorded by TraceElapsedTimeAction actions. This time is stored in the event payload of the after events. We discard events that do not have a payload, leaving us with just the after events. We can calculate the start timestamp by subtracting the payload time from the after event timestamp, taking care to convert to a common unit (the event timestamps are in milliseconds, but the payload times are in nanoseconds).

The start and end timestamps give us a timespan for the monitored methods. We build the event tree by treating timespans that are directly and wholly included in another timespan as children of those timespans.

The WLDF console extension can produce a similar event tree for the flow of a single request, within a server. While the console extension is great for quick browsing, our approach has a few of advantages. By using merge.xsl to merge events from multiple diagnostic archives, we can trace the flow of a request across multiple servers. The results are captured in an HTML report that can be published and distributed. The event tree is calculated using only timestamps and does not, for example, use the diagnostic context in its correlation. This makes the stylesheet quite general but means that events can be incorrectly marked as causes of other events. To avoid this, you may want to filter by diagnostic context. You can do this by specifying an appropriate WLDF query when you export from the diagnostic archive, or by supplying the stylesheet with a list of diagnostic contexts using its contexts parameter. In practice, you might find the diagnostic contexts of interest first by extracting all the diagnostic data into a CSV file, importing it into a spreadsheet, and looking for unusual (or perhaps typical) transactions.

The stylesheet expects an event data export file as input and takes a single, optional parameter, contexts, which is a list of diagnostic contexts to include from the source. If contexts is not specified, all events recorded by TraceElapsedTimeAction will be included.

```
<?xml version="1.0" encoding="utf-8"?>

<xsl:stylesheet xmlns:xsl="http://www.w3.org/1999/XSL/Transform" version="1.0"
xmlns:exslt="http://exslt.org/common"
xmlns:e="http://www.bea.com/ns/weblogic/90/diagnostics/accessor/Export">

  <xsl:output method="xml" indent="yes"/>

  <xsl:variable name="RECORDID" select="count(//e:ColumnInfo[e:Name='RECORDID']/preceding-sibling::*)
+ 1"/>
```

```
  <xsl:variable name="TIMESTAMP" select="count(//e:ColumnInfo[e:Name='TIMESTAMP']/preceding-
sibling::*) + 1"/>
  <xsl:variable name="CONTEXTID" select="count(//e:ColumnInfo[e:Name='CONTEXTID']/preceding-
sibling::*) + 1"/>
  <xsl:variable name="TXID" select="count(//e:ColumnInfo[e:Name='TXID']/preceding-sibling::*) + 1"/>
  <xsl:variable name="USERID" select="count(//e:ColumnInfo[e:Name='USERID']/preceding-sibling::*) +
1"/>
  <xsl:variable name="DOMAIN" select="count(//e:ColumnInfo[e:Name='DOMAIN']/preceding-sibling::*) +
1"/>
  <xsl:variable name="SERVER" select="count(//e:ColumnInfo[e:Name='SERVER']/preceding-sibling::*) +
1"/>
  <xsl:variable name="MONITOR" select="count(//e:ColumnInfo[e:Name='MONITOR']/preceding-sibling::*) +
1"/>
  <xsl:variable name="CLASSNAME" select="count(//e:ColumnInfo[e:Name='CLASSNAME']/preceding-
sibling::*) + 1"/>
  <xsl:variable name="METHODNAME" select="count(//e:ColumnInfo[e:Name='METHODNAME']/preceding-
sibling::*) + 1"/>
  <xsl:variable name="PAYLOAD" select="count(//e:ColumnInfo[e:Name='PAYLOAD']/preceding-sibling::*) +
1"/>

  <xsl:param name="contexts" select=""/>

  <xsl:template match="/">
    <xsl:variable name="sorted-nodes">
      <xsl:for-each select="//e:DataRecord[e:ColumnData[$PAYLOAD] != '' and
                                   ($contexts = '' or contains($contexts,
e:ColumnData[$CONTEXTID]))]">
        <xsl:sort select="e:ColumnData[$TIMESTAMP] * 1000000 - e:ColumnData[$PAYLOAD]"/>
        <xsl:copy-of select="."/>
      </xsl:for-each>
    </xsl:variable>

    <xsl:variable name="nodes" select="exslt:node-set($sorted-nodes)/e:DataRecord"/>

    <data>
      <xsl:call-template name="processLevel">
        <xsl:with-param name="nodes" select="$nodes"/>
        <xsl:with-param name="basetime" select="$nodes[1]/e:ColumnData[$TIMESTAMP] * 1000000 -
$nodes[1]/e:ColumnData[$PAYLOAD]"/>
      </xsl:call-template>
    </data>
  </xsl:template>


  <xsl:template name="processLevel">
    <xsl:param name="nodes"/>
    <xsl:param name="basetime"/>

    <xsl:for-each select="$nodes">
      <xsl:variable name="position" select="position()"/>
      <xsl:variable name="endMS" select="e:ColumnData[$TIMESTAMP]"/>
      <xsl:variable name="start" select="$endMS * 1000000 - e:ColumnData[$PAYLOAD]"/>

      <!-- Output the nodes that are not fully enclosed by others in $nodes.

           Nodes that overlap partially will all be output at this
           level - their contents may contain duplicates at lower
           levels.

           Where the times match exactly, break the tie using the
           document order. -->
      <xsl:if test="not($nodes[(position() != $position) and
                           ((e:ColumnData[$TIMESTAMP] * 1000000 - e:ColumnData[$PAYLOAD]) &lt;
$start and e:ColumnData[$TIMESTAMP] &gt;= $endMS or
                            (e:ColumnData[$TIMESTAMP] * 1000000 - e:ColumnData[$PAYLOAD]) &lt;=
$start and e:ColumnData[$TIMESTAMP] &gt; $endMS or
                            (e:ColumnData[$TIMESTAMP] * 1000000 - e:ColumnData[$PAYLOAD]) =
$start and e:ColumnData[$TIMESTAMP] = $endMS and position() &lt; $position
                           )]
                   )">

        <record start="{$start}" offset="{$start - $basetime}" duration="{e:ColumnData[$PAYLOAD]}"
                classname="{e:ColumnData[$CLASSNAME]}" methodname="{e:ColumnData[$METHODNAME]}"
                domain="{e:ColumnData[$DOMAIN]}" server="{e:ColumnData[$SERVER]}"
recordid="{e:ColumnData[$RECORDID]}"
                userid="{e:ColumnData[$USERID]}" txid="{e:ColumnData[$TXID]}">

          <!-- Recurse to include nodes in $nodes that we enclose. -->
```

```
            <xsl:call-template name="processLevel">
                <xsl:with-param name="nodes" select="$nodes[position() != $position and
(e:ColumnData[$TIMESTAMP] * 1000000 - e:ColumnData[$PAYLOAD]) &gt;= $start and
e:ColumnData[$TIMESTAMP] &lt;= $endMS]"/>
                <xsl:with-param name="basetime" select="$start"/>
            </xsl:call-template>
        </record>
      </xsl:if>
    </xsl:for-each>
  </xsl:template>

</xsl:stylesheet>
```

Formatting an Event Tree File

The event tree we've produced is just another XML file. Let's make it more comprehensible by rendering it in HTML. This stylesheet expects an event tree document as input, and takes no parameters.

```
<?xml version="1.0" encoding="utf-8"?>
<xsl:stylesheet xmlns:xsl="http://www.w3.org/1999/XSL/Transform"
                version="1.0">

  <xsl:output method="html"/>

  <xsl:template match="/">
    <html>
      <body>
        <table>
          <tr>
            <th></th>
            <th>Offset</th>
            <th>Method</th>
            <th>Duration</th>
            <th>Record</th>
            <th>User</th>
            <th>Transaction ID</th>
          </tr>
          <xsl:apply-templates/>
        </table>
      </body>
    </html>
  </xsl:template>

  <xsl:template match="record">
    <xsl:param name="indent" select=""/>
    <xsl:param name="level" select="1"/>

    <xsl:variable name="colour">
      <xsl:choose>
        <xsl:when test="$level=1">#F0D0D0</xsl:when>
        <xsl:when test="$level=2">#D0D0F0</xsl:when>
        <xsl:when test="$level=3">#C0C0E0</xsl:when>
        <xsl:when test="$level=4">#B0B0D0</xsl:when>
        <xsl:when test="$level=5">#A0A0C0</xsl:when>
        <xsl:when test="$level=6">#9090B0</xsl:when>
        <xsl:when test="$level=7">#8080A0</xsl:when>
        <xsl:when test="$level=8">#707090</xsl:when>
        <xsl:when test="$level=9">#606080</xsl:when>
        <xsl:otherwise>#505070</xsl:otherwise>
      </xsl:choose>
    </xsl:variable>

    <tr bgcolor="{$colour}">
      <td align="right">
        <font size="-1">
        <xsl:number level="any"/>
        </font>
      </td>
      <td>
        <xsl:value-of select="$indent"/>
        <xsl:text>+</xsl:text>
```

```
    <xsl:value-of select="format-number(@offset div 1000000, '0.00')"/>
  </td>

  <td>
    <xsl:value-of select="$indent"/>
    <xsl:value-of select="@classname"/>
    <xsl:text>.</xsl:text>
    <xsl:value-of select="@methodname"/>
    <xsl:text>()</xsl:text>
  </td>

  <td align="right"><xsl:value-of select="format-number(@duration div 1000000, '0.000')"/></td>

  <td>
    <xsl:value-of select="@domain"/>
    <xsl:text>:</xsl:text>
    <xsl:value-of select="@server"/>
    <xsl:text>:</xsl:text>
    <xsl:value-of select="@recordid"/>
  </td>

  <td>
    <xsl:value-of select="@userid"/>
  </td>

  <td>
    <xsl:value-of select="@txid"/>
  </td>
  </tr>

  <xsl:apply-templates>
    <xsl:with-param name="indent" select="concat('    ', $indent)"/>
    <xsl:with-param name="level" select="$level + 1"/>
  </xsl:apply-templates>
  </xsl:template>

</xsl:stylesheet>
```

The stylesheet formats a report like:

	Offset	Method	Duration	Record	User	Transaction ID
1	+0.00	MyServlet.service()	53.971	wldfdomain:AdminServer:2178	<anonymous>	
2	+38.67	wldfexample.SessionEJB_48sqxa_HomeImpl.create()	5.304	wldfdomain:ms1:2	<anonymous>	
3	+44.51	wldfexample.SessionEJBRemote.getTime()	8.466	wldfdomain:AdminServer:2177	<anonymous>	
4	+4.72	wldfexample.SessionEJBRemote.getTime()	3.749	wldfdomain:ms1:6	<anonymous>	
5	+3.64	wldfexample.SessionEJB.getTime()	0.104	wldfdomain:ms1:5	<anonymous>	

Figure 20.13: *A section of an example report produced by treeToHTML.xsl stylesheet*

The indentation indicates the parent/child relationships in the event tree. The Offset column gives the time in milliseconds since the start of the parent event. The Duration is in milliseconds. By modifying eventsToTree.xsl and treeToHTML.xsl other columns can be included or can be formatted differently.

This example explains how to bring the data collected by WLDF to life using a little bit of effort and some XSLT wizardry.

Summary

WLDF instrumentation and DYE injection provide a very powerful set of features to inject monitoring code into customer applications. WLDF provides out-of-the-box a large number of standard monitors and options. This chapter has provided an overview of the features.

DYE injection is the WebLogic feature which allows administrators to trace call routes throughout the system. This is a feature which usually is only available in external commercial products. WebLogic provides it as part of WLDF. Surprisingly this feature is very little known and used in the industry.

Please consult the Oracle documentation for a complete listing of features, standard monitors, DYE filters and more.

Part VII

Review and Appendices

Review and Comparison

Review and Comparison

WLDF is not the only possible solution for WebLogic. This section tries to do a high-level comparison between WLDF and JMX/WLST and also between WLDF and other commercially available products.

WLDF, WLST or JMX?

We need to make a distinction between WLDF, WLST and JMX. Here is a brief summary of each:

WLST

WLST is a scripted environment based on Jython. As such, the programming of those scripts is simpler to more "shell like" than JMX. For experienced UNIX admins this is a great benefit, especially as WLST simulates the MBean trees like a file system. WLST also offers file system like commands such as "cd", "pwd" and more for navigation. Despite of being a simplified approach it is a powerful environment with a great level of functionality. Embedding WLST in other programs is usually a pain as it is necessary to call an interpreter from Java. So in fact this means: Using Java to code free lines of text (with no test/debug abilities), call an interpreter which is then asked to translate these text lines back to Java and then execute the Java code.

WLST supports everything needed to monitor all aspects of WebLogic. From project experience there are a number of disadvantages for WLST here. The biggest disadvantage is the fact that parallel invocations to different admin server are not supported. You need to create an own Jython interpreter instance for each admin server connection. For dozens or even hundreds of admin server this is hardly possible due to the huge resource consumption. Furthermore a switching between those admin servers is too slow.

JMX

JMX is pure JAVA and based on the standard JAVA JMX API. Therefore this approach is much easier to understand and learn for JAVA developers who are e.g. supposed to write automation programs. Another big benefit is that JMX is native Java and does not need an interpreter. Therefore embedding JMX automation code in other programs is natural and logical. As JMX is not interpreted it is also faster. Reusing other Java libraries is easier.

For monitoring JMX is much better suited due to its ability to connect to many different admin server at the same time and use multithreading efficiently to collect data in parallel from different servers/domains. Speed, parallel invocations and easy integration in other monitoring tools are vital for monitoring and in this area JMX has proven to be the better alternative.

WLDF

WLDF is different because it is NOT a remote technology like JMX or WLST. One of the big benefits is that it is already implemented into WebLogic and therefore running inside the same process against MBeans or instrumented code in the same process. Therefore WLDF has very little to know impact on the network. WLDF exposes a large number of MBeans which wake it possible to do all configurations using WLST or JMS. Also runtime activities like downloading archives can be done using WLST or JMX.

Monitoring is made very easy with WLDF as everything is already implemented and must just be activated. A number of different notification types are already build into the system. The whole area of instrumentation is beyond any capabilities of JMX or WLST.

Alternatives to WLDF

Monitoring can be done using WLST or JMX pull implementations. It is also possible to write own monitoring applications which pushes monitoring data out (to avoid the pull). Albeit own solutions might be more flexible to provide what you need it is definitely more work to create and maintain them.

For instrumentation and also to re-implement dye injection AOP frameworks like Spring AOP or AspectJ could be used. But be warned that there is quite some work to be done to get to the level of support WLDF (and especially all the standard monitors) already provide.

WLDF comes with WebLogic free of charge. There are also other commercial solutions on the market which provide similar features. Keep in mind that WLDF is bound to the WebLogic version. Whenever you change to a different WLS version, WLDF will work as it is implemented in WebLogic. Other commercial products must be certified first on new WebLogic implementations.

There are many tools – open source and commercial – available which implement monitoring and troubleshooting. Almost all rely on accessing WebLogic remotely and querying data from MBeans. Tools like JConsole and Mission Control are coming with the JDK.

Summary

WebLogic provides out of the box a solution which is different to JMX and WLST as it does not require remote access. It comes with a rich feature set with regards to notification types, instrumentation monitors, archive and log file support and more.

There are other solutions and technology possible with WebLogic but it is always really worthwhile to examine first if WLDF can fulfill your monitoring requirements before investing in additional products or technologies.

References

References

This appendix provides a number of resources with complementary information about the different topics covered in the book.

References are provided for further reading and not as a list of resources used for this book.

Books

The following book provides a deep understanding of WLST and JMX. This is very useful as a foundation to get a better background about the source code used in this book.

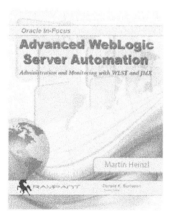

Title: Advanced WebLogic Server Automation
Administration and Monitoring with WLST and JMX
Publisher: Rampant TechPress
ISBN 13: 978-0-9916386-1-1
ISBN: 0-9916386-1-1

General Websites

Some web sites exists which do focus on WebLogic and also WLST. They provide a number of interesting examples. Well it is impossible to name all of them, therefore apologizes for those I am missing here.

- http://www.oracle.com
- http://wlstbyexamples.blogspot.de
- http://www.middlewaremagic.com
- http://weblogic-wonders.com
- http://wlatricksntips.blogspot.de/

Web Links

Oracle WLDF documentation:
- https://docs.oracle.com/middleware/1213/wls/WLDFC/toc.htm
- https://docs.oracle.com/middleware/1213/wls/WLDFC/architecture.htm
- https://docs.oracle.com/cd/E24329_01/web.1211/e24426/appendix_instrum_library.htm#WLDFC338

Other links:
- http://middlewaresnippets.blogspot.de/2014/01/automatic-scaling-application-using.html
- http://www.oracle.com/technetwork/articles/entarch/mining-wldf-xslt3-096004.html

DashBoard Links
- http://technology.amis.nl/2011/09/29/oracle-weblogic-extend-your-wldf-console/
- http://multikoop.blogspot.de/2010/04/monitoring-dashboard-in-wls.html
- http://docs.oracle.com/cd/E14571_01/web.1111/e13714/dashboard.htm
- http://www.albinsblog.com/2012/09/weblogic-monitoring-dashboard-to.html#.U3YwjXI-N0w

About the Author

Martin Heinzl is a senior/principal consultant in the areas of architecture, middleware and enterprise systems. Over the last 15 years, he has built up extensive experience in enterprise middleware technologies in distributed systems. His main areas of focus include architecture, integration, Java, J2EE, CORBA, distributed systems, integration approaches, and security. His project involvement has included analysis, design, architecture, SOA (like) systems, configuration, security, deployment, automation, management, and monitoring. This experience has given him a thorough knowledge of operations, automation, system architectures, development, and training.

Martin was also responsible for the automation of a complex web service security layer for an SOA infrastructure using single-sign on, SAML, and OWSM for a huge WebLogic farm (including Oracle service bus) with 500+ domains and 4000+ Managed-Servers. He was also responsible for the WebLogic infrastructure and monitoring concepts of in a high risk/high volume financial system. He is currently working in the middleware platform hosting team of a global bank.

In 2013, Martin joined the Oracle Customer Advisory Board for WebLogic and he always tries to be up to date on middleware technologies by attending conferences and taking part in beta programs. Martin is located in the Frankfurt/Main area in Germany, and you can reach him at wls_automation@mh-enterpriseconsulting.de.

Index

X

www.ingramcontent.com/pod-product-compliance
Lightning Source LLC
Chambersburg PA
CBHW080153060326
40689CB00018B/3956